PANCHAYATI RAJ AND RURAL DEVELOPMENT

PANCHAYATI RAJ AND RURAL DEVELOPMENT

SUBHASH KANSAL

CYBER TECH PUBLICATIONS
4264/3, Ansari Road, Daryaganj, New Delhi-110002 (India)
Ph.: 011-23244078, 011-43559448 Fax: 011-23280028
E-Mail: cyberpublicationsdelhi@yahoo.com
Website: www.cybertechpublications.com

PANCHAYATI RAJ AND RURAL DEVELOPMENT

SUBHASH KANSAL

First Edition 2011

Published by :

G.S. Rawat for **Cyber Tech Publications**
4264/3, Ansari Road, Daryaganj, New Delhi-110002 (India)
Ph.: 011-23244078, 011-43559448 Fax: 011-23280028
E-Mail: cyberpublicationsdelhi@yahoo.com
Website: www.cybertechpublications.com

Preface

In order to ensure that Panchayati Raj Institutions function as instruments of local government, it is important that their functional and financial autonomy is guaranteed and transparency in their functioning is ensured This has to be accomplished in most of the States. The role of the Gram Sabha is, perhaps, the most important in ensuring the success of Panchayati Raj Institutions at the village level. The role of local people in conducting social audit and fixing responsibility on panchayat functionaries will be effectively ensured with Gram Sabha becoming active. It is essential that the village community perceives meetings of the Gram Sabha as useful. The most important factor for that is the empowerment of the Gram Sabha.

Another important factor for the success of the Panchayati Raj system is the need for transparency in the functioning of these bodies. Panchayats being closer to the people, their right to information and accessibility to the panchayats must be ensured This issue was discussed in the Chief Ministers Conference held on 2nd August, 1997 and the Committee of Chief Ministers as well. The Ministry had written to the States. The Hon'ble Prime Minister too, in his letter to the Chief Ministers, had urged that all relevant information on development schemes taken up by the Panchayat along with the budget for them should be displayed prominently in the Panchayat Office. Relevant records should be made available for inspection by members of the public. Photocopies of documents such as muster rolls, vouchers, estimates etc. can be made available to the public on payment of a nominal fee. Technical manuals may be prepared for execution of various works at the Panchayat level so that transparency can be ensured The Ministry convened a Conference of State Ministers of Rural

Development and Panchayati Raj on May 13, 1998. This meeting was inaugurated by the Hon'ble Prime Minister.

The resolutions adopted in the Conference held on 13.5.98 are - (i) a Task Force for studying the structure and functioning of the Panchayats should be set up; (ii) provisions of 73rd Amendment Act and Central Act 40 will be complied with; (iii) Gram Sabhas should be convened on a single pre-determined day every quarter and (iv) care should be taken to respect the autonomy and independence of each tier of PRIs and to build up capability of the village level Panchayats. In pursuance of the resolution, a Task Force was constituted under the Chairmanship of the then Minister of State (Independent Charge), Ministry of Rural Areas & Employment to study the structure and functioning of PRIs. The State Governments have been requested to ensure that the Gram Sabha Meetings are convened once in each quarter preferably on - 26th January-Republic Day; Ist May-Labour Day; 15th August-Independence Day and 2nd October-Gandhi Jayanti.

—Author

CONTENTS

1

Panchayati Raj

Panchayats have been the backbone of the Indian villages since the beginning of recorded history. Gandhiji, the father of the nation, in 1946 had aptly remarked that the Indian Independence must begin at the bottom and every village ought to be a Republic or Panchayat having powers. Gandhiji's dream has been translated into reality with the introduction of the three-tier Panchayati Raj system to ensure people's participation in rural reconstruction.

73RD AMENDMENT ACT, 1992

The passage of the Constitution (73rd Amendment) Act, 1992 marks a new era in the federal democratic set up of the country and provides constitutional status to the Panchayati Raj Institutions (PRIs). Consequent upon the enactment of the Act, almost all the States/UTs, except J&K, NCT Delhi and Uttaranchal have enacted their legislation. Moreover all the States/UTs except Arunachal Pradesh, NCT Delhi and Pondicherry, all other States/UTs have held elections. As a result, 2,32,278 Panchayats at village level; 6,022 Panchayats at intermediate level and 535 Panchayats at district level have been constituted in the country. These Panchayats are being manned by about 29.2 lakh elected representatives of Panchayats at all levels. This is the broadest representative base that exists in any country of the world – developed or under-developed.

The main features of the Act are – (i) a 3-tier system of Panchayati Raj for all States having population of over 20 lakh; (ii) Panchayat elections regularly every 5 years; (iii) reservation of seats for Scheduled Castes, Scheduled Tribes and women (not less than one-third of seats); (iv) appointment of State Finance Commission to make recommendations as regards the financial powers of the Panchayats and (v) constitution of District Planning Committees to prepare development plans for the district as a whole. As per the Constitution (73rd Amendment) Act, the Panchayati Raj Institutions have been endowed with such powers and authority as may be necessary to function as institutions of self-government and contains provisions of devolution of powers and responsibilities upon Panchayats at the appropriate level with reference to (a) the preparation of plans for economic development and social justice; and (b) the implementation of such schemes for economic development and social justice as may be entrusted to them.

FINANCIAL POWERS OF PANCHAYATI RAJ INSTITUTIONS

Article 243-G of the Constitution of India provides that the States/UTs may, by law, endow the Panchayats with such powers and authority as may be necessary to enable them to function as institutions of self-government and to prepare plans for economic development and social justice and their implementation including those in relation to the matters listed in the Eleventh Schedule.

As per Article 243-H of the Constitution, State Legislatures have been empowered to enact laws;

(i) to authorise a Panchayat to levy, collect and appropriate some taxes, duties, tolls and fees;

(ii) to assign to the Panchayat, some taxes, duties, tolls levied and collected by the State Government;

(iii) to provide for making grants-in-aid to the Panchayats from the Consolidated Fund of the State; and

(iv) to provide for constitution of such funds for Panchayats for crediting all money received by or on behalf of Panchayats and also the withdrawal of such money therefrom.

CONSTITUTION OF STATE FINANCE COMMISSIONS

Article 243-I of the Constitution provides for constitution of a State Finance Commission to review the financial position of

Panchayats and to make recommendations to the Governor regarding the principles governing the major issues mentioned in Article 243-H. All the States/UTs barring Arunachal Pradesh constituted State Finance Commissions and all the SFCs except Bihar have submitted their Reports to the respective State Governments. The States of Assam, Karnataka, Kerala, Madhya Pradesh, Punjab, Rajasthan, Tamil Nadu, Tripura and West Bengal have accepted most of the recommendations of the SFCs. Andaman & Nicobar Islands, Dadra & Nagar Haveli, Daman & Diu and Lakshadweep Islands have received Reports of the Finance Commission which will be placed on the table of Houses by the Ministry of Home Affairs being the nodal Ministry. States such as Andhra Pradesh, Himachal Pradesh, Haryana, Karnataka, Kerala, Madhya Pradesh, Maharashtra, Rajasthan, Sikkim, Tamil Nadu, Tripura, Uttar Pradesh, Assam, Punjab, Orissa and West Bengal have constituted second generation of State Finance Commissions. The Finance Commission for the four UTs has also been constituted by the Central Government. Constitution of State Finance Commission is now due in Goa, Manipur and Gujarat.

Eleventh Finance Commission

The Eleventh Finance Commission recommended Rs. 1600 crores per annum for rural local bodies. Out of total grants, an amount of Rs.197.06 crores was earmarked for development of data base on the finance of the Panchayats and an amount of Rs.98.61 crores for maintenance of accounts of Panchayats as the first charge on these grants. The Commission also recommended that in cases where elected local bodies are not in place, the Central Government should hold the grants for local bodies in trust on a non-lapsable basis during 2000-05 and that the Central Government would withhold a part of the recommended grants in case of such bodies to whom functions and responsibilities have not been devolved. Besides, the Commission recommended that Audit of accounts of the local bodies should be entrusted to the C&AG who may get it done through his own staff or by engaging outside agencies on payment of remuneration fixed by him and an amount of half-a-per cent of the total expenditure incurred by the local bodies should be placed with the C&AG for this purpose, and the report of the C&AG relating to audit of accounts of the

Panchayats should be placed before a Committee of the State Legislature constituted on the same lines as the Public Accounts Committee.

The Ministry of Finance releases Grants recommended by the Eleventh Finance Commission

- Towards realizing the vision of Mahatma Gandhi of every village being a republic through 3- tier system of Panchayati Raj.
- 2,32,278 Panchayats at village level; 6,022 Panchayats at intermediate level and 535 Panchayats at district level manned by about 29.2 lakh elected representatives, the broadest representative base that exists in any country.
- Panchayati Raj Institutions (PRIs) empowered to function as institutions of Self Government and to prepare plans for economic development and social justice and their empowerment. Panchayati Raj Institutions constitute the bedrock for the implementation of most of Rural Development Programmes.
- Strengthening of Gram Sabha as a vibrant forum of decentralized democracy and effective instrument for ensuring social audit, 1999-2000 observed as the 'Year of Gram Sabha'
- An All India Panchayat Adhyakshas Sammelan was held on 5th and 6th April, 2002 to get a feedback from the Adhyakshas in order to revitalize and strengthen Panchayati Raj Institutions in a time bound manner. In the Sammelan, a 'National Declaration' was adopted by consensus, resolving that State Governments would ensure the implementation of the Provisions of Constitution (73rd Amendment) Act, 1992 and Provisions of Panchayats (Extension to Schedules Areas), Act, 1996 in its true spirit by December, 31, 2002. (EFC) to the States. For the year 2000-2001 ad-hoc grants of Rs.57,186 lakhs were released to the States on "on Accounts" basis to the extent of 50% of allocated grants. EFC Grants were not released during 2000-2001 to the States of Andhra Pradesh, Assam, Bihar, Gujarat, Jharkhand and Punjab as elections were due. During the year 2001-02, funds were released to the tune

of Rs.2,06,944 lakhs. However, these grants were withheld for the States of Arunachal Pradesh, Jharkhand, Jammu & Kashmir and Punjab due to pending Panchayat elections. During the current year, an amount of Rs.3,56,822 lakhs has been released as on 4.12.2002.

INITIATIVES TAKEN BY THE MINISTRY

A Conference of the Chief Ministers on Panchayati Raj was held on 2nd August, 1997 at Vigyan Bhavan, New Delhi, under the chairmanship of Hon'ble Prime Minister to review the functioning of the Panchayati Raj Institutions where the outstanding issues like devolution of powers/ functions and responsibilities upon PRIs, setting up District Planning Committees; implementation of the reports of the State Finance Commissions, linkage of DRDAs with Zilla Parishads, training to Panchayati Raj elected representatives/functionaries were discussed in great detail. The Conference also called upon the concerned 8 States to enact the required State Legislation on the Provisions of the Panchayat (Extension to the Scheduled Areas) Act, 1996 before 23rd December, 1997.

Based on the detailed discussions, the Conference recommended setting up of two Committees – (a) the Committee of the Panchayat and the Tribal Development Ministers of the 8 States covered under Schedule V of the Constitution under the then Chairmanship of Minister (RA&E) to examine and to give their recommendations to enact the State legislation in consonance with the Central Act, 1996 before the cut off date i.e. 23rd December, 1997; and (b) the Committee of the Chief Ministers under the Chairmanship of Prime Minister to examine the issues regarding the devolution of powers, functions and responsibilities upon PRIs and to recommend measures to streamline the Panchayati Raj system.

The reports of the Committee of Panchayat and Tribal Development Ministers of the Schedule V States and the Committee of Chief Ministers under the Chairmanship of the Prime Minister have been circulated to the States for appropriate action. The important recommendations of the Committee of Chief Ministers were:

- Leave selection of beneficiaries to Gram Sabha.
- Waive requirement of Technical sanction for works upto Rs. 10,000.
- Innovate to provide adequate manpower support to the Gram Panchayats.
- Delegate total control over such manpower to Gram Panchayats.
- Zilla Parishad Chairpersons be made the Chairpersons of DRDAs.
- Provide reasonable opportunity of hearing to the PRIs before suspension/dismissal.
- Gram Panchayat President to be accountable solely to Gram Sabha.
- Expeditious constitution of District Planning Committees.

In order to ensure that Panchayati Raj Institutions function as instruments of local government, it is important that their functional and financial autonomy is guaranteed and transparency in their functioning is ensured This has to be accomplished in most of the States. The role of the Gram Sabha is, perhaps, the most important in ensuring the success of Panchayati Raj Institutions at the village level. The role of local people in conducting social audit and fixing responsibility on panchayat functionaries will be effectively ensured with Gram Sabha becoming active. It is essential that the village community perceives meetings of the Gram Sabha as useful. The most important factor for that is the empowerment of the Gram Sabha.

Another important factor for the success of the Panchayati Raj system is the need for transparency in the functioning of these bodies. Panchayats being closer to the people, their right to information and accessibility to the panchayats must be ensured This issue was discussed in the Chief Ministers Conference held on 2nd August, 1997 and the Committee of Chief Ministers as well. The Ministry had written to the States. The Hon'ble Prime Minister too, in his letter to the Chief Ministers, had urged that all relevant information on development schemes taken up by the Panchayat along with the budget for them should be displayed prominently in the Panchayat Office. Relevant records should be made available for inspection by members of the public. Photocopies of documents such as muster rolls, vouchers, estimates etc. can be made available to the public on payment of a nominal fee. Technical manuals may be prepared for execution of various works at the Panchayat level so that transparency can be ensured

The Ministry convened a Conference of State Ministers of Rural Development and Panchayati Raj on May 13, 1998. This meeting was inaugurated by the Hon'ble Prime Minister. The resolutions adopted in the Conference held on 13.5.98 are - (i) a Task Force for studying the structure and functioning of the Panchayats should be set up; (ii) provisions of 73rd Amendment Act and Central Act 40 will be complied with; (iii) Gram Sabhas should be convened on a single pre-determined day every quarter and (iv) care should be taken to respect the autonomy and independence of each tier of PRIs and to build up capability of the village level Panchayats. In pursuance of the resolution, a Task Force was constituted under the Chairmanship of the then Minister of State (Independent Charge), Ministry of Rural Areas & Employment to study the structure and functioning of PRIs. The State Governments have been requested to ensure that the Gram Sabha Meetings are convened once in each quarter preferably on - 26th January-Republic Day; Ist May-Labour Day; 15th August-Independence Day and 2nd October-Gandhi Jayanti.

The Government of India decided to observe the year 1999-2000 as the "Year of Gram Sabha". This is in recognition that the Gram Sabha is potentially the most significant institution for participatory and decentralised democracy. On 17th March, 1999, all Chief Ministers/Administrators have been requested to initiate measures to energise Gram Sabha in tune with the Seven Point minimal package during the 'Year of Gram Sabha':

A conference of Ministers of States in - charge of Panchayats Raj was held on 11th July, 2001 in New Delhi to discuss measures for strengthening Panchayati Raj Institutions towards implementation of the Constitution (73rd Amendment) Act, 1992. The major recommendations adopted in the Conference included:

Panchayat elections should be regularly held every 5 years.The States would issue detailed executive instructions devolving specific and substantial executive powers in respect of the 29

Subjects listed in the 11th Schedule, upon each tier of Panchayats by 31st March,2002.

- A task Force comprising senior officers from the Ministry of Rural Development and the State Governments would be set up suggesting how to operationalise administrative decentralization of powers and submit its report by 31st August, 2001.
- District Planning Committees would be set up by the remaining States/UTs by December, 2001.
- The State Acts would be amended (by 31st March, 2002) to bring them in conformity with the provisions of Panchayats (Extensions to the Schedules Areas) Act, 1996.
- The scope of State Government's intervention and control over the PRIs should be minimized and if there is any specific complaint against any Panchayat, it should be referred to a body similar to the "Ombudsman" in Kerala.
- The parallel bodies, if any, set by the States, should work under the supervision of Panchayats and the Gram Sabha.
- It was resolved that the following Four-point strategy for strengthening of Gram Sabhas will be implemented by the States:
  a) Awareness through print and electronic media, street plays and training to the elected Panchayat representatives.
  b) Participation of the community in the preparation of need-based action plans, their execution and monitoring.
  c) Transparency by displaying all relevant information on a bill board regarding estimates, availability of funds and expenditure on the works taken up by the Panchayats, making available relevant records for inspection by the public, and providing photocopies of documents, on demand , on payment of nominal charges.
  d) Social Audit should have binding legal outcome so as to curb corruption and misutilisation of funds.

The Chief Ministers of the States and Administrators of Union Territories were advised to implement the resolutions of the

Conference within the time frames agreed upon during the discussion.

In pursuance of the resolution of the Conference of State Ministers incharge of Panchayat Raj held in July, 2001 in Delhi, a Task Force on Devolution of Powers and Functions upon PRIs was constituted on 11th July, 2001 under the Chairmanship of Additional Secretary & Financial Advisor in the Ministry of Rural Development consisting of State Secretaries in-charge of Panchayati Raj in Assam, Chhattisgarh, Kerala, Karnataka, Uttar Pradesh and West Bengal and concerned Joint Secretary in the Ministry. The Task Force submitted its report on 31st August, 2001 within the time frame. The recommendations of the Task Force included:

(i) interse distribution of the 29 Subjects into activities/ tasks to be performed by different tiers of Panchayats,

(ii) enhancement of the financial resources of Panchayats,

(iii) provision by the State Government of "Untied" grants to enable Panchayats to utilise the same in conformity with local needs and priorities,

(iv) mandatory Social Audit by Gram Sabhas and

(v) availability of qualified/trained personnel, at various level, to assist Panchayati Raj Institutions in day-to-day working.

The Chief Ministers of States and Administrators of UTs were requested to initiate appropriate steps, keeping in view of recommendations of the Task Force, towards the completion of devolution of powers upon Panchayats by the end of March, 2002.

An All India Panchayat Adhyakshas Sammelan was held on 5th and 6th April 2002 in New Delhi with a view to getting a feed back from the Adhyakshas and revitalizing and strengthening the Panchayati Raj Institutions in the country in a time-bound manner. The discussions in the Sammelan focussed on the topics namely, i) Devolution of Powers & Functions to Panchayats, ii) Functioning of the Gram Sabha, iii) Planning for Development at the Grass-root Level, iv) Social Audit, v) Resource Mobilisation by the Panchayats and vi) Awareness Generation for the Rural Development Programmes and Capacity Building. Besides the Panchayat Adhyakshas, Union Ministers, State Ministers in-charge of Panchayats, Central and State Officials and representatives of

NGOs and International Organisation attended this Sammelan, which was inaugurated by the Prime Minister and also addressed by the Leader of Opposition. The National Declaration adopted by the Sammelan indicate, inter-alia that the States and Union Territories would initiate, by the end of December, 2002, the necessary measures :-

- to hold regular and timely Panchayat elections,
- to devolve funds, functions and functionaries to Panchayats,
- to constitute District Planning Committees and make them functional,
- to set up Ombudsman (to be headed by a retired Judge) to look into the complaints against the Panchayats,
- to ensure Parallel Bodies function under the guidance of the Panchayats,
- to amend the State Legislations to provide Panchayats adequate control over natural resources like, land, water, minor forest produce and minerals,
- to make legal provisions for accountability and transparency in the functioning of Panchayats in accordance with the 4-Point strategy -Awareness, Participation, Transparency and Social Audit and
- to strengthen the Gram Sabhas and Gram Panchayats.
- to devise an appropriate mechanism to provide significant non-budgetary resources in the form of loans with adequate maturities to PRIs, specifically to be used for such developmental projects as are planned and executed by PRIs themselves.
- to put in place an appropriate structure of incentives to recognise and encourage the Panchayats for outstanding performance, especially in respect of improvements effected in accepted Social Development Indicators.
- to discuss the need for an appropriate new Amendment to the Constitution to bring about speedy and effective devolution of financial and administrative powers to PRIs and to quickly initiate the process of bringing in the much needed new Constitution Amendment. The Sammelan also urges all the Political Parties and Members of Parliament

to pass the Amendment and thus usher in the era of Second Generation of Panchayati Raj Reforms.

The Ministry of Rural Development is currently considering ways of securing mandatory devolution of atleast some of the administrative and financial powers to Panchayati Raj Institutions by the State Governments.

The Ministry had introduced the Constitution (Eighty-seventh Amendment) Bill,1999 in the Parliament on 17.12.1999 to amend Article 243-C(2) and (5) of the Constitution to enable the State Legislatures to decide the methodology for election of members and chairpersons of Panchayats at the intermediate level and the district level.

It was decided to have wider consultations with all the political parties and the State Governments on the Bill. Accordingly, the comments of all the State Chief Ministers were sought in this behalf.

A meeting of Leaders of all Political Parties in the Parliament was held under the Chairmanship of the Hon'ble Prime Minister on 19th May, 2001 to seek the approval of all Political Leaders in respect of the Constitution (Eighty-seventh Amendment) Bill, 1999. Since no consensus was arrived at in the Meeting, it was decided to defer the Bill and to study further in wider context of Panchayati Raj in the country.

The provisions of the Panchayats (Extension to the Scheduled Areas) Act, 1996

This Act which came into force on 24th December, 1996, extends Panchayats to the Schedule-V areas of States such as Andhra Pradesh, Chhattisgarh, Jharkhand, Gujarat, Himachal Pradesh, Maharashtra, Madhya Pradesh, Orissa and Rajasthan. It intends to enable tribal society to assume control over their own destiny to preserve and conserve their traditional rights over natural resources. The State Governments were required to enact their legislation in accordance with the Provisions of Act before the expiry of one year i.e. 23rd December, 1997. All the States barring have enacted State Legislation to give effect to the provisions contained in The Provisions of the Panchayats (Extension to the Scheduled Areas) Act, 1996.

Issues Arising Out Of Implementation Of Part-IX of the Constitution and PESA, 1996

While the State Panchayati Raj Acts have been enacted, State Election Commission and State Finance Commissions have been set up and regular Panchayat elections have been held providing reservation for SCs/STs/Women in Panchayats, the results of actual implementation of the Constitution (73rd Amendment) Act, 1992 have fallen far short of expectations on the ground level.

- Though the political decentralisation has been largely successful, with elections held regularly and with ample participation of people, there is only minimum administrative and fiscal decentralisation, which remain de facto under the control of the State Governments.
- Panchayats have not given adequate responsibilities to levy and collect taxes, fees, duties or tolls. Panchayats should have been granted appropriate powers to generate their own resources.
- Recommendations of State Finance Commissions have been either accepted partially or implemented half-heartedly.
- Powers given to the State Election Commissions vary from State to State. These Commissions should have been given powers to deal all matter relating to Panchayat elections namely, delimitation of constituencies, rotation of reserved seats in Panchayats, finalislation of electoral rolls, etc.
- Gram Sabhas have not been empowered and strengthened to ensure people's participation and transparency in functioning of Panchayats as envisaged

There are certain problems, both with certain Central laws and State legislations as have been passed in pursuance of Act 40 of 1996. Certain crucial issues arise:

- Definition of Minor Forest Produce - the Indian Forest Act, 1927 defines timber as including within its definition, bamboo as well as cane. The Ministry of Environment and Forests define Minor Forest Produce to exclude bamboo and cane. While doing so, they have decided to adopt the definition of timber as given in the Indian Forest Act, 1927. (According to which timber includes not only trees but also bamboo and cane). In most States, tribals have been traditionally depending on bamboo and cane for their livelihood. However, for the last many years, Forest Corporations and Forest Departments have prevented tribals from having access to bamboo and cane while at the same time giving these to private industry at highly concessional rates. In many cases, tribals have been driven to desperation on account of this policy of State Forest Departments. It is felt that the definition of timber in the Central Act, 1927 is neither scientific nor equitable, and goes against the spirit of the provisions of Act 40 of 1996.

- Ownership of Minor Forest Produce :- There are also issues arising from the interpretation by the Ministry of Environment and Forests of the intention of Parliament regarding vesting of ownership of Minor Forest Produce in Gram Sabhas. The proposals made by the Ministry of Environment and Forests interpret the intention of Parliament as giving not ownership per se, but making available to the Gram Sabhas, residual profits of State Forest Corporations/ Federations. This necessarily means that according to the Ministry of Environment and Forests, State Forest Corporations/Federations will continue to trade in Minor Forest Produce and if there is any surplus, that surplus will be given to the Gram Sabhas. This Ministry has already taken up these issues with the Ministry of Environment and Forests.

Research & Development Work

A Research Advisory Committee headed by the Secretary (Rural Development) approves proposals from voluntary organizations/institutions on Action Research studies related to Panchayati Raj. The Ministry has commissioned several such studies on issues such as Performance of Panchayats, women empowerment, Awareness Campaign, implementation of PESA, 1996, etc.

TRAINING OF PANCHAYATI RAJ INSTITUTIONS

Under the Scheme Panchayat Development and Training (PD&T) central assistance is provided to the States, NGOs and other institutions for their efforts to impart training to the elected and official functionaries of the Panchayati Raj Institutions. The funding pattern under the scheme is as follows:

(a) 20% funding is provided for lodging and boarding and 50% for reproduction of training material and other items to State Governments;

(b) 100% Central assistance is provided to NGOs and other institutions.

The elements of support by Ministry of Rural Development under this scheme include the following:

* Expenditure on participation for training of elected representatives of Panchayati Raj Institutions including awareness generation programmes.
* Cost of expenditure on accommodation/ hiring of rooms.
* Audio/ Video training equipment expenditure.
* Workshops/Seminars, awareness generation campaigns on Panchayati Raj.
* Support for Mobile training facilities for training in Panchayati Raj.

Proposals received under the scheme are considered by the Training Research and Advisory Committee (TRAC) headed by the Secretary (RD). With the reallocation of work relating to capacity building of PRIs, to Training Division the proposals relating to capacity building of PRIs are being processed by Training Division for consideration by TRAC.

The Plan Outlay for this scheme for the year 2002-03 is Rs.5.00 crore.

The Central Outlay for training of Panchayati Raj Institutions during the Ninth Plan was Rs. 17.00 crores. During 2002-2003 an amount of Rs. 3.85 crores was allocated but it has been kept at Rs.1.98 crores only for the current year at RE stage for the Action Research Study/Workshop component.

2

Rural Housing

Housing is one of the basic requirements for human survival. For a normal citizen, owning a house provides significant economic security and dignity in society. For a shelterless person, possession of a house brings about a profound social change in his existence, endowing him with an identity, thus integrating him with his immediate social milieu.

There is a clear correlation between the poverty and the housing condition. The poor person either does not have a house or lives in an unserviceable kutcha house. According to the 1991 Census, around 3.1 million households are without shelter and another 10.31 million households reside in unserviceable kutcha houses.

Considering the magnitude of the problem, the Central Government announced in 1998 a National Housing and Habitat Policy which aims at providing 'Housing for All' and facilitating construction of 20 lakh additional housing units (13 lakh in Rural Areas and 7 lakh in Urban Areas) annually with an emphasis on extending benefits to the poor and the deprived. Government is committed to the goal of ending all shelterlessness by the end of the Xth Plan Period. For achieving these objectives a comprehensive Action Plan for Rural Housing has gone onstream.

INDIRA AWAAS YOJANA

The Government of India is implementing the Indira Awaas Yojana since the year 1985-86 with the objective of providing assistance primarily to the below poverty line (BPL) rural households belonging primarily to the Scheduled Castes, Scheduled Tribes and freed bonded labour categories. From the year 1993-

94, its scope has been extended to cover non-scheduled castes and scheduled tribes rural BPL poor subject to the condition that non SC/ST households shall not receive more than 40% of the IAY allocation. Benefits of the scheme have also been extended to the families of the ex-servicemen of the armed and paramilitary forces killed in action. 3% of the houses are reserved for the BPL physically and mentally challenged persons living in rural areas.

The ceiling on construction assistance under the Indira Awaas Yojana currently is Rs. 20,000/- per unit for plain areas and Rs. 22,000/- for hilly/ difficult areas. The ceiling on upgradation of a kutcha house to semi-pucca/pucca is Rs. 10,000/-. Under the IAY, Gram Sabha is empowered to select the beneficiaries. Further, the allotment of dwelling units should be in the name of female member of the beneficiary household. Alternatively, it can be allotted in the name of both husband and wife. Sanitary latrine and smokless chullah are the integral part of an IAY house. The construction of the house is the responsibility of the beneficiary. The IAY house is not to be constructed and delivered by any external agency such as government departments, NGOs, contractors, etc. Since inception of the scheme till December, 2002 about 92 lakh houses have been constructed under the IAY by incurring an expenditure of Rs. 15839.83 crores approximately.

The Action Plan for Rural Housing consists of the following elements:

I. Provision for upgradation of unserviceable kutcha houses in the Indira Awaas Yojana (IAY) in addition to the new construction.

II. Credit-cum- Subsidy Scheme for Rural Housing.

III. Innovative Stream for Rural Housing & Habitat Development.

IV. Rural Building Centres.

V. Samagra Awaas Yojana.

VI. Enhancement of equity contribution by Ministry of Rural Development to HUDCO.

VII. National Mission for Rural Housing & Habitat.

Physical and Financial Achievements under the Indira Awaas Yojana since inception till date

Year	Expenditure (Rs. In Crore)	Number of houses built
1985-86	57.93	51252
1986-87	149.18	160197
1987-88	235.37	169302
1988-89	149.65	139192
1989-90	188.50	186023
1990-91	213.07	181800
1991-92	263.01	207299
1992-93	238.81	192585
1993-94	481.00	372535
1994-95	500.38	390482
1995-96	1166.36	863889
1996-97	1385.92	806290
1997-98	1591.48	770936
1998-99	1803. 88	835770
1999-2000	1907.63	925679
2000-2001	2185.80	1170926
2001-2002*	2149.55	1171081
2002-2003**	1172.31	640829
Total	15839.83	9236067

* provisional

** up to 31.12.2002

Criteria of Allocation under Indira Awaas Yojana.

Allocation of funds under Indira Awaas Yojana to the States/ UTs is made based on the poverty ratios as approved by the Planning Commission and the rural housing shortage as per the Census 1991. Both parameters are given equal weightage.

Credit-Cum-Subsidy Scheme for Rural Housing

The Credit-Cum-Subsidy Scheme for Rural Housing was launched w.e.f. 1st April, 1999. The Scheme targets rural families having annual income upto Rs.32,000/-. While subsidy is restricted to Rs.10,000/-, the maximum loan amount that can be availed is Rs.40,000/-. The subsidy portion is shared by the Centre and the

State in 75:25 ratio. The loan portion to be disbursed by the commercial banks/Regional Rural Banks, housing finance institutions etc. Since inception of the Scheme upto 2001-2002, against the Central allocation of Rs. 288.00 crore, about 85564 houses were constructed by incurring an expenditure of Rs. 77.79 crore.

From the year 2002-2003, the Central allocation under IAY and CCSS has been combined.

Innovative Stream for Rural Housing and Habitat Development*

During 1999-2000, a Rural Housing Scheme namely Innovative Stream for Rural Housing & Habitat Development was launched with an objective of promoting and propagating the cost effective and environmental friendly construction technologies, materials, designs, etc. for suitable rural human settlements consistent with agro-climatic variation and natural disaster proneness. The Scheme is being implemented on project basis. Among those who may apply for assistance under the Scheme include recognized Educational/Technical Institutions, Corporate Bodies, Autonomous Societies, State Governments, Development Institutions and Credible NGOs with proven track record and experience in the field of Rural Housing. The maximum permissible assistance in case of an NGO/autonomous society is Rs. 20.00 lakh and for Government Agencies is Rs. 50.00 lakh. During 2002-2003, an amount of Rs. 10.00 crore has been allocated and Rs. 5.11 crore has been released so far to implement the projects. Since inception of the Scheme till date, 125 project proposals have been approved.

Setting up of Rural Building Centres*

The objectives of establishment of the Rural Building Centres are: (a) Technology transfer and information dissemination (b) Skill upgradation through training and (c) Production of cost effective and environment friendly materials/components. For setting up a Building Centre, a one time grant of Rs.15 lakh is provided. During 2002-2003, Rs. 3.00 crore has been allocated and 22 RBC proposals have been approved. Since inception of Scheme till date, 77 project proposals have been sanctioned. It is a project based demand driven Scheme.

SAMAGRA AWAAS YOJANA

Samagra Awaas Yojana is a comprehensive housing Scheme launched in 1999-2000, with a view to ensuring integrated provision of shelter, sanitation and drinking water. During the first phase of its implementation, it has been decided to take up Samagra Awaas Yojana in one block each of 25 districts of 24 States and one Union Territory which have been identified for implementing participatory approach under the Accelerated Rural Water Supply Programme. The existing schemes of housing, drinking water and sanitation follow the normal funding pattern. However, a special central assistance of Rs.25 lakhs is provided for each block for undertaking the overall habitat development and Information, Education and Communication (IEC) activities with 10% contribution coming from the people. During 2002-2003, an amount of Rs. 0.43 crore has been released. Since inception of the Scheme, 33 proposals have been approved.

PRADHAN MANTRI GRAMODAYA YOJANA (GRAMIN AWAAS)

Pradhan Mantri Gramodaya Yojana : Gramin Awaas (PMGY:GA) was launched from the year 2000-2001. The implementation of PMGY has been reviewed by the Planning Commission. As a follow up action of this review as well as the feed back received from the States, Planning Commission has decided to directly manage the Programme once again as was being done under the earlier Basic Minimum Services (BMS) programme from the year 2002-2003.

Equity Support to HUDCO

To meet the housing requirement of economically weaker households in rural areas and to improve the outreach of housing finance in rural areas, equity support to HUDCO has been hiked from Rs.5 crore in the Eighth Plan Period to Rs.350 crore during the Ninth Five Year Plan period and the entire amount has been released to HUDCO. As per information received, HUDCO has sanctioned 23.54 lacs dwelling units under 2 million housing programme in last 4 years i.e. an average of 5.89 lacs dwellings per year. Above sanctions were in addition to a sanction of

Rs.1136.39 crore as against HUDCO's allocation for normal rural housing in last 4 years of Rs. 873.70 crore. This loan has helped to sanction a further 26.65 lakh dwelling units. On an average HUDCO has sanctioned approx. 12.54 lakh rural dwellings per year in the last 4 years, as against approx. 9-10 lacs dwellings to be sanctioned based on the MoU signed with the Ministry.

During 2002-2003, an amount of Rs. 50 crore has been allocated for Equity support to HUDCO.

National Mission for Rural Housing and Habitat

A National Mission for Rural Housing and Habitat has been set up by the Ministry of Rural Development to facilitate the induction of science and technology inputs, on a continuous basis, in the sector and to provide convergence to technology, habitat and energy-related issues in order to provide affordable shelter for all in the rural areas, within a specified time-frame, and through community participation. Towards this end, an Executive Council under the Chairmanship of the Minister of Rural Development and an Empowered Committee under the Chairmanship of Secretary (Rural Development) has been constituted. A Working Group was constituted by the Empowered Committee to specify the aims and objectives of the Mission, firm up specific time framework to achieve these aims and objectives, formulate a road map to facilitate the entry of private capital in Housing development in the rural areas, shortlist the agencies which could undertake the task of preparing a techno-legal regime for rural planning for consideration by this Ministry etc. The Action Plan prepared by the Working Group is under consideration.

Training Programmes

From the year 2000-01, it was decided by the Ministry that State Specific programmes will be organized through HSMI with the objective of promoting State specific technologies, materials, designs etc. for cost effective rural housing. Besides, the HSMI will also conduct Training of Trainers (TOT) for SIRD at regional level. During the current financial year 2002-2003, one training programme on Rural Housing project formulation for the States of Jammu & Kashmir, Uttaranchal and Himachal Pradesh has been conducted by the HSMI at Shimla from 24.12.2002 to 28.12.2002.

NATIONAL WORKSHOP ON RURAL HOUSING AND HABITAT DEVELOPMENT-2002

A "National Workshop on Rural Housing and Habitat Development" was organized by the Ministry of Rural Development in collaboration with CAPART on 18-19th October, 2002 at New Delhi.

The purpose of the Workshop was to sensitize the Government and the Non-Government Agencies about opportunities and fund availability under the various Rural Housing Schemes being implemented by the Government of India. It also provided a platform for increased Government-NGO interaction and to identify critical issues (both at policy and implementation levels) which require immediate attention of the Ministry, the State Governments and NGOs. Discussions generally structured around the concept papers covering a variety of subjects in the Rural Housing Sectors such as:

1. Networking, training and capacity building of Voluntary organizations
2. Financing options in rural housing sector
3. Cost-effective Innovative Housing in rural areas
4. Public – NGO – Private Partnership in rural housing
5. Calamity resistant technologies, building material, appropriate designs and structures. The recommendations of National Workshop on Rural Housing and Habitat Development are: · Traditional techniques, methods and skills in building construction in rural areas should further be improved/developed and promoted.

- Rural Building Centres should be developed as an enterprise.
- Artisans connected with housing should be trained further in the use of innovative technologies, materials, methods etc.
- In case, the use of innovative technologies increases the cost of the house, incremental/skeleton concept may be allowed
- Housing without habitat is incomplete. Habitat Development should be made an integral part of housing.

NEW INITIATIVE TAKEN UNDER THE RURAL HOUSING SCHEMES

Provision of 5% allocation for Natural Calamities and other emergent situation under the IAY.

With the approval of the Cabinet, it has been decided to earmark 5% of the allocated funds in a financial year to meet contingencies arising out of natural calamities and other emergent situations under the Indira Awaas Yojana. The Guidelines to this effect have already been circulated to all States/ UTs.

DEVELOPMENTS FOR WOMEN WOMEN AND PANCHAYATI RAJ

In the history of Panchayati Raj, April 23, 1993 is a landmark day. As on this day the institution of Panchayati Raj was accorded constitutional status through the Constitution (Seventy-third Amendment) Act, 1992, thereby seeking to transform Mahatma Gandhi's dream of Gram Swaraj into reality. The UPA government has made Panchayati Raj as one of the pivots of the Common Minimum Programme. A full fledged Ministry status was accorded to Panchayati Raj with the two key functions of economic development and social justice.

Panchayati Raj (local self-governance) holds the key to garibi hatao (alleviation of poverty). This can come about only if the institutions of Panchayati Raj are strengthened at the grassroot level. The Government has identified 16 major dimensions to this whole process adding two more rural business hubs and IT enabled e-governance, as also 100 different steps that need to be taken to strengthen this process. It's a movement from empowerment to entitlement and then on to enrichment, according to the Minister of Panchayati Raj, Shri Mani Shankar Aiyar.

A fresh national impetus has been given to the devolution of powers, responsibilities and finances through the Seven Round Tables of State Ministers of Panchayati Raj which arrived by consensus, at 150 recommendations pertaining to 18 dimensions of Panchayati Raj.

Women hold a key place in making Panchayati Raj effective. It is clear that women have been able to enlarge their representation beyond a minimum 33.33 per cent prescribed by the Constitution.

In Karnataka 45 per cent of the elected offices are occupied by women and in Uttar Pradesh 54 per cent of the Zilla Panchayat Pradhans are women. Similarly in Tamil Nadu 36 per cent of the chairpersons of gram panchayats are women. In promoting the larger social objectives through PRIs, States have been sensitized to issues of gender empowerment so that unintended consequences of such policies do not diminish the role of women in Panchayati Raj.

The Centre has the responsibility for implementing in letter and spirit, the provisions of the Constitution relating to Panchayats and Nagarpalikas. Efforts are being made towards evolving the Local Self Government institutions in States and Union Territories as a role model. Considerable progress has been made in this regard in Damn and Diu and Nagar Haveli.

The Indian voter is one and indivisible. The principle of parity between parliamentary and assembly elections, on the one hand and panchayat elections, on the other, must therefore be maintained, especially as it is noticed that peoples participation in panchayat elections is substantial and generally equal to or higher than in parliamentary/assembly elections. While all matters relating to panchayat elections have been vested by the Constitution in State legislatures/governments, there is a need to work towards commonality, if not uniformity, in election procedures and provisions.

In the southern part, Karnataka shines as an example in implementing and strengthening PRIs. Karnataka has initiated implementation of 77 of the 106 recommendations of the Round Tables. The amendments made to the Karnataka Panchayat Raj Act in October 2003 and the subsequent steps taken to strengthen the Grama Sabha; create and empower Ward Sabhas; complete Activity Mapping; and rationalize and simplify schemes entrusted to the Panchayats are examples to be emulated countrywide. The monitoring of the actualization of devolution by the Legislative Committees is a significant step in the strengthening of Panchayats in the State.

The entrustment of schemes by the State Governments to Panchayats in the current year's budget is a giant step forward in matching the functional transfer with funds. Through this process, the Panchayats now handle in excess of Rs. 3,500 crore of Plan funds per year.

West Bengal has been at the forefront of the empowerment of Panchayats from 1973 onwards. In 1994, it enacted its State Panchayat Legislation to conform to the 73rd Amendment to the Constitution, so as to establish Panchayats as institutions of local self-Government in the letter and spirit of Part IX of the Constitution. The steps taken in this State to institutionalise peoples' participation through Panchayati Raj, stand testimony to its sustained commitment towards Panchayati Raj.

The panchayat system appears to provide a systematic training ground for the people who will take top leadership positions in the country in the future. Women are making impressive strides in this quest for leadership. It appears that the leadership of the ordinary people is being established in West Bengal. Through the panchayat system, the voiceless seemed to have gained the voice.

With commitment to democratic decentralization, these bodies are on their way to becoming truly self-governing institutions.

Through the experience of the Indian Panchayat Raj Institutions (PRI) 1 million women have actively entered political life in India. The 73rd and 74th Constitutional Amendment Acts, which guarantee that all local elected bodies reserve one-third of their seats for women, have spearheaded an unprecedented social experiment which is playing itself out in more than 500,000 villages that are home to more than 600 million people. Since the creation of the quota system, local women-the vast majority of them illiterate and poor-have come to occupy as much as 43% of the seats, spurring the election of increasing numbers of women at the district, provincial and national levels. Since the onset of PRI, the percentages of women in various levels of political activity have risen from 4-5% to 25-40%.

According to Indian writer and activist Devaki Jain, "the positive discrimination of PRI has initiated a momentum of change. Women's entry into local government in such large numbers, often more than the required 33.3 %, and their success in campaigning, including the defeat of male candidates, has shattered the myth that women are not interested in politics, and have no time to go to meetings or to undertake all the other work that is required in political party processes...PRI reminds us of a central truth: power is not something people give away. It has to be negotiated, and sometimes wrested from the powerful."

Contrary to fears that the elected women would be rubber stamp leaders, the success stories that have arisen from PRI are impressive. A government-financed study, based on field work in 180 villages in the states of Uttar Pradesh, Rajasthan and Madhya Pradesh, and coordinated by the Center for Women's Development Studies in New Delhi, has found that a full two-thirds of elected women leaders are actively engaged in learning the ropes and exercising power. Says Noeleen Heyzer, executive director of UNIFEM, "This is one of the best innovations in grass-roots democracy in the world."

Women leaders in the Panchayati Raj are transforming local governance by sensitizing the State to issues of poverty, inequality and gender injustice. Through the PRI, they are tackling issues that had previously gone virtually unacknowledged, including water, alcohol abuse, education, health and domestic violence. According to Sudha Murali, UNICEF Communications Officer in Andhra Pradesh, women are seeing this power as a chance for a real change for them and for their children and are using it to demand basic facilities like primary schools and health care centres.

The PRI has also brought about significant transformations in the lives of women themselves, who have become empowered, and have gained self-confidence, political awareness and affirmation of their own identity. The panchayat villages have become political training grounds to women, many of them illiterate, who are now leaders in the village panchayats. Says Sudha Pillai, joint secretary in India's Ministry for Rural Development, "It has given something to people who were absolute nobodies and had no way of making it on their own. Power has become the source of their growth."

By asserting control over resources and officials and by challenging men, women are discovering a personal and collective power that was previously unimaginable. This includes women who are not themselves panchayat leaders, but who have been inspired by the work of their sisters; "We will not bear it," says one woman. Once we acquire some position and power, we will fight it out...The fact that the Panchayats will have a minimum number of women [will be used] for mobilizing women at large." It is this critical mass of unified and empowered women which will push forward policies that enforce gender equity into the future.

An observation by Deepak Tiwari in This Week, India's No.1 Weekly News Magazine, displays the promising future made possible by the PRI. He notes, "'Learning politics' is the latest fad for young village girls, who dream of joining the growing band of women panchayat representatives, 164,060 at last count, in the state."

It is a story about 330,000 women who have entered the arena of formal politics. This number will soon rise to more than 1 million women. These are women who have been elected to local councils by the processes of classical democracy: universal adult franchise; political party campaigns in a multi-party system; and mandatory elections every five years. As elected members of local government, the power these women have is real. This includes the power to decide both the direction and pace of local development and also to administer and monitor the implementation of those decisions.

Significantly, the remit of these local councils mirrors the themes of the World Summit for Social Development, held in Copenhagen in 1995: poverty eradication (usually economic programmes targeted towards the poor); social security programmes such as welfare for children, the old and the disabled; and the social sectors of education, health, women and development. The success story of the women of India is that they are beginning to translate these global themes into policies and programmes at the local level. The story begins with a law passed in 1983 in the southern state of Karnataka. This law included a clause that 25 percent of the seats in local councils would be reserved for women. The elections to these councils were held in 1987. On 1 May 1987, the Janata Dal (the party that won the elections) called a convention of all the 56,000 elected representatives, of whom 25 percent were women. It was a wonderful sight to see 14,000 women in the audience, shining bright, 80 percent of whom were participating in politics for the first time, thrilled with their victory at the hustings. Even those who had passed the law, and advocated for its positive discrimination in the interests of gender equity, were stunned.

By 1995, the presence of women in local government had increased by many multiples, as the whole nation had introduced this political/ administrative change to reserve seats in local councils for women through the 73rd and 74th amendments to the Constitution. In India, we call this new system the Panchayat Raj Institutions system (PRI). The women whom PRI has brought into politics are now governing, in the formal sense of the word. They are the government for their area, be it one village, or a larger area such as 100 villages or a district.

The entire process of restructuring the national political and administrative system started as recently as January 1994. It is, therefore, too early to assess how far women's entry into formal structures of government as a result of PRI has changed the direction and practices of development, especially in relation to sensitive packages of social and economic security, the reduction of inequality, the safeguarding of livelihoods and the environment, and the reduction of domestic violence and other forms of oppression of and discrimination against women; in other words, all the elements of a feminist agenda for social and economic progress.

The 73rd Amendment to the Constitution of India

This Amendment, dated 24 April 1993, directed all state legislature to amend their respective Panchayat legislation to conform to the Constitution Amendment, within one year. All the states complied and adopted new Panchayat legislation by 23 April 1994. By April 1995 all the states were expected to complete decisions on new Panchayats-and those who delayed ran the risk of losing central government assistance, as announced by the Prime Minister.

Why?

The Constitution of India was adopted in 1950. It had envisaged (Article 40) that "the State shall take steps to organise village Panchayats and endow them with such powers and authority as may be necessary to enable them to function as units of self-government." This provision of the Constitution was primarily advisory. In the following four decades, some sporadic and indifferent steps were taken by some of the state governments to organise Panchayats; but they were invariably denied any meaningful powers and authority and, worst of all, the elections were seldom held at 5-year intervals as required. This deplorable state of affairs was an affront to the Constitution (Article 40) and there was growing demand in the country for a definite constitutional mandate to secure periodical and regular elections to Panchayats just as in the case of Parliament and State Assemblies.

The features of the Act in brief are:

- Panchayats shall have a uniform five-year term and elections to constitute new bodies shall be completed before the expiry of the term. In the event of dissolution, elections will be compulsorily held within six months.
- In all the Panchayats, seats shall be reserved for Scheduled Castes(SCs) and Scheduled Tribes(STs) in proportion to their population and one-third of the total number of seats will be reserved for women. One-third of the offices of chairpersons of Panchayats at all levels shall also be reserved for women.
- Offices of the chairpersons of the Panchayats shall be reserved in favour of SCs and STs in proportion to their population in the State.
- The Gram Sabha will be a body comprising all the adult members registered as voters in the Panchayat area.

It is too early to assess how far women's leadership of local development has facilitated a more just and peaceful society. Nevertheless, we have some indications of women's impact on the administration and on their male colleagues' attitudes towards women's priorities and women's capabilities, which this paper will discuss. To make this assessment as quantifiable as possible, we must address both the national and the state level. As the PRI process came into effect nationally only in 1993, the information on impact is still not adequate, although there is some preliminary and anecdotal evidence on which to draw. A more detailed assessment may be made at the state level, and this paper will discuss the evidence from the state of Karnataka, which is one of the two states that has experienced a full 5-year term of this new administrative and political regime (1987-1992), with about 14,000 women in the development councils. With this in mind, I have prepared this paper to:

- bring to you the voices of the women concerned, in assessing the impact of the constitutional change;
- draw from this experience some inferences regarding the characteristics of women's leadership at the grassroots;
- comment on the outcome, especially the indications of success;
- argue the case for political restructuring, for a widening of representation, as a key to sustainable development with equity;
- identify some interventions, by both international agencies and the global movements committed to the elimination of inequality and poverty, which could strengthen grassroots women leaders; and
- relate my own involvement in this story, not as evidence of personal achievement, but rather to indicate the role of an individual in collective action.

But the measures of this success must be somewhat different from the indicators that are commonly used to identify success stories. Examples of such commonly used indicators include the capability (vision, insight, commitment) of organisations of women, or NGOs, to establish movements which generate ideas and prototypes for people-led development activities (e.g. the Green Belt Movement in Kenya and the Sewa Movement in India), or the success of organised advocacy and pressure groups, such as the "Support Stockings" in Sweden and the National Women's Coalition of South Africa, in transforming political representation by putting direct pressure on the State from outside.

But in this story, the success of PRI lies in the possibility of women transforming the State from within. I argue that this new arrangement provides the first step to converting grassroots leadership into State leadership, which many feel is the key to ushering in equitable, people-led development. What appears to be happening is that as women enter the structures of governance in large numbers, they are changing these structures so that they reflect more closely the concerns of women. This is different from the usual process by which a small number of grassroots representatives are elected and can easily be isolated and forced to make compromises. The sheer

number of women that PRI has brought into the political system has made a difference. But the difference is also qualitative, because these women are bringing their experience in governance of civic society into governance of the State. In this way, they are making the State sensitive to issues of poverty, inequality and gender injustice. Measuring and assessing these qualitative changes is not easy, however. Furthermore, the immeasurable is sometimes invaluable. Thus, while much in this document is subjective and preliminary in character, it gives a strong indication of positive outcomes for gender-equitable governance, and is very suggestive of areas for future research.

Who are these women?

The women who have entered politics through PRI are from local areas, representing various backgrounds; rich and poor, dominant and oppressed social classes, educated and illiterate, working and not-working. In a survey of elected women in Karnataka between 1987-89, the following picture emerged (Shashikala et al 1989):

- Age: They were usually young women, 25-45 years old (more than 50 percent were 25-35 years old, while 75 percent were below 45 years of age). The explanation given is that older women still feel a reluctance to go into public office. Elected men, on the other hand, were usually of an older age-group. It was noted that experience in political work was an advantage for all candidates, from which men were more often able to benefit.
- Political Experience: 20 percent of the women, compared to 80 percent of the men, had previous political experience.
- Caste: The pattern of caste representation was the same as before the constitutional change. 60 percent of the elected representatives, whether men or women, were from the dominant castes. However, a reservation for the

"downtrodden" castes and minorities added a margin of representation for these groups.

- Education: Most of the women elected were illiterate. Here too the variations were striking between men and women, with 20 percent of men being professionally-educated compared to 5 percent of women.
- Occupation: The majority of women declared themselves as homemakers. However, we know that this is a broad category which includes heavy work, including income-generating activity.

POSITIVE DISCRIMINATION WORKS

The percentages of women at various levels of political activity has shifted dramatically as a result of this constitutional change, from 4-5 percent before PRI to 25-40 percent after PRI. At the local level, the numbers of women representatives have increased from no more than 6 in each assembly, usually less than 1 percent in these bodies and that too as nominated or co-opted members, to a total of 330,000 and a presence sometimes in excess of the mandatory one third, the highest proportion being 43 percent. In other words, in some cases women have moved out of reserved constituencies.

Could these women have entered these elected bodies in such large numbers, without the reservation of seats, and the considerable pressure it put on the parties to field women candidates? There is evidence to suggest that women would not have entered these councils in these numbers were it not for this constitutional mandate. It was the pressure of national law, combined with the political imperative of winning elections, that changed political parties' perception of women's limited capacity for public office.

In this regard, it is interesting to note the genesis of the constitutional mandate. The legislative action which enacted the reservation of seats for women did not result from any significant campaign by the women's movement, nor from an unusually gender-sensitive leadership of a political party. There may have been some pressure from the women's wing of the Janata Dal party, in which there was a history of demanding more places for women in the allocation of constituencies for the central parliament. But this was less significant than the fact that, at that time, the leadership of the Janata Dal party was projecting an image of being "people-led" and progressive and whose political philosophy (which could be deemed an amalgam of democratic socialism and Gandhian philosophy) regarded the issues of justice between the genders as a part of their broader concept of justice. By contrast, in west Bengal, where decentralised government was also introduced at the same time, the political party in power (namely, the Marxist CPI(M) party) did not make this special accommodation for women in the first phase. In other words, PRI cannot simply be equated with progressive politics, as there was not a special place for gender within a Marxist political analysis of the class struggle.

Thus the story I am telling is a complex one. Its plot-line is not a conventional tale of excluded women fighting to gain entry into bastions of male power. Women's entry in large numbers into local government arose from a mixture of political opportunism and an ethical sensibility that regarded the implications of gender as integral, rather than peripheral, to the creation of a more just society. Critically, it arose from the actions of both women and men.

Nor should the effects of the PRI system be described simplistically. Increasing the representation of women has not automatically led to a more gendered analysis of the issues confronting local government. Nor has it necessarily raised the profile of women's needs and interests in the policy agenda, particularly as surveys indicate that most of the women were elected because of the status of their husbands, fathers or sons and that such women often act as proxies for men's views at the councils, being advised by their male relatives. However, as one woman elected through PRI has noted:

> It is true we came through our men the first time and are often proxies for them, but we know what it is about and will come on our own next time.

Thus, the positive discrimination of PRI has initiated a momentum of change. Women's entry into local government in such large numbers, often more than the required 33.3 percent, and their success in campaigning, including the defeat of male candidates, has shattered the myth that women are not interested in politics, and have no time to go to meetings or to undertake all the other work that is required in political party processes.

PRI has also highlighted the intersection between gender interests and social class, for its reservation of seats has enabled poor and marginalised women to demonstrate their deep political consciousness and interest in obtaining power. For them, politics and elections are very practical routes out of poverty and instruments of social change. The next two sections will explore the ways in which PRI is beginning to transform both women and the system of governance itself.

The History of Women's Inclusion in Political Representation in India

1946 There were 16 women out of 150 members in the Constituent Assembly.

1957 When Panchayat Raj was first introduced, the concept was to co-opt two women "who are interested in work among women and children" (Balwantrai Mehta Committee Report).

1961 Maharashtra Zilla Parishad and Panchayat Samiti Act of 1961 provided for the "nomination of one or two women" to the Panchayat bodies "in case women were not elected".

1973 West Bengal Panchayat Act, also provided for co-opting 2 women.

1976 The Report of the Committee on the Status of Women (CSWI) demanded representation of women in Panchayat as well as the establishment of "All-Women Panchayat at village level".

1978 In Maharashtra Panchayat, only 6 women were elected although 314 were nominated. In most parts of India, women were brought into Panchayat only through co-option.

1983 As many as 25 percent of seats were reserved for women in the Karnataka Zilla Parishads, Taluk Panchayat Samitis, Mandal Panchayat and Nyaya Panchayat Act of 1983. Elections under this Act were delayed for various reasons and could only be held in 1987. Some 14,000 women were elected out of 30,000 candidates who contested.

1988 Elections were held in Uttar Pradesh for 74,000 village Sabhas, the first elections for 22 years. There was provision made for the co-option of only one woman.

In Panchayat elections, less than one percent of women came through elections.

1991 Orissa Panchayat Samiti provided for "not less than one third of the total number of seats to be reserved for women". Elections were held in 1992 and over 22,000 women were elected. In Kerala Districts Councils elections, while 30 percent seats were reserved for women, 35 percent seats were won by women.

1993 About 71,000 women candidates contested elections and with 33 percent seat reservation, 24,900 women came in through the ballot box.

1994 In Madhya Pradesh 150,500 women were elected to village, block and zilla Panchayats.

33 percent of seats were reserved for women in village Panchayat and women captured 43 percent of the seats.

Transforming Women

Women's experience of PRI has transformed many of them. The elements of this transformation include empowerment, self-confidence, political awareness and affirmation of identity.

Empowering women

Women have gained a sense of empowerment by asserting control over resources, officials and, most of all, by challenging men (Jain 1980; Anveshi 1993). Men and their habits, long outside the realm of female influence, seem to be a major concern of elected women. For example, Deviramma, a 50-year-old woman from the "Golla", or cowherd community, kept cattle and sold curd until recently. Today, she is president of the Yeliyur Gram Panchayat, one of the 5,611 Gram Panchayats constituted in December 1993 under the Karnataka Panchayat Raj Act 1993. As quoted by Rai et al (1995), she states:

If we are outspoken, they-the men-call us brazen and dub us shameless. But now we don't care because we know we have access to people who will have to hear us. The day we have our

Gram Panchayat meeting, the men and the people at home mock us-that's when we bring out books and show them what we know.

Nevertheless, Deviramma reports that: "Our secretary, who is a male, doesn't let us talk at the meetings", a complaint that she has already made to the Deputy Commissioner. Similarly, 50-year-old Sibamma has now become an articulate Scheduled Caste member of the Brahamasandra Gram Panchayat. She says (Rai et al 1995):

The men have always ridiculed us, and perceived us as incapable of the management of public affairs. We now make up one third of the councils. This adds to our sense of strength. We must be 50 percent or more. We must overpower them with our numbers.

Women are also aware that their strength comes not only from their numbers but also from their knowledge and skills, for example literacy. Thus, women see training as an important part of their empowerment. Many NGOs have seized on this as a fundamental issue and have begun to focus on the training of women. Clearly this is necessary, but the danger of too narrow a focus is to suggest that it is only women who need training. What the presence of women politicians has done is to invert the conventional hierarchies as to who are the teachers and who are the taught. Such women are making it clear that it is the male extension officers who need training, and not just the female representatives. This is an important message for donors and other funders of training, who have tended to assume in the past that the objects of their support must be women.

Women's empowerment challenges traditional ideas of male authority and supremacy. It is unsurprising, then, that PRI has been opposed by some men. Ratanprabha Chive (Ratna) is the sarpanch(head) of the seven halets(hamlets) that comprise the Ghera Purandar Panchayat. Ratna was beaten up as soon as she assumed office by her rival who could not accept the fact that a female had outwitted him (Rai et al 1995). Today Ratna puts forward proposals in this male-dominated office and poses questions when she is unsatisfied. She says:

Whenever there is any tension in the villages, they come to me and I have learnt how to sort out the problem. Many people have realised that it is indeed a waste of time to make a complaint to the police chowki(station).

She has launched programmes for adult education, digging wells for drinking water and repairing school buildings. She seems to have tackled the political and bureaucratic system which is complicated for a women who has studied only up to Standard 7 (the public education system runs from Standard 1-12). As Ratna says:

It is not the education that matters so much here. It is the grit and determination, which a woman has in plenty.

Self-confidence gained through belonging to local organisations seems critical to enabling women to step out of unequal relationships (Antrobus 1985; ISST 1992). This sense of freedom is even more profound when the group to which women belong is the PRI. This freedom is carried into the very activity of politics by these women. There is a visible difference, a sense of excitement, in the women of rural India.

We are better representatives than men, as we can always be found at home in the kitchen or in the nearby fields. Men wander about, they are either in the town or the beer shops.

Nagamma was an elected member, from a reserved constituency, but she won against a male Scheduled Caste member, which was a very unusual occurance in the Panchayat Raj elections. The villagers in the area who were interviewed during this study were unanimous in their view that this woman was the most effective among all the female elected members of the mandal, a view which was also shared by the Pradhan(the head of the village).

Not all men have opposed PRI and the changes it has brought. Kultikori, a big village in West Bengal, elected an all-woman Panchayat in 1993. When it was time to decide on party candidates for the May 1993 elections, all the members of the male-dominated body stepped down.

They asked their party, the CPI(M), to field the young women of the Ganatantrik Mahila Samiti (the women's wing of the party) who had done remarkable work in eradicating illiteracy in the village. The CPI(M) fielded women candidates in all 11 seats of the Panchayat, and they won (Rai et al 1995).

PRI has given many women a greater understanding of the workings of politics, in particular the importance of political parties. Vijayalakshmi was a Congress-I member of the Mandal, a homemaker, of Munnuru village. She wanted party politics to operate in the elections to Mandals because the party bureaucracy (at the State level) usually controls its members in the Mandals. Without the party, no one else would be able to control them.

The party functionaries and the leaders are well-informed of the activities of the Mandal members, and they take some care to see that they function in such a way as not to jeopardise the outcome of elections, which, since 1993, means that female members must be respected. Kamalamma is a Scheduled Caste member and belonged to the Janata Party. She used to roll beedis to earn some money, and remained at home most of the time. She says that the influence of the political parties is such that now persons from deprived groups have a better chance of being elected members. Earlier, only persons with money and of the upper castes could be elected to any position of importance.

On the other hand, some women's involvement in PRI has helped them affirm their identity as women with particular and shared experiences. A woman at a Panchayat meeting in Karnataka stated (SSF 92):

When we meet we work together as women, for our lobby. We don't take much notice of our party identities.

Such women seem to be drawn to an identity above caste or party. This self-perception arises from two sources: from women's own sense of their shared experience and from attitudes and imagery imposed on them by the men. The men see these new political actors as women not as party colleagues. Party politics, a necessary condition for classical democracy, is competitive, but the women bring a non-competitive or cooperative ethic as they are drawn to work together across party lines and seem to have similar interests. Gender can supersede class and party lines. Women have opened up the possibility for politics to have not only new faces but a new quality.

PRI has helped to change local government beyond simply increasing the numerical presence of women. There is now a minority of women who are in politics because of their leadership qualities or feminist consciousness, for example, the women who were formerly part of the Sanghas of the Mahila Samakhya Programme, an awareness-raising, group-based programme. Visible changes in the articulation of ideas and leadership qualities exhibited by this minority were noted in the survey between 1987, the first year, and 1990 (ISS 1994). The difference women are making to local government is becoming evident in different priorities and different values (Jain L.C. 1994).

Some of the ways in which women, through PRI, are changing governance are evident in the issues they choose to tackle; water, alcohol abuse, education, health and domestic violence. For example, forty teams of women in Sonbhadra (Uttar Pradesh) area had carried out systematic yatra, or processions, covering ten villages each, or 400 villages in all, to explain the salient features of the 73rd Amendment and the place given in it to women. In the discussions that took place during these yatras, women voiced clear priorities. For nearly 90 percent of the women, the top priority was water. They expressed a need for clean water for fields, for their cattle and for their families. They said life was unbearable and cultivation impossible without developing the water resources of the area. Even as they were determined to prevent the outflow of water from their areas, they were equally determined to prevent the inflow of liquor into their area.

We have been ruined by liquor. We are being ruined day after day. The day's wages are drunk by the men-folk. There is no money for groceries, hence no cooking.

Alochana, a centre for documentation and research of women in Pune, found that only two of the nine members in Bittargaon could sign their names. However, in this village which has a 16,000 population, Alochana found out that the women have "learnt to keep accounts from the local school teachers and the gram sevaks(rural workers). They have put an end to gambling and have come down heavily on liquor dens." The policy they adopted was to "shut the door on every drunken husband." Any protest made by them or children is met by physical assault.

We will not bear it. Once we acquire some position and power, we will fight it out. We know that it is not going to be easy because this battle will be carried out in each home. But the fact that the

Panchayats will have a minimum number of women we will use that strength for mobilising women at large and keep liquor out, as a priority.

Women are also taking action against child marriage and child domestic labour, whilst promoting girl-child education, as is evident from the many success stories from Nellore, the heart of the successful anti-arrack struggle (Rohde 1994; Anveshi 1993).

We want education for our children. There are schools and teachers who draw their salaries regularly. They mark the attendance of non-existence students in their registers. But they scarcely come to the schools. With this sorry state of affairs, how can you have education for your children? We are going to tell those teachers: either teach or go. As with education, women have used their elected authority to address quality health care as a critical issue. In Maharashtra, the Indian School of Political Economy organised 60 workshops at Pune under the project of "Leadership Training for Rural Women". The chief conclusion of these workshops was that family planning, drinking water, schools and bio-gas plants are the priorities of women, rather than the TV set or temple (Mahipal 1994). Women, too, have brought domestic violence onto the agendas of political campaigns. In these and other ways, the issues women choose differ from conventional political platforms, which are usually caste/ethnic/religion-based.

But not only do women choose different issues, they appear to choose less corrupt practices as well. Kogendranath Mohato, Panchayat secretary of Kultikori, says:

The men I had worked under formerly passed on their expenses in cigarettes and paan (bread) to the panchayats. But the didis (sisters) here are not only clean on this score, they are more dedicated.

Women value proximity, whether it be to a drinking water source, a fuel source, a creche, a health centre, a court of justice or an office of administration. Poor women have to walk to access these facilities, which is exhausting and consumes valuable time. Moreover, when there is an attack, a rape, a burning, a witch hunt or other violence against a woman, seeking redress from Councils, which are located far away, may not be feasible. But if these Councils and the people in them are near, the chances of redress and effective action are greater. The decentralisation of government structures has, however, been regarded with suspicion and anxiety by progressive groups. Decentralisation can exacerbate lack of local resources and perpetuate regional disparities. It has often been misused by central government to offload social security provision. It has also been misused politically by dictators or single authority regimes to control from the centre through decentralised mechanisms.

But the enormous expansion of women's representation in decentralised government structures has highlighted the advantages of proximity, namely the redress of grievance and (most important of all) the ability to mobilise struggle at a local level where it is most meaningful, for example, the anti-arrack movement. Thus women are helping to radicalise local government. If the critique of macro-economic policies is about equity, then what better response can there be but to put political power in the hands of those most inequitably treated, namely women? In this sense, PRI may be conceived as a macro-political adjustment whose effects are felt at the micro-level.

Women are beginning to change not only the issues and values of governance but are also adopting different methods to those of men. They do not let official protocol stand in their way. Narayanan (1993) recounts the story of one Panchayat official, Suman.

According to them (the officials) the area was not a catchment area and hence not suitable to construct a tank. They could not think anything beyond that. But Suman wanted to keep up her promise to the electorate of reviving the old tank. She mobilised necessary resources through other sources, and was able to fulfil her promise. After a good monsoon, the tank was flooded with water much against the scientific thinking of the bureaucracy.

Many obstacles to the realisation of PRI's transformative potential remain. Scepticism about decentralisation persists in many quarters. There continues to be a resistance to really devolving power and funds from centres of (male) power to the periphery. Women still face considerable handicaps to their involvement in politics; for example, inadequate education, the burden of reproductive and productive roles, a lack of self-confidence and the opposition of entrenched cultural and religious views. There are also administrative obstacles to be overcome. The current administration framework has a departmentally-administered sectoral funding pattern which conflicts with the women-led, area-derived programmes arising from PRI. There is a need to cut through the existing system of development finance to find more flexible approaches capable of responding to the new priorities that are being expressed. United Nations and other donor agency funding for central government inadvertently supports this regressive national budgeting process (Jain 1994b, 1995a).

PRI is beginning to transform the processes and priorities of local government in India as well as the women who have been brought into politics. But sustaining this transformation is a significant challenge, given the inertia and resistance of patriarchal institutions and values. Those women elected through PRI need specific kinds of support which go beyond technical training. They need support to build solidarity amongst women, through strengthening links between women's organisations and elected bodies. They need information about innovative organisations which enhance women's lives such as health providers, credit institutions and so on. Many women's NGOs are already providing these kinds of support to women representatives (Jain 1994a).

There is, however, a major gap in this woman-to-woman support which needs attention by the world-wide women's movement and local feminist groups. This is the need to build feminist consciousness, and strengthen women's sense of common identity, by articulating the elements of a feminist consciousness and presenting it as the special quality of women's leadership. These qualities of women in leadership are becoming well-known, especially as they continue to emerge from the collective struggles of poor women (Jain 1995b, 1995c). Such qualities include: avoiding conflict, pre-empting injustice, responding to issues of basic needs for the family, learning through doing, consulting, sharing, caring, undoing hierarchies and rebuilding informality. The question remains as to whether it is possible to assist women both to recognise these qualities as being valuable and unique and to identify with such qualities as being constitutive of the way they see themselves.

The emphasis from the women's movement today is to demand more opportunity for women to lead, to demand more power for women (translated, for example, into demands for fixed percentages in all decision-making bodies, or legal and educational programmes for women's empowerment). But there has been insufficient elaboration of what that leadership has to offer which distinguishes it from men's leadership and which commends it as something special (Jain 1992). Such an elaboration through feminist discourse and action is essential for this revolution to deliver the promise it holds.

PRI has created an opportunity to take forwards this feminist discourse and action in order to elaborate the qualities and benefits of feminist leadership in local governance. If they are to seize this opportunity and not only take power but also transform the values and priorities of India's political and cultural space, women must raise their own consciousness of the quality and content of feminist leadership.

An Action Agenda

How can women raise their own consciousness and sustain the transformations of PRI? The support of the women's movement in India is critical. Many sections of the movement were initially sceptical about the real value of this "revolution". However, as they have become more familiar with these elected women, they have been overwhelmed by the vitality and the enthusiasm of the women and are now offering both moral and material support. This process is of central importance, and must be continued and reinforced.

There is also a need for a more enabling environment, which would allow PRI to become a process for the empowerment of women, not to mention other social groups who have been left out of participation in representative governance. Such an environment would include legal frameworks and services as well as packages of technical support.

Multi-lateral and bi-lateral development assistance also needs to be re-thought. UN agencies, for example, are often obstacles to efforts to shift power structures from the civil service to the citizens. The procedures of donor bureaucracies require the continued presence of central government and central machineries for negotiation and accountability.

Their division into subject sectors also inhibits the establishment of integrated support services such as social development services, to be designed and accessed by women at the local level. Ironically, it is development assistance agencies which often provide vigorous examples of patriarchal obstruction to people-led development. Finally, careful research is required to substantiate the claims made by supporters of the PRI movement.

CONCLUSION

Deep poverty is a social and political phenomenon as much as an economic problem and thus requires political and social change, particularly within the sites of power. The quest for equity cannot come about without wider representation of all groups, especially those currently denied access to power, and the presentation of all points of view in the process of decision-making. Revision of the current administrative and political structures, and their rules, is necessary in order to facilitate this broader representation and its translation into political power for those who are currently marginalised.

PRI reminds us of a central truth; power is not something people give away. It has to be negotiated, and sometimes wrested from the powerful. Enshrining political change within the law has forced both the pace and direction of such change. Democratic politics is, in reality, the interplay of vested interests and PRI's great achievement has been to mandate a vested, and mutual interest, between women and the political process. The lesson of PRI is clear: if the wisdom of grassroots organisations, especially the courage and clarity of women, is to become policy, it will not be through the art of intellectual persuasion but by the arrangements made within a political system for their voice to have power.

Bringing women into power is thus not only a matter of equity, of correcting an unjust and unrepresentative system. The World Summit for Social Development, Copenhagen 1995, addressed itself to the removal of poverty, the achievement of full employment and social integration. Many believe that these questions cannot be effectively addressed without the kind of democratisation of the representative process that has been discussed in this paper. Political restructuring is key to economic growth with justice. PRI is also demonstrating that transforming local councils into representative bodies means they are likely to be more environmentally protective, as the new members have a greater stake in their local natural resources.

PRI in India offers an opportunity to women to change the face of political leadership. But we still have to ensure that these are spaces where women can go to negotiate for power. Other questions that arise at a conceptual level are:

- Is this model a valuable method of restructuring the State?
- Does local government with special reservation to ensure the participation of "subordinated" groups as discussed here, bring a form of convergence between the State and civil society?
- In our discussion of alternative economic models, do institutional arrangements provide the safeguard for economic equity by changing power structures?
- At the level of discussion on macro-economic policy, especially structural adjustment programmes, does local self-government of this kind provide the necessary challenge to the imposition of economic policies which reinforce inequity and exploitation?

But I am not one to end with questions. Many of these questions can be answered through actively supporting the restructuring of politics as a key to economic growth with justice. The international community, which participated with such solidarity and clarity at the Social Summit in Copenhagen and the Fourth World Conference on Women in Beijing, should see these types of arrangements as a means of moving beyond postulating goals and providing critiques, to offering a substantive, viable alternative for action.

3

Panchayati Raj and Reservation

In India and Bangladesh, the recent Constitutional Amendments have brought a considerable number of women into the mainstream political arena, bringing to the fore a range of issues involving not only women's rights but their role in politics. It had enabled women to come to power, but not actually empowered them in the political sense of the term.

However, there was a considerable status enhancement among women and has made a difference in the perception among the men in the society with regard to their credibility in politics. The attitude of a large number of men towards women in politics has been changing from one of hostility and underestimation to reconciliation and trust.

The empirical study of the Panchayati Raj Institution and the Union Parishad has brought to the fore some emerging leaders among women at the grassroots level.

The reservation given to women seemed to be quite inadequate as far as their empowerment was concerned since the number of women who came to power exceeded even the 33 percent mark in most of the states in India. However, in Bangladesh the one-third mark in the Union Parishads was more of a move in the opposite direction and a disabling factor since as against men who contested from one ward, a woman had to cover three wards with all odds stacked against her to contest for one position.

As far as the inspiration factor behind joining politics was concerned, majority of women and men revealed that it was because of a sincere urge for public service and for developing the village that they took such a step despite the fact that family response towards their joining politics were sometimes negative. Politics as a profession was not worthy, because of the dominance of muscle and money power, and that there was too much threat of violence.

It was evident that lack of effective and timely planning, lack of political background, absence of suitable socio-economic and political environment, lack of appropriate organizational framework, lack of skill and training put women behind in proving their competencies compared to their male counterparts. It had been identified that women had limited scope to exercise political rights, lack of control over resources and had a limited choice in decision-making.

The hurdles faced by women in participation started at the nascent stage itself, especially in Bangladesh where most of the women were not even allowed to vote due to religious fatwas by the fundamental groups. The Indian scenario is not diametrically opposite, but to a great extent still witnesses a great deal of forced silence among the elected women representatives. The women Panchayat members were the worst hit and the most peripheral in this 'silent revolution.'

Most of the women emphasized the fact that their participation could be better if they had functional education and also training on the various intricacies involved in the political field.

The process of globalization has led to discourses on development having different perspectives. One of the major upcoming development discourses puts gender and governance on the forefront of these. In this context, the governments of India and Bangladesh have amended their laws for fair representation of gender in the local government to ensure good governance. Not withstanding the fact that constitutional support and legislative measures are necessary for bringing about social change, but this, however, cannot be achieved single-handedly. Constitutional efforts are needed to strengthen and consolidate them for meaningful empowerment. The question is whether an intervention like the constitutional amendment is able to ensure women's empowerment or whether the patriarchal structures, manifested in the household and the state, will continue to dominate.

In recent times, there has been a common realization in Bangladesh and India, that a strong and effective local government is one of the essential preconditions for ensuring good governance. It is generally agreed that an empowered local government is the key foundation on which the success of any democratic nation rests.

In this regard, one of the significant goals set out by the Fourth World Conference on Women, 1995, in Beijing was adequate representation of women in all decision-making bodies (Beijing Platform for Action, 1996). It was suggested that in any representative body there should be a 'logical balance' of men and women to voice the concerns of the society en masse. Good governance means being participatory, accountable, predictable and transparent which reasonably calls for a gender balance in political decision-making. It is believed that women's insights and values of governance can enhance and enrich the overall decision-making process. It is also generally observed that women at the local level are more sensitive to community issues.

Local government is part of overall governance. Local government institutions, being nearer to people, can involve them in various ways:

- planning and implementation of projects supervision of educational institutions, hospital and other government financed units
- mobilization of support for new initiatives like campaign against dowry, child labour etc. enforcement of laws regarding gender discrimination, violence against women, environment protection
- mobilization of resources in the form of taxes, fees, tolls etc. Popular participation also assumes importance because of its potentials for holding the local government institution accountable to the community.

On the other hand, local government institutions as the representative organization of the people can enforce accountability the central/national government authorities. The more aware, vigilant and active the community becomes through their participation in local government bodies, the greater is the pressure on both local government institutions and the government authorities to become transparent and responsive.

The potentials of local government institutions can be realized more effectively where there is decentralization and devolution of powers. Accountability, transparency, participation, empowerment, equity and all other attributes of good governance can be in full play and become a part of the daily work of both the government and local government bodies when decentralization and devolution take place. Without decentralization and devolution, local government bodies remain paper organizations without any effective role. It will be no exaggeration to say that it is in a decentralized local government system that most of the attributes of good governance have a chance to survive and prosper. Strengthening of local government institutions can, therefore, be seen as a positive trend towards good governance.

All successive governments in Bangladesh, since its independence, felt the need to have viable local government for ensuring effective governance. As a result, we have seen 'decentralization' as an important policy agenda of all governments. Thus, reforming local government is not a new phenomenon in Bangladesh. The repetitive process of local government reform has been handed down to the sovereign state of Bangladesh from Pakistan as a postcolonial extension. However, the necessity to reform the existing structure of local government by various successive government in Bangladesh indicates their failure to create effective institutions for enhancing local democracy and delivering development programmes.

In Bangladesh there have been five major attempts to reform local government under five different governments. The objective of all, at least at the level of rhetoric, was to introduce participatory and accountable local governance through decentralisation of functions and powers to locally elected institutions. All these governments also recognised the relevance and important of the role of decentralised local institutions in planning and implementing need-based development projects for poverty alleviation and reduction of socio-economic inequality. However, the objectives were not realised and the governments failed to keep their commitment towards grassroots democracy and to devolve power to the people at lower levels to manage their own affairs. Consequently, the primary goal of poverty reduction, economic equity and gender balance remained unfulfilled (Khan, Z.R., 1999).

One of the important reasons why women have not received adequate benefits from years of planning and development was their inadequate representation, non-participation and non-involvement in the preparation and execution of plans for their economic development and social justice through decentralized institutions.

In Bangladesh, Article 9 of the Constitution promotes the special representation of women in local government. In recent years, a constant pressure on the Union Parishad from the academia, citizens and women's groups, a protected process, to provide adequate gender representation has lead to the Union Parishad Amendment Act 1997. This is, in itself, a remarkable initiative for providing adequate representation to women.

The Constitution of Bangladesh provides for equality of men and women. There is no legal barrier to women contesting or voting for any elective office, including that of the head of the State. Article 9 of the Constitution promotes the special representation of women in local government (Constitution of the People's Republic of Bangladesh, 1972). Although the constitution grants equal rights to all citizens in all spheres of life, there have been very few women in local government. In 1976, provision was made for two nominated female members in addition to nine elected members and one chairperson in each Union Parishad, which increased to three nominated women members in 1983. In 1992, it was changed to indirect election where three women members in each local government body were supposed to be elected by the chairperson and other elected members. This process of filling women's seats in the local councils totally ignored the scope of women's active participation and role in these political organizations where policies are decided and crucial plans for local development are formulated. The nominated women could not play more than the role of a 'yes' person of the chairperson and members, who were predominantly men (Khan, Z.R., 1998).

In 1997, the Union Parishad Ordinance of 1983 was amended and through this Amendment, for the first time, provision was made for direct election for the female members to three reserved seats for women in the Union Parishad (The Local Government Union Parishad Amendment Act, 1997).

In 1997, again for the first time in the history of Bangladesh direct election for women representatives was provided in the local government at the lowest tier, the Union Parishad. Much enthusiasm has been observed among the women centering Union Parishad election. The number of voters was 50 million and the most striking feature of the election was the overwhelming participation of women voters. About 210,334 candidates including 45,000 female candidates contested in the Union Parishad election. A total of 13,000 women candidates were elected in the election to represent women's reserved seats (The Daily Janakantha, 15 December 1997). The whole process was a major breakthrough for the rural women in Bangladesh.

These are indeed, unique experiments in the world of democracy, wherein women at grassroots level of Bangladesh, irrespective of their educational, occupational and socio-economic background, have been found suitable enough to occupy political positions and participate in decision-making and economic development through local governance.

In Bangladesh, though the female chairpersons and members have gained enough confidence in their ability to discharge administrative duties, the discriminatory attitude of their male counterparts has been the main stumbling block. According to the Local Government Ordinance, elected women Union Parishad members will act as chairperson in at least three of 12 standing committees of the Union Parishad. But in reality it is found that in many of the Union Parishads, the Standing Committees have not yet been formed. Moreover, where they are formed, the women members have no responsibilities despite their inclusion in the committees (Shamim, I., 1999).

Women, however few, have been articulating and trying to sensitize local and national leaders and decision makers of the need for women's participation in the political process. Efforts are underway to take political scene more democratic, participatory, accountable and transparent so as to ensure a just, humane and equitable society. The urgency for political empowerment of women has therefore, increased manifold. There is a need to enable women to be more effective members of local government bodies. Two aspects of effectiveness need to be considered, i. e. effectiveness in participating in overall Union Parishad operations and their involvement in the development issues.

The Indian Constitution has been committed to introduce socio-economic and political transformation. The initiatives of empowering women and the marginalized sections are the reflection of its democratic spirit that can be noticed from a number of amendments in these fields. Especially, the 73rd and 74th Constitutional Amendment Acts provide for an opportunity for women's entry into political spheres. These Amendment Acts provide for a 33 percent reservation of seats for women in the governance of local bodies (rural and urban) with aspiration of good governance and fair representation in the development process at grassroots level. The 73rd Constitutional Amendment Act is an important landmark in the history of Indian women's participation in the formation of democratic institutions at grassroots level. Not only do they have one-third membership, they also head, as chairpersons, one-third of the Panchayats. According to the estimates, three would be a total of 7.95 lakh women in leadership roles in three tires of the Panchayati Raj alone. In fact, in Karnataka, 43.88 percent of seats were won by the women in the 1994 and 1996 elections, much beyond the stipulated 33.3 percent in the Constitution. The new government system in India has shown that given an opportunity, women too can perform very well in public life.

The most significant aspect is that the gender representation in the decision-making has been taken into account. Although, the Acts have enabled women to participate in the PRI as members, Sarpanch, Block and Zilla Panchayat Adhyakshas throughout the country for over five years, an urgent need is felt to strengthen them.

The reservation in Panchayats have provided for the erosion of the traditional gender, caste, class roles and hierarchy but it is a long and difficult process. Women not only have to fight for their right to be more than proxy members but also to break the barriers of gender division of labor, illiteracy, low level of mobility, seclusion, lack of training and information, which still continue to exist without enough support from the power structure. Women's low self-esteem at the household level and their new role in local politics where they are now expected to function as leader creates a contradiction between women's role at home and in local government.

It has only been four years for Bangladesh and about a decade for India since the enactment of these constitutional changes. This however, is too short a period to modify the dominant patriarchal structure of society that has continued to exist for last many millennia via the historical processes and social formations. The process of empowerment in the local government institutions will enable women to re-examine their lives, recognize the source and structure of power and of their own subordination and initiate action to challenge the existing ideology as well as structures and institutions.

By contesting and getting elected to local government, women have shattered the myth of their own passivity-that women are not willing to enter politics. However, women's representation in the decision-making positions with monitoring power, is still negligible. The present rules of the game and decision-making procedure do not allow a greater participation of women and in the absence of women, there is no effort to recognize or change the game. The very absence of women at these levels thus leads to preservation and reinforcement of male-oriented and male benefiting types of decisions.

Objectives

The study is broadly an attempt to analyze the emerging scenario of women leadership at local politics by focusing on the elected women representatives of Union Parishad of Bangladesh compared to their counterparts in Panchayats of India. More specifically, the study will focus on the views, opinions, activities and training of the local government representatives in the following areas:

- Understand the grassroots level democracy, the decentralization of power and women's political participation

- Examine the role of gender in the functioning of local political institutions and focus on a comparative perspective on the experiences of India and Bangladesh
- Constraints and problems faced by women and men in the electoral process and as representatives in the local bodies
- The extent of devolution of power and active participation in the various committees
- The role of family networks, political parties and government and non-governmental organizations in their attainment of power
- Their participation in developmental works and programs
- Gender related obstacles encountered by women and men while undertaking development programs
- Strategies to overcome the barriers
- Needs, level of awareness and training as well as initiatives taken by the government and non-government organizations in those areas.

THEORETICAL FRAMEWORK

In recent times, the process of 'globalization' of goods, market expansion, liberalization, commercialization of agriculture and market-oriented growth has been profoundly influencing the rural areas. The fact remains that whether in terms of 'food security', feminization of poverty', the rising environmental crisis, the import of worldwide economic and political change falls most heavily on women, especially rural women.

There can be no second opinion about the fact that national development cannot occur without broad based rural development and for rural development to happen there is an urgent need to empower the rural people, especially the rural women-politically, socially and economically. In this regard, it must be stated that the framework employed here shall work within the parameters of the 73rd Constitution Amendment Act, Schedules 5 and 11 of the Constitution of India and Article 9 of the Constitution of Bangladesh.

The new leadership that has emerged at various levels, especially at the level of local government seems to have posed a serious challenge to the traditional power structures. The women emerging from their traditional household roles and demonstrating their capacities of decision-making, administration and execution at the local level have been observed in different forms in the two countries under study. These examples are few and far between and yet they reflect a great degree of hope for a positive change.

The main problem that concerns us here is whether the representation of such a large number of women in the local government institutions has made any significant departure to affect the existing gender biased social structures and norms. These changes need to be assessed in terms of:

- Whether recognition of such constitutional structures, especially leadership of women for collaboration and joint efforts have been accepted by the traditional power structures
- Whether the new Amendment of the Union Parishad Act of Bangladesh and 73rd CAA in India have led to the overall empowerment of elected women and other marginalized sections of the society
- Whether the bodies of local self-governance have been liberated from acting as line agents of the State and empowered with functional autonomy
- Whether women have been able to bring in any new developmental alternatives as far as the local governance is concerned.

Relevance of the Study

The present study will be of some great significance as it is one of the few studies that attempt at linking gender issue with that of local governance. The study gains further importance due to the fact that it is a comparative study of two similar, neighboring countries and yet encrusted with significant differentials. As far as women at the grassroots are concerned, the study intends to give a new perspective on the prevalent notions of 'women are not interested in politics,' 'women do not have the qualities and capacities to run local governing bodies,' that the really marginalized women will not be able to benefit from the new set of arrangements since the upper caste/class women will usurp all the new forms of devolved power, etc. The study will be extremely relevant in the growth of some comprehensive models and encourage further research within academia as well as the voluntary sector. Some of the significant features are noted below:

- To provide suggestions for the effective performance of both men and women as political leaders by understanding the constraints as well conducive factors in the process
- To bring out the needs and requirements of men and women leaders and suggest necessary measures
- To evaluate the necessity of training for them
- To analyze the need of reservation to involve a large number of women in decision making institutions at the local government level
- To focus on the change in attitudes and opinions of the people at large about women from one of hostility and underestimation to reconciliation and trust.

Methodology

The study focuses on the gender issues in the reconstituted local government system in Bangladesh and India and the extent of devolution of power to women and men in the latest amendments of the two countries.

The methodology for the study of local governance in Bangladesh and India differed to some extent because of some contrasting socio-cultural and political characteristics found in these two countries. These broad dissimilarities pertain to the domination of religion in Bangladesh and that of caste in India. The study was limited to six districts of Bangladesh and two districts of India given the availability of time and resources. The primary sources of data were a combination of qualitative and quantitative methods such as interview using structured interview schedule, Focus Group Discussion, case studies and observation. Statistical information were processed, analyzed and presented in tables and graphs to present the major findings.

SELECTION OF THE STUDY AREA IN BANGLADESH

Six districts were purposively selected from six divisions of Bangladesh. A total of 202 Unions have been selected randomly from 34 Upazila of six districts. Since the districts have unequal number of Union Parishads, the number of sample Unions was unequal. A sample of 602 women and 399 men Union Parishad members were selected randomly from the list of Union Parishad members. These men and women members were selected from the sample Union Parishads.

SELECTION OF THE STUDY AREA IN INDIA

Uttar Pradesh (UP) and Madhya Pradesh (MP) were selected for the Indian study, which are very large states that have a very large number of districts and population within their territory. The selection of the districts was based on the nature and level of development with reference to literacy, health, life expectancy, sex ratio, access to basic amenities, etc. Indore and Varanasi were the most developed districts within their respective states, while Etawah and Chhatarpur are among the most backward ones.

The target group, i.e., elected representatives was selected on the basis of sex and elected hierarchy in the Panchayati Raj structure. They were members and chairpersons of the Gram Panchayats, Block and Zila level Panchayats of Madhya Pradesh (Indore and Chhatarpur) and Uttar Pradesh (Varanasi and Etawah). The sample included 600 women and 400 men.

Organization of the Study

The study is divided into five chapters. The first chapter is the introduction with the statement of the problem and the methodology used in the study. Chapter two focuses on the local governance in South Asia and the institutional background of local government system in Bangladesh and India.

Chapter third is on the socio-economic profile of local representatives, both men and women with special emphasis on the emerging women leaders in local self-government. Electoral democracy at grassroots level is the focus of the fourth chapter which includes women's political participation as candidates, motivation for joining politics and problems faced during elections and overall obstacles encountered by women representatives, as well as training needs and interventions for capacity building.

HISTORY OF THE LOCAL SELF-GOVERNMENT AND THE SILENT REVOLUTION

Local Government System in South Asia

The different countries in South Asia followed different paths towards political, social and economic development. India became a republic, a democratic and secular nation with a mixed economic setup that was overtly centralized, top-heavy and bureaucratic, besides taking recourse to import substitution and state sponsored industrialization. The state of Pakistan had experiments with the democratic form of governance at various intervals but remained largely and intermittently a military state where the State itself was the biggest producer of goods and services. Sri Lanka took the democratic road with great emphasis on social development. Bangladesh became a hostage to military rule for a while but settled on a democratic political system with increasingly greater emphasis on exports along with regional and global integration. The huge size at which the various activities were undertaken by these countries, viz., nation-building activities, development planning, economic stability, multi-level reforms and pressure for improving the quality of life led them largely to neglect their own local government systems at the micro-levels.

In India, Bangladesh and Sri Lanka, as well as in Pakistan the national political scenario as well as the national economic initiatives have generally tended to over-centralize resulting in the gross neglect of their own grassroots governance (Rahman, S., 2000.). A recent study of local government system in Bangladesh concluded that although the constitution provides for an autonomous local government system the provisions have not been implemented. The local government system has been subject to many changes and experiments, which has not only destabilized the system, but has caused the community to distance itself from the local government which it was supposed to serve (UNDDSMS, 1996).

Women and Local Governance in South Asia

Women leaders in South Asia had and have been occupying the highest positions in their in their respective governments, e.g., from Indira to Sheikh Hasina, Khaleda Zia and Benazir Bhutto to

Sirimavo Bandaranaike and Chandrika Kumaratunga. And yet, the statistics tell a different story. The vast majorities of South Asian women are illiterate, in poor health, invisible in the system of national accounts, and suffer legal, political, economic and social discrimination in all walks of life. Women in South Asia also have the lowest rates of participation in their governance structures. Except for India where more than 33 percent members of local government are women (Mahbub ul Haq Human Development Centre, 2000).

The 1999 Report on Human Development in South Asia advocated that if governance is to promote human development, it has to go beyond being pro-people or people-centered. It has to be owned by the people. Women account for half the population of South Asia, yet they remain mostly invisible in all governing institutions. Women hold the top positions in major political parties of the region, yet these powerful positions have not translated into positive outcomes for the majority of South Asian women. Most political parties do not even maintain data on their women membership and few women are granted party tickets for elections. In some countries, women are more visible in local governance structures than in any other governing institution. Most gains have been made in India, where one-third of the seats in Panchayats is reserved for women. However, gender bias pervades at all levels of governance in South Asia, which may be one of the reasons for the region's governance crisis (Mahbub ul Haq Human Development Centre, 2000).

Organization at the grassroots level allows people to contribute significantly to the governance of their communities. For women, successful grassroots experience has meant a chance to form coherent voice, to be heard and to make a difference in their communities. Across South Asia, the experience of women in local government has been varied, with some countries being more successful than others in attaining greater women's participation.

With the exception of India and Bangladesh, women's representation within local bodies in South Asia remains minimal. But even in Bangladesh, female representation barely rises above 20 percent. In 1992, the Government of India passed the 73rd and 74th Amendments to the Constitution of India. Termed the 'silent revolution', these Amendments paved the way for women's entry into local governance by reserving 33 percent of seats for them in the Panchayats at all the levels, including that of the chairperson's seat. In most states, reservation of seats has met with success, with female representation exceeding the 33 percent quota in states such as Karnataka, Kerala and Manipur.

Experience over the last decade has shown that women who have gained access to the Panchayats and Municipalities have performed well. Some of them have already established excellent records of service and even won distinguished awards for their performance. Being mostly illiterate, a large number of them have placed a high priority on acquiring literacy to be able to perform better at their jobs. Substantial numbers of teachers, lawyers and other functionaries at the grassroots level have been able to win elections and become members of the Panchayats.

In Bangladesh, women have been incorporated into local governance through reservation at the Union Parishad level. Bangladesh has experimented different forms of local government throughout its political history-sometimes at the village level, the Gram Sarker and sometimes at the sub-district level, the Upazila. But the Union Parishad, which consists of representatives from several villages, has remained the most effective local body at the local level. Currently there are about 4,276 Union Parishads in Bangladesh. Since 1997, a quota of three seats or one-fourth of the total has been reserved for women in the Union Parishads. This has brought up women's representation from a very few to over 20 percent. However, reforms suggested for one-third female participation at the sub-district and district levels remain unimplemented.

Local government is also an integral part of the Nepalese governance system. Since adopting a policy of decentralization, local governing bodies have over the years acquired increasingly greater authority in Nepal. The Local Self-Governance Act of 1999 is by far the most progressive Act in terms of devolving authority from central to the local governing bodies. Local governing institutions now have some taxation authority at the local level as well as limited judicial authority to tackle local level disputes. However, female representation in local governing institutions has been very limited in Nepal. Currently, there is less than 10 percent of women in the District Development Committees (DDC) and Village Development Committees (VDC) combined. Not a single woman is the chairperson of a DDC or mayor of any municipality. Out of 3,913 VDCs, there are only 13 chairpersons who are women. On the positive side, one of every five seats in each ward of a VDC and municipality that is reserved for women candidates has ensured the participation of an additional 36,023 women at the ward-level governance of VDCs and municipalities.

Sri Lanka's Current System of Governance Consists of Three Tiers-the Municipal Councils, Urban

Councils, and the Pradeshiva Sabbas. While total membership of these councils exceeds three thousand, less than 3 percent are women. In the last bodies' elections, held in 1997, only one woman was elected mayor of a municipal Council in the province of Jaffna. Unfortunately, in 1998 she became the victim of political assassination. In the Urban Councils, while there are currently two female Vice-Chairpersons, women occupy none of the 36 posts for Chairperson. At present, three of the Chairpersons and two Vice-Chairpersons in the Pradeshiya Sabbas are women. Despite this, women represent only 1.72 percent of the total membership of the Pradeshiya Sabbas. Currently the government has also put forward a recommendation for fixing a quota of 25 percent for women in local government.

Until recently, female representation in local governance in Pakistan was negligible. The current government has scheduled fresh elections, starting December 2000, for local government at three levels-the Union Council, the Tehsil Council and the District Assembly. Fifty percent of seats at the union level have been reserved for women. At the Tehsil and district levels, women will be allocated 5 and 10 seats respectively, forming roughly about 15 percent of the total seats.

Since politics is traditionally a male domain and all financial, economic, commercial and political negotiations conducted outside the home are by males, South Asian women have very limited access to decision-making process, and they have a severe lack of access to and control over financial resources. This effectively reduces women's chance of contesting elections. Political equality is still elusive in most South Asian countries, though some progress has been made. As men have control over assets and have relatively better education, they have a dominant position in terms of political power remain surrogate actors in the political process. Tokenism is more evident and problematic at the local level than at higher levels of government. Women councilors may not necessarily be educated. Lack of awareness leads to situations where they may become dependent on male councilors or political parties, focusing more on issues of men's interest than on women's concerns. In some cases women are elected as councilors without actually participation in the functioning of local bodies. Most women lack any effective power or influence in local governance structure. Many of them do not have the necessary skills to present ideas effectively. Lack of awareness of the possibilities of political participation means inadequate contribution to public affairs on the one hand and women's empowerment at the other. Women councilors themselves recognize these problems.

Local bodies, if properly utilized can vehicle of women's active participation when it is effectively mainstreamed. Since these institutions function at the grassroots level, representatives, both men and women, are more aware of, and can be more responsive to the needs of women and children as well as to the problems of rural communities. Tapping into the latent capacity of women is essential to substantially enchanting the socio-economic development of South Asia. Decentralization is thus a prerequisite for effective mainstreaming of women's concern in development. However, unless existing mechanisms and attitudes that deny women equal chances in decision-making are not modified, simple devolution of power will not be enough to ensure greater female participation in decision-making (Mahbub ul Haq Human Development Centre, 2000).

The history of local government in Bangladesh goes way back to the British Colonial period. It can be traced back to the Bengal Local self Government Act of 1855, which established the three-tier system: District Board, Local Board and Union Committee.

During the British period, several acts were passed to promote local-level self-rule and people's participation in the administration was almost absent (Siddiqui, K., 1994). A study of local government system in Bangladesh concludes that although the constitution provides for an autonomous local government system these provisions have not been implemented resulting in a local government system that is not functioning properly. The local government system has been subject to many changes and experiments, which has not only destabilised the system but also caused the local government system to distance itself from the community it is supposed to serve (UNDDSMS, 1996).

Local Government Upazila Parishad Act was passed in Parliament in December 1998, providing for creation of an elected council at the Thana/Upazila level. In the new Upazila Parishad system, the chairman to be elected directly by the people, will head the Parishad and have the executive power. Chairmen of the Union Parishads and municipalities will be the members of the Upazila Parishad. One third of the total number of women members of the Union Parishads and municipalities concerned will be the members of the Upazila Parishad. The women members of the Union Parishads (UP) and the municipalities will elect them (The Local Government, Upazila Parishad Act, 1998).

According to the Local Government, Union Parishad Ordinance 1983, a Union Parishad shall consist of one chairman, nine elected members and three nominated women members. The Union Parishad Act, 1993 has brought about some changes in the composition of Union Parishad. The Union Parishad shall be divided into 9 wards and 9 members, one from each ward shall be elected by the voters of the concerned wards. Instead of nomination, the 3 women members will be indirectly elected by the Chairman and members of the concerned Union Parishad.

The right to vote in local bodies was dependent on the possession of property, tax payment and education. Women ordinarily being deprived of property and educational opportunities were automatically left out of this voting right, which in a way amounted to discrimination. Till 1956, women were not even able to cast vote in the election to rural local bodies, when for the first time election was based on the basis of universal suffrage. However in 1997, on the basis of the recommendations of the Institutional Review of the WID Capability of the

Government of Bangladesh and the Local Government Reforms Commission, direct election for women representatives was provided in the Union Parishad. According to the new law, a Union is divided into wards. One member will be elected from every ward. Furthermore every Union comprising 9 wards has been divided into three parts for women members who will be elected through direct vote.

It would be least incorrect to state that none of the successive governments at the Centre or at the State levels went beyond paying a ceremonial lip-service of promising empowerment to the Indian women and took no serious measures to alter the existing power relations to bridge the gender-gap. It took almost half a century for the Indian Parliament to understand the rationale behind providing reservations for women at the Panchayati Raj level. In fact, there appears to be little difference between the attitude of the British colonial regime (whose one the deliberations with regard to the franchise of Indian women vide the Act of 1919 was that it was a matter to be settled by the legislative councils of India through legislation) and that of the makers of the COI. The Constitution of Independent India, similarly, after quarantining equality to all women in all spheres, left their political representation to their own willingness, opportunity and support even while providing for reservations for Scheduled Castes and Scheduled Tribes.

As far as the Panchayats are concerned the question of reservation for women sounded meaningless, once the enactment about PRIs was pushed into DPSP. Like the Act of 1919, the Constituent Assembly also left the issue of reservation for women to the various state legislatures.

The decade of the 1980s was one that saw a movement and a general consensus building up towards reservation of seats for women of not less than 33 percent. But before the much required corrective via the 73rd Constitutional Amendment Act (CAA) came, another bill in 1989 had been tabled before the Indian Parliament, known as the 64th Amendment Bill, seeking "as nearly as may be" up to 30 percent seats in favor of women in the membership of Panchayats at all the three levels, including in the provided for SC/ST and in the total seats. However, it did not provide for reservation among chairpersons. It is important to mention here that after the 64th Amendment Bill fell and before the 73rd CAA was passed, several States initiated some correctives in their Panchayat laws in order to bring reservation for women as if in sheer anticipation of the 73rd CAA. These States were Orissa, which provided 30 percent reservation for women in the membership of the Panchayat; Maharashtra, which introduced a 30 percent reservation for women in the membership of the Panchyats in 1991; and Kerala, which also late did before 1992. The most crucial difference between the 73rd CAA and the earlier 64th Amendment Bill was the fact that there was not provision for reservation for the seat of chairpersons in the 64th while the 73rd contained it.

In India, the government functions at three levels-the federal, the state or regional leveland grassroots level, called the Panchayati Raj. The Panchayati Raj system covering thevillage, tehsil and district has brought government to the doorsteps of the masses.

In 1992, the government of India enacted the 73rd and 74thAmendments to the Constitution of India toprovide for one-third representation of women in local government. By 1993 all states except Bihar hadratified these amendments. Previously, Panchayats were governed by State Panchayat Acts, which allowedthe nomination of only two or three women. As a consequence, in all the 223,000 Panchayats across India,only 13 percent members were women.

However, with the onset of the silent revolution in the form of theseConstitutional Amendments, the numbers of women rose to 33 percent or one million. Presently, there are 655,629 women members in the Gram Panchayats, 37,523 in the Panchayat Samitis and 3,161 in the ZillaParishads. Under the Constitutional Amendments, women can be members as well as Chairpersons of theselocal government institutions. Elections under this system have already been held once, and some states arepreparing for a second round. The experience has been positive in states such as Gujarat and West Bengal but hosts ofissue still remain. Resistance from male power centers to devolution, discrimination on thebasis of class and casts and opposition from religious elements are just some.

Whatsoever might have been the logic behind zeroing in on not less than 33 percent figure, the number was inadequate to represent women. Unfortunately, a 33 percent only for all the states, on the one hand, and on the other, even this 33 percent was not vertically maintained to the level of various quorums of Panchayat meetings where the most crucial decisions regarding Panchayats were taken.

It can be concluded that despite some advances, both in terms of devolution and delegation to the local government system of South Asia, with a fair degree of certainty the local government systems are generally handicapped and ill-governed. Most of them lack technical as well as functional know-how, and in the absence of adequate financial resources to undertake the activities within their domain they still continue to be largely dependent on the Central and State government. As a matter of fact, dependence on grants from higher levels of government has increased overtime instead of declining. A prime example of such micro-management and intervention is the practice of deputized central administrators to the local government systems. There is also a strongly prevalent myth across the subcontinent that local governments are incapable.

The Constitutional Amendment Acts of both India and Bangladesh have brought in a large number of women into the realm of politics at the local level, which was unthinkable earlier. Before these Acts women did take part in the political process at the national, regional and local levels but their presence was negligible. This glaring lack of representation can be attributed as a spin off factor of the larger socio-cultural and politico-religious dimensions of the South Asian structural reality. This then meant that in a democratic setup where numbers tend to be crucial, women and their issues were always marginalized. The emerging trend of women's leadership in the local self-government shows that a large number of women were young, married, illiterate/literate, and agriculturist by occupation and equally divided between very poor, poor and middle-income groups in India. Secondly, there were two elections in India as against Bangladesh where there was only one election. In India, about 83.4 percent women were first timers in local politics. On the other hand, 16.6 percent women had contested and won posts in Panchayats at different levels even for the second time, especially when the seats were not reserved.

Socio-Economic Profile

Women leaders' socio-economic profile provides the background the representatives have come from. When we take a gender perspective in political leadership, the socio-economic profile becomes even more important standard to analyze the impact of women's political leadership, whether their background is a hurdle/barrier or a major constraint for quality functioning.

Age

In Bangladesh, majority of the women members were in 25-34 years age group, in contrast to 55-64 years 65 years & above majority of men members who were in 35-44 years age group. However, 16 percent among men members were in the age group of 55-64 years, while there was only one percent among women who belonged to the same age group. Moreover, it is interesting to note that men continued to be involved in local politics even when they were above 65 years of age. On the other hand, there was no elderly woman member of that age. Only 4 women members were below 25 years of age. It might be explained by the fact that men members were in politics for longer time, but women began their political career at the local level in 1997 after the amendment of the Ordinance.

In India, there were hardly difference in percentage of men and women of the different age groups. Nearly 10 percent of women members were below 25 years of age. They were not only new to politics, but were also new to the functional maintenance of society. However, overwhelming majority of 84 percent of women were of the age group of 25-50 years who were expected to bring change in village development. The same was true for men (82 percent). Women once taken as the maintainers of status quo were now expected to be the 'change agents.'

Marital status signified a change in perception and attached honor and responsibility of the representatives for community work, whether married or not made a tremendous difference in a traditional society. While a married woman was considered to be responsible, the single woman was taken on a tentative basis. As long as she was unmarried, she was considered to be irresponsible, while the stigma on a widow was appalling in our society. The level of participation in such hostile circumstances does affect quality representation.

Marital status played an important role for participation in politics at the Union Parishad level in Bangladesh. An overwhelming majority of both men and women were married, with higher percentage for men (97 percent) compared to that for women (91percent) as married people were more accepted as political leaders in rural Bangladesh due to maturity and stable family life.

Only one man was a widower, while 43 females were widows was significant because they were usually the heads of their households and hardly received support from other men members of their in-law households. Only 2 percent of both men and women members were unmarried, as they were less acceptable due to their age as well as their lack of experience.

The same trend was found in India where nearly 90 percent women were married which was nothing, but a mere reflection of kind of women socially accepted as representatives. As such, there were only a few single men and women at local level politics.

Moreover, in both India and Bangladesh we find the practice of child marriage quite prevalent. Nearly 54 percent of the women in India said that they were married before they were 18 years of age, which is quite alarming although the government is continuously trying to make it obvious that child marriage is illegal.

Religion had been a major source of enforcing the gender-gap in our society. In Bangladesh the number of Muslim women representatives was almost 83 percent, while in India, 96.3 percent women representatives were from the Hindu religion.

It was assumed that women could not fare well in politics since they are neither literate nor exposed. In Bangladesh, majority of the members both women and men were educated up to the secondary level. In India, 30 percent women were illiterate compared to only 7 percent men.

Women were found to be at the receiving end of the patriarchal set up since only 5 percent were found to be graduates in India. However, majority of women as well as men had primary and secondary education. However, interestingly in both the countries, some of the women were graduates and masters degree holders despite class, caste and religious fundamentalist forces in these countries.

In Bangladesh 82 percent women were housewives and had the strict sense of purda culture, which made their quality representation impossible owing to lack of exposure and movement. Unlike their Indian counterparts, they had only the domestic chores to deal with while the Indian women representatives were more involved with outside work as well as for their livelihood as they were mostly from below poverty line families. Men were mostly farmers and businessmen.

In the rural area, the economic set-up is characterized by land holdings that are 'inherited' through male line. Women are excluded from owning any land/property. Access to land control over material and economic resources, especially land, the single most important means of production in rural Bangladesh and India, women were ingeniously removed. They are merely working on it but not owing it. However they do earn, especially for their family's livelihood.

In India, housewives were only 7 percent. Majority men as well as women were involved in agriculture-related work and agricultural laborers, while very few were involved in business, non-agricultural work, different professions and service.

Monthly income of women representatives was an important indicator of economic solvency as well as economic empowerment. In Bangladesh, there were sharp differences between the level of income of women and men members. Majority of the women members (84 percent) had income below taka 4,000 per month, while the men members (89 percent) were in higher income brackets of taka 4001 and above. Moreover, 32 percent of women members earned as low as taka 500 per month. Women were mostly dependent on their husband's incomes and her income was perceived as a supplement to the household income. As such, women members were dependent on family decision for contesting in the election and getting financial support. In India, women as well as men were mostly in the lower income category, hardly earning 2000 rupees a month, while only a few had a viable income. However, case studies from all over India revealed that Panchayat work had not suffered because of their poor economic status.

In Bangladesh as well as in India, majority women members were above the age of 25 years and married. It seemed that maturity of the members was a very significant criterion not only during election campaigns but also as an important factor to have an impact on the decision making process. Maturity in age and honor attached to marriage were yardsticks to be acceptable to the members of the community. Level of education was very depressing for both men and women, but for women it was even worst. For example, about 30 percent women were illiterate in India.

However, in Bangladesh, they could at least sign their names owing to NGO programs related to adult literacy. Occupational status of women in India and Bangladesh were different. In Bangladesh, majority of women representatives were housewives, unlike in India where they were more involved in agriculture work and laborers outside their home. In both the countries, women earned far less than men. Given the deprived socio-economic status, women had to face more hurdles than men during elections and as members of the local self-government.

Political participation is one of the major ways to ensure women's empowerment, to increase decision-making power and greater ability and to influence matters that affect their lives in the community and the larger society. In the broader sense, participation in politics goes far beyond electoral politics, such as voting and election to public office. Women's empowerment begins with their consciousness-perceptions about herself and her rights, her capabilities and her potentials, awareness of her gender and socio-cultural, economic and political forces that affect her. Women's political empowerment and equal representation in all decision-making institutions are critical inputs in their struggle for freedom from patriarchal subjugation. Local government bodies have a vital role in the developmental processes. Therefore, importance of local level government to women and men is twofold.

First, decisions made at the local levels have implications for the distribution of resources and opportunities between women and men. Second, the lower tiers of government are also arenas in which individuals gain experience and knowledge and a political base for seeking office at higher levels. Within local bodies, women are generally, expected to represent women's interests. That is, women's development is seen as women's business rather than the responsibility of both men and women members. Allied to this is the perception that women serving at the local level should focus on women and children's issues rather than the full range of issues at the grassroots level.

In 1976, provision was made for two nominated women members in addition to nine elected members and one chairperson in each Union Parishad, which was increased to three nominated women members in 1983. The nomination system in local government was changed in 1992 to indirect election where three women members in each local government body will be elected by the chairperson and other elected members.

There was an extremely low level of women's presence in the most important local council, the Union Parishad. No woman was elected in the local government elections of 1956 and 1969. One woman was first elected as chairperson in 1973. Although in 1992, the number increased to thirteen women, Union Parishad chairpersons being elected and subsequently twenty in 1997, still in the case of local government bodies, women were grossly under represented. However, the process of filling women's seats in the local councils totally ignored the scope of women's active participation and role in these political organizations where policies are decided and crucial plans for local level development are formulated. The nominated women could not play more than the role of a 'yes' person of the chairperson and members, who were predominantly men. In addition, such nomination also takes away the credibility and acceptability of the women to the women's constituencies whose causes they represented. Once again, in the provision of reserved seats for women to be filled through nomination reflects the male biases in policy making with the net result that the elected bodies become extremely male dominated (Khan, Z. R., 1998).

The 'selected' or nominated women members usually came from a rural elite group. In the nominating process-status, kinship and especially the relationship with the chairman were considered. The constituents, especially the rural women, had no way of 'electing' their own representatives. As the 'selected' representatives do not come through the election process, they usually do not know or care about their role and functions as people's representatives. Even most of the women voters do not know who their representatives are in the local government and what responsibilities and duties the representatives have towards constituents.

Therefore, the nominated female representatives are far less accountable to than those elected. In fact, they are more accountable to the men who have 'selected' them, if they wish to retain their posts, than to the electorate or the people who should really matter (UNDP, 1994). Hence in 1997, direct election for women representatives was provided in the local government at the lowest tier, the Union Parishad.

In India, reservation for women in political bodies became necessary, considering the social conditions in which women of the country lived even after the constitutional guarantee of their rights to equality and political participation it became necessary for the state to remind the political institutions at different levels, particularly the Panchayat level (district, block, village) to give adequate representation to women. The 73rd Amendment envisaged a significant structural change by decentralizing power and redressing the gender imbalance in the institutions of self-governance. Once the bastion of upper caste/class male power structure is now forever changed. What reservation has basically done is to give the other half of the state, i.e. women a say in the political system in a country, albeit at the grassroots. If we see it in another way, once these women taste power at the local level and understand its intricacies, they could very well enter national politics, with or without reservation, provided the political parties give party tickets to the women participants. After all, in a plural society like India, the political system has to ensure a modicum of equality between all the groups and communities if history's longest oppression is to be seriously tackled.

The 73rd CAA has certain intricacies. The Act suggests that the constituency at each election keeps rotating, the constituency reserved for women will be chosen by lottery, with those that have just been reserved excluded. Consequently it would damage both women and the parliamentary system. For women, since the fixed reserved constituency would mean ghettoisation, they would forever keep campaigning only against other women.For parliament, it would be destabilizing since with a minimum of two-third of the sitting members are due to change at every election (The Hindu, May 20, 2000).

Another argument is that if a particular constituency is declared reserved for women for more than one term it would end up in the hands of those with vested interests. The rotation system gives more women the opportunity to participate (The Deccan Herald, October 22, 2000). But the purpose of reservation is not only giving an opportunity to women in politics but also for the betterment of the society and to quicken the process of development; the whole purpose behind decentralization of power. This could happen only when those participating are for a longer term in the office and are experienced in the art of politics.

The discussion on reservation after almost a decade needs to appraise the impact on the society at large and in particular its effect on the village power structure. While the positive side shows women's alacrity in participating, in managing funds, on developmental works and last but not the least in cutting across the class-caste-gender barriers. The other side has a grim picture, where once the male bastion of power/status is challenged, changed and given a new meaning, 'full-fledged democracy', led to averse male response leading to violence, public ridicule, defamation, no-confidence motion, etc.

The aversion was not only because women have entered their space but also because women's work procedure is different compared to the men counterparts. Moreover, women laid emphasis on development works to be planned and executed-a phenomenon not appreciated by many who had been in the past siphoning off the development funds by showing most of the works on paper (The Deccan Herald, January 1, 1997). It was assessed that women in politics would affect development in a profound manner. A global assessment of women in politics arrived at three conclusions. "Firstly women choose issues of importance to themselves using a variety of meanings in different cultural contexts.

Secondly, no issues are tied solely to one political context and a condition and thirdly the political problems, facing women cluster into four topics: personal safety, security and autonomy, reproductive rights and maternal and child health problems, equalizing access to public, communal and market resources for problem solving and empowerment, and remaking the political and legal rules of the game" (Sharma, 1998). Women are closer to the environment and demand facilities that affect their immediate surroundings like drinking water facilities, healthcare, education, etc.

The emerging women's leadership and the making of the Sarpanch-Pati was a pattern emerging among the young, new, development-seeking men and women with constraints that hampered their work, but it was the women who were bigger losers at the present state owing to the guile of their men folk. The flow chart given below explains the whole process of how men have become Sarpanch-Pati.

So that their own wife/ mother/ daughter may occupy the post and they may command via proxy rule and once the reserved seat becomes vacant they may retrieve the seat or get elected to it by virtue of their work during the proxy rule.

How?

Women are concerned about the development in their area and are committed to public service.

What motivates and encourages them?

But why such young and married women are encouraged/ allowed to leave homes and join politics when they themselves note that 'perception of politics' and 'neglect of family front' is a constraint

But why should they encourage?

A large number of young women are joining politics and getting elected.

EMERGING WOMEN'S LEADERSHIP

Even after all these mechanisations by male counterparts of the elected women members, a considerable number of them (13.5 per cent) came back for a second time.

Women's Political Participation

What participation means is the functioning of the whole array of public institutions and forces which are involved in molding the lives of the people by way of decisions and policies that impinge on their relations with one another (Kaushik, 1992). Participation of women in the local bodies would include:

- Women as voters
- Women as members of political parties
- Women as candidates
- Women as elected members of local government bodies taking part in decision-making, planning, implementation and evaluation
- Women as members of women's organizations, their association with voluntary organizations
- Women in developmental works and dealing of priority issues in the village level.

Gender empowerment is determined by the degree to which women and men participate actively in economic, professional and political activity and take part in decision-making. Women's political participation was hindered by a system of social relations in the male-dominated society, reflecting the orthodox male-centric mentality like religious fundamentalism. Only men were consistently educated and trained for leadership, while very few rural women had the opportunity to pursue their education because of tradition. Women themselves had been strongly influenced by male-dominated village communities and had little faith in their own capacities to take on leadership roles.

In India, among the women who became Sarpanches, elected Panchayat members, intermediaries in Panchayati Samitis and chairpersons at Zilla Parishads, nearly 83 per cent of these women

Public service were first timers in politics and 74 per cent of the women stood independently. About 23 per cent stood as party candidates. These women were predominantly married, illiterate/literate and from very poor families. This trend focuses on whether these rural women, always in veil, inarticulate and ignorant of the rules of the political game would be able to make even a dint in their self-identity.

While in Bangladesh, most of the women members attained school level education and were married. Though these women had attained some school level education, they were not employed thus leading to dysfunctional educational syndrome. This was one of the major reasons for the lack of effective participation among these women in Union Parishads in Bangladesh. But we still find some sporadic cases among these women who have made a mark in the Parishad cutting across the gender-class-traditional bias of a primarily Islamic society.

MOTIVATION FOR JOINING POLITICS AND ELECTION PROCESS

The level of participation could be understood from the reasons to get interested in politics in the first place and what were the issues promised in the election manifesto and their success and failures in implementing them.

Both men and women who became representatives of the Panchayat, i.e. 40 percent men and 38 percent women were interested in village development, while 27 percent men and 28 percent and women respectively were interested in public services. The assumption that only women take up social development issues and men opting for infrastructure development was grossly mistaken.

Improvement Inwomen/social Welfare

The way a man aspired for a link road closest to the city was also a woman's aspiration. The difference was that women's priority lies in the development of the immediate surroundings due to the fact that they were the ones who suffered the most without the civic amenities, water supply, fodder and fuel sources and access to credit. It was clear from the election promises the men and women candidates had made before the elections. In Bangladesh, women who contested elections were usually motivated by NGOs or came from families having political background where male family members were active in local level politics. Very few entered politics as replacement after their husband's death.

There were hardly any differences in priority areas and election promises between men and women candidates. Education and improvement in civic facilities were commitments of an overwhelming majority of men and women candidates in both Bangladesh and India. In India, nearly 34 percent women as well as men contesting elections had priority areas such as women development and social welfare. The myth that women only feel about women's needs and problems no more holds true.

Issues Hindering Election Process

In Bangladesh, lack of economic resources was a major obstacle because most of the candidates were not very well off. It was more true in the case of the women candidates. Women candidates hardly had viable income or landed property of their own and were usually dependent on their husbands' earnings. As such, they also encountered social constraints and lack of family support. However, social security, especially during campaigns seemed to be a major problem, irrespective of gender and it was mostly threats from opposition. In the case of a woman candidate, opposition even tried to convince the candidate to withdraw her nomination paper. Lack or lower level of education of candidates also played a negative role during campaigns and receiving votes. Women candidates often suffered from lack of self-confidence. However, an overwhelming majority of the candidates did not face any problems during the election, 82 percent among women and 84 percent among men candidates.

Problems Faced During Elections

In Bangladesh, professionals stated that campaign for votes at night were difficult and risky for the women candidates, especially because women could not move easily as men did. Moreover, women candidates had to face some social and religious constraints during their campaigns. They also faced financial problems due to lack of political support. It was very difficult for women candidates to campaign throughout the constituencies under three wards. Violence was more pronounced due to the fundamentalist forces by not even allowing the women to vote. The major fact that cannot be ruled out while discussing of women's participation in the Panchayats in India is the "violence" in the Panchayats that rather increased with the 73rd CAA. Violence against women, which in the villages was usually confined to their houses and of course inter-community violence had now spread its diabolic tentacles in the socio-political arena. During elections and decision-making also in everyday matters, violence against women was ever present. Beating up these women or their husbands, sexual harassment in public and molestation were imploring the society's equality front. Women due to the very patriarchal structure were as it was submissive and could not speak freely. Violence was the only aspect impeding women's ultimate overt participation in the Panchayats. Apart from overt violence, the fear of violence was something that had severely impaired women from actively participating in the Panchayat activities.

Fulfilling Election Promises

As to the extent of fulfilling election promises, both men and women in India initiated debates on the issue or persuaded these with higher authorities. But, unfortunately a vast majority did not response, which may be owing to the fact that they could not accept the work on their terms and complete it or maybe they did not understand the questions.

In Bangladesh, majority of the members had no problems in fulfilling the commitments they gave during election campaigns as they had not many priority areas except expansion of education and infrastructure development which were also priority areas of the annual development plan of the local government. However, both men and women could not fulfill some promises due to their own economic impoverishment, social and family problems, lack of education and security and last but not the least threats from political groups.

Though a large proportion of women and men in India mentioned that lack of funds had tied their hands, lack of knowledge, coordination, planning strategy and confrontation of party politics lead to hindrances. The main reason behind decentralizing the power structure was that corruption would not/could not reach the grassroots. Here comes the effective role of women, who were considered to be less corrupt in management.

There were some common obstacles that had hindered women's political participation in Bangladesh and India. Some were socio-economic, while others were mainly political.

ATTENDANCE AND PARTICIPATION IN MEETINGS

Attendance of meetings is not only an important indicator for active participation but also a forum to discuss development activities and decision-making. Moreover, active participation of members and the level of acceptance at meetings were important indicators of their involvement in development activities at local level.

In Bangladesh, an overwhelming majority of 96 percent among men members and 88 per cent among women regularly attended the meetings. But the majority of the women members who attended the meetings could not play effective roles in the decision-making process except giving support to their male counterparts.

In India, nearly 68 percent women attended the meetings regularly, against 72 percent men. At least 32 percent women were either irregular or never attended the meetings. This was also true of 28 percent men. 88% 12% Regular

Unfortunately in Bangladesh, there were about 12 percent women and 3 percent men members who were irregular at meetings. Majority of them explained that they did not get notices of the meetings in time (39 percent women and 43 percent men). A few members reported that although they did not attend the meetings, their signature in the resolution book and attendance registers were collected after holding the meeting. As for other reasons, there was a difference between men and women members. For example, 18 percent women members complained that they were not given any responsibility, and that was why they lacked the interest in attending meetings regularly. Sickness was another factor for irregularity, which was as high as 21 percent among men and only 8 percent among women. Family problems were another valid reason for 10 per cent women such as household work, lack of cooperation of in-laws and husbands, child rearing responsibilities, etc. A few women members about 4 per cent did not trust the chairmen. In Bangladesh, an overwhelming majority of 83 percent women were active participants against 92 percent men who attended the meetings. Partial participation and non-participation were very low among both men and women. In Bangladesh, there were several reasons for the acceptance at meetings. Women members reported that their opinions were accepted because their

With regard to partial and non-acceptance of the opinions of women at the meetings, majority of women reported that because they had minority representation in the Union Parishad, their voices were not heard. It was also pointed out by a large number of women (56 percent) that their identity as 'women' worked as barrier for their opinions to be accepted at meetings. Among other reasons given by women was the chairman's ignorance of women's opinions and reluctance of men members to allow women colleagues to speak. On the other hand, men's opinions were fully accepted more than partial acceptance. Their opinions were only rejected when they did not have a good relationship with the chairmen.

Problems Encountered at the Local Level

Active participation not only included their attendance at meetings, level of participation in the meetings, how acceptable were their opinions, but also the hindrances while undertaking development works at the local level. At the same time, their election promises were important indicators of whether they were able to fulfill them and if not what were the obstacles.

As far as women and their new relationship with politics is concerned, there were two kinds of women representatives in the Panchayats: those who had and are facing problems, and those who have had a smooth entry.

Smt. Dhan Devi, a Panchayat member of Bahadurpur Luhiya Gram Panchayat, Basrehar Block of EtawahDistrict said, "In our Nyaya Panchayat the Pradhan and other officials work according to their personalwhims and fancies. Though we attend the meeting but deliberately keep quiet. In my locality not even a brick lane has been made and the common passage that existed earlier has been closed down indefinitely.We women have been made

Panchayat members only to behave as passive 'yes' people sans respect and importance whatsoever."

Women representatives faced problems when she did not have any political or organizational affiliations, did not have any family members in politics and fought independently without any party support for which she had to contest elections. On the other hand, women who were associated with political parties, claimed to have a family member in politics, accepted party ticket for election and was elected without contesting and did not even made any promises had hardly any problems. Moreover, 79 percent women did not face any election violence due to the fact that they had political backing and about 49 percent women were encouraged by the male members of their families. While 40 percent opined that just being a woman, male dependency, dual responsibilities and purdah were some of the social problems that women had to live up with. The above analysis clearly indicates that women who were active in party politics had support from political groups and gained more recognition in the Panchayat meetings. On the contrary, women who were independent of party affiliation had to struggle on their own to establish their rights and get things done because their voices were hardly considered in the local level meetings.

In Bangladesh women had some schooling, still there were orthodox fundamentalist patriarchal men in the Union Parishad. A case in retrospect was of Saleha Khatun, an elected Union Parishad Member of Sukhpuria Union of Chougcha Thana under Jessore district. She faced various problems while performing her duties. Saleha knew that according to Union Parishad Ordinance, each female Union Parishad member should preside over at least one project. She also learnt that they had the right to participate in one-third of development programs. However, the chairman did not respect the Ordinance and left women out of development activities. Moreover, he threatened women if they raised their voices. There were no arrangements for holding monthly meetings. As a result, women failed to participate in the decision-making process and undertake development activities.

Thus we find that the Bangladeshi counterparts faced a stronger opposition in participation itself, while in India women representatives did participate but their voices got submerged in the men's groups where the actual decisions were taken, as it was a forbidden space for women.

In Bangladesh, professionals opined that communication was the main problem that they faced. Women were unable to communicate with all the people of the three wards. Sometimes their men colleagues ignored them. Social and religious barriers, non-cooperation from husbands and small honorarium were among other problems. Chairman, politicians and others mentioned that communication with voters, family affairs, illiteracy, physical incapability, insecurity, disturbance by miscreants, etc. were faced by women members. Housewives observed that financial crisis was the main problem that women members faced as honorarium given to them were not enough. Moreover, their husbands did not cooperate with them.

The problems of men as Union Parishad members were different from their women counterparts. Problems were encountered by 47 percent men Union Parishad members, which was 60 per cent in the case of women members. Majority of the women who faced problems mentioned that chairmen did not allocate development works for them and men members opposed females' involvement in development activities. Women members also mentioned problems of non-cooperation from local people, for example people did not give land for road construction work to women members. Other problems included corruption of higher authority and men colleagues, less allocation to female, less value given to women, lack of security, etc.

About 53 percent men did not face any problems at all in performing Union Parishad activities. Men who faced problems reported that they did not get cooperation from local people while land acquisition was necessary for road construction, as well as chairman's negative attitudes towards allocating work and money to members. Other problems faced by men members included political interference, irregular meetings held by the chairman, delay of receiving project money and so on. Women Problem with chairman regarding allocation of development work & funds Problems faced from men members who opposed women members, to get work and laugh at them Villagers do not cooperate

Corruption at the higher level Lack of fund/less allocation for development work Lack of education, confidence, security, honorarium and financial problem Women members were not informed about their rights & duties.

The reasons faced by both men and women members while undertaking any development work in the Panchayat of India were numerous. But for women, household workload, the attitude toward the caste and gender were the most dominating factors. Nearly 49 percent women representatives were ignorant of the power and duties specified to them, while 31 percent of the women representatives were not able to participate properly owing to the heavy workload at the house. Other obstacles faced by women were lack of information and mobility. While these were also handicaps of men representatives, they do not have the household to deal with. Apart from the impediments faced by them, some of the women and men felt that the decisions were usually taken and influenced by the rich and influential people.

- The women did not allow me to attend meetings
- I am not given an opportunity to speak at the meetings
- Women did not have any recognition in Saifai Gram Panchayat
- We did not have any rights except for the fact that we were members of the Panchayat.
- We did not get assistance from the Block

COOPERATION RECEIVED AT LOCAL LEVEL

Although women and men faced various types of problems both at the household level and in the community, still they could carry out their activities with the support and cooperation they received from other groups and people. Moreover, election promises can only be materialized when there was cooperation from the community from where the members have been elected. Level of cooperation received by members also helps in understanding the success of carrying out the work successfully.

In Bangladesh, Union Parishad members received cooperation from colleagues, family members, relatives, members of the community, Union Parishad chairmen and NGOs to carry out their development activities. Local government representatives elected from the grassroots level received cooperation mostly from the community people, 36 percent women members and 44 percent men members. Regarding other sources of cooperation, there was different scenario by gender. Women members rⁿceived the highest cooperation from their women colleagues (38 percent), compared to 14 percent from their men members. On the other hand, only 4 per cent men members reported to have such cooperation from their women colleagues. Regarding cooperation from the men colleagues, 14 percent women and 44 percent men reported in favor. On the other hand, only negligible 4 percent women members got support from their husbands. The same trend was true of men members, where men got more cooperation from men colleagues (44 percent) than from their wives who were hardly involved or consulted by their husbands. Support from the NGOs was also very low in the case of both among women and men members.

There were not many proxies in the Panchayats, but on the other hand nearly 33 percent of women were helped by their husbands in the Panchayat work. Initially, most of these women were helped by their husbands and men colleagues, but once they understood the intricacies on the work front, they took charge. The community members cooperated with 29 percent of the women members and 38 percent of the men members. This would lead to better coordination and also speedy development through the group effort.

CAPACITY BUILDING THROUGH TRAINING INTERVENTIONS

The need of training and awareness could bring women representatives in a better position not only in the participation level but also at the decision-making levels. The assistance given by the NGOs through the various training programs and general awareness programs is worth noting. The need for training of women does not mean that women were incapable of undertaking development at local level perceived by men politicians, but for qualitative input in development works taken up by the government, which did not reach those who actually needed it. Training has been identified as an important tool to carry out development activities. Training is essential, especially for women because their participation in local government and in the public sphere is a new phenomenon

In Bangladesh, 71 percent women members received training from government and NGOs, compared to only 45 percent men members. Training received by women members from government organizations were mainly on health, sanitation and family planning. Women Union Parishad members also received training on fisheries, poultry, dairy farm and horticulture activities, child rights and early marriage.

In India, the scenario of training was minimal. However, the Panchayat representatives had identified some major areas in which they need training. Most of them emphasized planning procedures, as developmental issues could be dealt successfully only when the planning agendum was taken up with full conviction. The next priority was education, as owing to lack of training, people do suffer in taking quick and emphatic decisions.

The governments of India and Bangladesh provided a major opportunity to include provisions to ensure greater participation by women in local government and greater responsiveness of local government authorities to women's interests and needs. In India, reservation for women in the Panchayat level had basically given women a say in the grassroots political system. On the other hand, the emerging women's leadership, there evolved the Sarpanch-Pati where women may occupy the post but the men may commend via proxy rule. Women's political participation in the local bodies included mainly women as voters, as candidates, as elected members taking part in decision-making, planning and implementation.

In India, the problems faced by women during the election and while implementing development works in the Panchayats were mostly caste/class factors, while in Bangladesh, it was the religious fundamentalist and the purdah restriction.

The women representatives were designated as change agents for rural development, but unfortunately they did not have enough knowledge or training on development and organizational issues to provide a support system for rural women.

CONCLUSION AND RECOMMENDATIONS

The essence of good governance lies, on one hand, the inclusion of local level planning in the national government and on the other hand, the success of a local government depends on peoples' participation. It is the grassroots level people who could contribute significantly to the governance of their communities. However, unequal participation of women and men in the government planning works as a barrier to ensure good governance in both Bangladesh and India. After three decades of research focused on gender equality, it is clear that there is a crucial need for a gender-specific development paradigm into all areas of policy making and planning so that women's needs can be met and their participation ensured. Decentralization has been identified as one of the important prerequisite to ensure gender balance into development process.

The present study was an attempt to review the participation of women at grassroots level democracy in Bangladesh and India. The study examined the role of government of Bangladesh and India to ensure gender balance at local level policy planning. In Bangladesh women's participation at local level politics has been recently ensured through the constitutional reform, while in India it had been for sometimes. It has been found in both the countries that although a large number of women were elected as local representatives, obstacles related to women's gender identity refrained them to play their roles effectively. It was evident that lack of effective and timely planning, lack of political background, absence of proper socio-economic and political environment, lack of appropriate organizational framework, lack of skill and training placed women behind to prove their competencies compared to their men counterparts. It had been identified that women have limited scope to exercise political rights, lack of control over resources and limited choice in decision-making. However, women had been trying to overcome the barriers through their active participation in the local level policy-making.

Attempts had also been taken to sensitize communities as well as local and national leaders and policy makers to the need for gender balance in the political process. Efforts are going on to make politics democratic, participatory, accountable and transparent so as to ensure a just, humane and equitable society. The urgency for political empowerment of women has therefore increased manifold. There is a need to enable women members to be more effective members of local government bodies. Two aspects of effectiveness need to be considered: effectiveness in participating in overall operations and effectiveness in stimulating attention to women's development issues.

That being the case, the foremost task is to reach out to women to make them politically aware and conscious. This task requires to be taken up on a mass and intensified scale. Coordination and cooperation of both government and NGOs are necessary to achieve this goal. Political parties have a significant role to play as well.

At the same time it must be acknowledged that the effort becomes even more difficult when precautions have to be taken to make governance more streamlined, empowering and development oriented while at the same time ensuring that the plurality of the multilayered cultural complexes enmeshed and intertwined with centuries of constructive accretion are not disturbed in any simplistic and radical manner.

Recommendations

Suggestions and recommendations are under three heads, viz., the role of government, role of political parties and role of NGOs and civil societies.

Role of Government

Election rules and regulations to be restructured: Both in India and Bangladesh, election rules should be restructured in the light of facilitating women's participation in the electoral processes, i.e. right to choose their representatives, freedom to express their views and opinions, freely allowed to cast their precious vote, strict ban on use of violence in elections, limits on expenditure and its strict implementation.

Representation of women members at the local level committees: Both in India and Bangladesh, at the local level, planning and decision-making committees should comprise at least 50 percent women. Social programs should be introduced to encourage women's effective participation in such activities.

Fair representation of minorities: The Bangladesh government should also let the minorities like Hindus and Christians be represented in the decision-making process, which could be facilitated by the help of reservation or through fair entry basis.

Information and training to women members of local bodies: The government along with the NGOs imparting training should provide information and training to women members of local bodies to increase their knowledge of local government, responsibilities and functions. This could be through information manuals, mobile training program and through audio-visual mediums. Women should be given various opportunities for leadership training and education in order to encourage them to take up political and leadership position in all fields. Supportive services should be provided to allow women to participate in local bodies.

Exchange of information and experience: Through the Local Government machinery, program or project should be developed that would allow for meetings for the exchange of information and experience on the ways in which women members can pursue issues of women's equality and development as members of local government.

The effectiveness of all Union Parishad and Panchayat members must be increased in promoting women's development. Training materials and courses for members of local government bodies should be revised to include components on women's equality and development. This should include components on changing attitudes to women's participation in decision-making bodies as well as components on assessing programs and projects to ensure that women benefit.

Literacy in legal rights and politics: In all formal and non-formal schools, proper training and exposure to the legal and political rights of women should be given to bring about attitudinal changes among both men and women.

Improvement of motivational programs: To create greater awareness among women about their low status in society and the need to improve it, motivational programs for expanding opportunities for education, health care and employment should be launched.

Participation of women in all activities: To ensure participation of women in development and social activities equal importance should be given to their opinions. To ensure an active participation of women in all activities of Union Parishad and Panchayat, government should monitor that women representatives are given their due respect to undertake and participate equal partners with men in development works at the local level.

Implementation of all kinds of activities: To ensure suitable training on proper implementation of all kinds of development activities and for the proper advancement of grassroots level poor community.

ROLE OF POLITICAL PARTIES

Need for democratization from within: If women are to come even without reservation, as was not approved by some sections of the women's groups and the academia, the foremost responsibility should be that of the political parties who should recognize the capability and success of women and give party tickets to those who are interested to stand for the said post.

Party manifestoes and constitutions should include gender equity as one of their goals and have a plan of action for its achievement.

The present system of reserved seats is a necessary evil that may continue until greater representation of women is achieved. However, political parties in Bangladesh should work together to amend the system of nomination to direct election of women to the reserved seats for the Parliament as well.

Conscientisation to Women's Issues: To raise the political consciousness of the people and to sensitize them about women's issues, political parties should organize workshops, dialogues, discussions and mass meetings. Political parties should also sensitize party leaders and party workers about women's issues by organizing discussion sessions.

Maintain Linkages with Voters: Political parties should encourage their women candidates to maintain a continuous linkage with the voters, with special emphasis on women voters, so that they are not misled by the male members of their families.

Fair Elections at All Levels: Political parties should work towards free and fair elections so that women candidates can contest. Awareness programs for the voters should be undertaken so that they can cast their vote in favor of eligible candidates.

Stand against Factionalism: Political parties should take a positive stand against factionalism, fundamentalism and misinterpretation of religious beliefs, which stands in the way of women's political participation. In order to develop political awareness and consciousness, women should be involved in social, economic and political activities.

Implementation of Legal reforms and UN Conventions: Political parties should ensure the implementation of legal reforms and UN Conventions relating to women.

To Change the Policy of Political Parties: Women belonging to all political parties have to take organized steps to change the discriminatory policy and approach political parties in the matter of financial support to women candidates in elections. Political parties should provide financial allocations for the campaign expenditure of women candidates.

ROLE OF NGOS AND CIVIL SOCIETY

NGO Agenda: Political empowerment of women should be incorporated in the NGO agenda. They should consciously make an effort to emphasize the issues of gender equity and women's empowerment in its right perspective. Both men and women leaders at the grassroots and national levels must be sensitized to women's issues, and form pressure and advocacy groups for the realization of gender equity. Women should be made aware of their potential political power and their contribution to the political process as voters.

Networking: To facilitate the inclusion of women's issues in the political and public agenda, networking between the women's organizations and women politicians, in particular, is necessary. Curriculum and media should be adequately utilized so as to change patriarchal social values and encourage women towards leadership roles and activities.

Organize Pressure Groups: To support women candidates and mobilize funds for increasing women's participation in politics,

NGOs should organize support groups and raise the political consensus of women through seminars, workshops, orientation training, mass media, etc. To lobby for increasing women's participation in politics, pressure groups should be formed within and outside the Parliament.

Participation in Political Parties: To increase the number of women in the rank and file at all levels of political parties, grassroots women's organizations should mobilize women at all levels. They should also highlight the potentials of women and their competence as candidates.

Knowledge about the functions of Panchayats and Union Parishads: Most of the women members had lower levels of education. Their training may be conducted by the relevant training institutes or by the respective district authority with the financial support of the government or assistance from the donor agencies/ development partners. A training or instructional handbook on women's power, rights, functions and management of the Union Parishad should be provided to them after being elected as women members of the Union Parishad.

To participate in the local bodies meeting: In order to ensure proper participation in the local bodies, the government may undertake the membership of women members in the different committees, specially the committees dealing with family planning and women's development. A mechanism should be developed to ensure regular attendance of the women members at the meetings.

Selection procedures of party's candidates: Rural women do not have a clear appreciation and adequate awareness of the issues faced by the women because of the respective environment. Women members, whatever may be their selection procedure, are recognized as leaders at the grassroots level by the government and by the local community. They should, therefore, be given adequate training and exposure to the issues, which stand in the way of the integration of women with the socio-economic life of society.

4

Pradhan Mantri Gram Sadak Yojana (PMGSY)

The Pradhan Mantri Gram Sadak Yojana (PMGSY) was launched on 25th December, 2000, and has now been under implementation for just over two years. It is a 100% Centrally Sponsored Scheme which primarily aims to provide single all weather road connectivity to over 1.60 lakh eligible Unconnected Habitations at an estimated investment of about Rs. 60,000 crore. The works are executed by the State Governments and monitored by the Ministry of Rural Development through the National Rural Roads Development Agency (NRRDA), set up for the purpose.

MAIN FEATURES OF PMGSY

Based on the experience gathered during the last two years of implementation of the PMGSY and the feedback received from the Field Engineers, States and Public Representatives, the Guidelines of PMGSY have recently been revised and issued on 7th January, 2003. The Revised Guidelines have become effective from 15th January, 2003.

The salient features of the PMGSY are as under:–

l Preparation of Rural Roads Plan and Core Network – All roads under PMGSY are to be prioritised out of the Core Network keeping in view the priorities as per the Guidelines in respect of population size and giving preference to New Connectivity. l Roads specifications – Roads are to be built as per the specifications given in Rural Roads Manual published by the Indian Roads Congress (IRC:SP20:2002). It may be noted that the Rural Roads

Manual allows for a carriageway of 3.0m where traffic intensity is less than 100 motorised vehicles per day and where the traffic is not likely to increase due to situation, like, dead end, low Habitation and difficult terrain condition. To ensure economy in respect of link roads, the carriageway width may be restricted to 3.0m

PMGSY- AT A GLANCE

Objective

A 100% Centrally sponsored scheme launched with effect from 25th December,2000 to provide connectivity to all Unconnected Habitations (around 1.60 lakh) with all weather roads. All Unconnected Habitations with a population of 500 *persons (or more) to be provided connectivity by the end of Tenth Plan Period (2007).*

Estimated Expenditure

Rs.60,000 crores

Execution of Works and Monitoring

- *Works to be executed by the State Governments. Project proposals are to be based on the District Rural Roads Plan and identified Core Network.*
- *No new Agency/Consultants to be created for execution only.*
- *Roads are to be built as per the specifications given in Rural Roads Manual published by the Indian Roads Congress. Ensuring the quality of the Road is primarily the responsibility of State Governments/Union Territories.*
- *District Monitoring and Vigilance Committee set up by the Ministry of Rural Development also monitors the Progress under the Scheme.*

Maintenance

- *The responsibility of maintenance of roads is of State Governments. The scheme envisages* performance guarantee for five years by the Contractor; thereafter the roads may be transferred *to Panchayati Raj Institutions for maintenance.*

Progress

- *In the last 24 months, project proposals worth Rs.7553.77 crore pertaining to all 28 States and 6 Union Territories clearedOver 37000 Habitations are likely to be benefited and about 56000 km. of roads would be constructed on completion of projects already cleared*
- *A sum of Rs.4925.00 crore released to States /UTs till November, 2002 and an expenditure of Rs.3321.59 crore has already been incurred till December, 2002 on the works done.*
- *11,572 road works already completed.*
- *85% of roads works cleared in the year 2000-2001 have already been completed. Likewise, 52.73% of the funds released to the States for the road works cleared in the year 2001-2002 have been utilized upto December, 2002.*

NATIONAL RURAL ROADS DEVELOPMENT AGENCY (NRRDA)

- *Registered under the Societies Registration Act, 1860 to extend support to Programme through advice on technical specifications, project appraisal, appointment of part time Quality Control Monitors etc.*
- *Became functional in 2002.*

In all such cases with corresponding reduction in roadway width etc. as per the Rural Roads Manual.

District level Programmes – Once the Core Network is prepared, it is possible to estimate the length of roads required for New Connectivity as well as Upgradation for every District. The State's Allocation will henceforth be distributed among the Districts giving 80% on the basis of road length required for providing connectivity to Unconnected Habitations.The District-wise allocation of funds would also be communicated to the Ministry/NRRDA every year by the State Government.

Scrutiny, Approval and Clearance – The proposals prepared by the District Panchayats are to be approved by the State level Standing Committee, whereafter Detailed Project Reports will be prepared for those roads and scrutinised by the State Technical Agencies (STAs) nominated by the NRRDA (Annexure-XV). The

STAs have been selected from among the Indian Institutes of Technology, Regional Engineering Colleges and Government Engineering Colleges of repute.

Proposals are to be sent to NRRDA for clearance based on the scrutiny completed by STAs. Project clearance and Release of funds – Projects will be cleared by the Empowered Committee of the Ministry of Rural Development and 25% of the estimated cost will be released at the time of clearance. Subsequent releases for all road works will be subject to utilisation of 60% of earlier released funds as well as completion of 80% of the approved road works upto (but not including) the year previous to the current year and other standard conditions.

Fund management in State – Each State will identify/create a State level Autonomous Agency to maintain and operate Bank account to receive project funds. This account will be operated by the District Programme Implementation Units (DPIUs). Execution – No new Agency/Consultants will be created for execution only. Tendering – The works will be tendered as per Standard Bidding Document being circulated to the State Governments by NRRDA. Projects will be completed within 9 – 10 months except in the case of Hill States where upto 18 months is allowed. Cost escalation, if any, due to changes in design or time-overruns or tender premium will be borne by the State Governments. Monitoring and Quality – Ensuring the quality of the road works shall primarily be the responsibility of the State Governments/ Union Territory Administrations, who are implementing the Programme. In addition, District Vigilance and Monitoring Committee set up by the Ministry of Rural Development will also monitor the progress under the Scheme.

Computerisation – An Internet based software has been developed by C-DAC, Pune and installed alongwith hardware in all States and Districts. Training has also been provided to staff. It is expected that data regarding proposals and projects as well as detailed information regarding execution of new road works will be regularly entered into data base. Regular updating of the software (called OMMS) is an essential requirement for continued funding of projects under PMGSY and failure to do so will affect releases.

l Maintenance – Roads under PMGSY are required to be maintained by the State Governments. State Governments have to communicate a satisfactory mechanism for the maintenance of rural roads under PMGSY in order to be able to receive Programme assistance. The Scheme envisages Performance Guarantee for five years by the Contractor whereafter the road may be transferred to Panchayati Raj Institutions for maintenance.

NATIONAL RURAL ROADS DEVELOPMENT AGENCY (NRRDA)

The National Rural Roads Development Agency (NRRDA), registered under the Societies' Registration Act, 1860 to extend support to the Programme through advice on technical specifications, project appraisal, appointment of part time Quality Control Monitors, management of monitoring systems and submission of periodic reports to Ministry of Rural Development, became functional during the year 2002. A number of Workshops on Maintenance of Rural Roads, Accounting and Audit System for PMGSY, Quality Control Handbook, Standard Bidding Document and Core Network were organised by the NRRDA during the year. Details are given at Annexure-XVI. Further, several studies were sponsored and Manuals, Handbooks and other publications were brought out by the NRRDA during the year. These included, inter alia, the Quality Control Handbook, the Quality Control Registers, User Manuals, publications on progress of works etc. Details are at Annexure-XVII.

Progress of works

In the last two years, the Ministry have cleared project proposals to the tune of Rs. 7553.77 crore pertaining to all 28 States and 6 Union Territories. Over 37,000 Habitations are likely to be benefited and over 56,000 km. of roads will be constructed upon completion of the road works already cleared under the PMGSY. This includes about 9500 Habitations being covered and 8650 kms. being constructed through completion of incomplete road works started under the erstwhile Basic Minimum Services Programme (BMS) for which a sum of Rs. 672.26 crore was provided in the year 2000-01 under the Programme.

A sum of Rs. 4925.00 crore has been released to the States/UTs till November, 2002 and the value of work done/expenditure of Rs.3321.59 crore has been incurred till December, 2002 and 11,572 road works have been completed. The Statements showing physical and financial progress under PMGSY in the years 2000-01 and 2001-02 are given at Annexures XVIII & XIX. 85% of road works cleared in the year 2000-01 have been completed and 82.50% of the funds released have been spent upto December, 2002. Likewise, 52.73% of the funds released to the States for the road works cleared in the year 2001-02 have been utilised upto December, 2002 and all the road works are likely to be completed by May-June, 2003.

A review of performance reveals that 18 States and Union Territory of Pondicherry have by and large completed all road works of 2000-01. These are Andhra Pradesh, Arunachal Pradesh, Goa, Gujarat, Haryana, Himachal Pradesh, Karnataka, Kerala, Maharashtra, Meghalaya, Mizoram, Nagaland, Punjab, Rajasthan, Sikkim, Tamil Nadu, Tripura and Uttar Pradesh. All other States, except Bihar and Jammu & Kashmir, are expected to complete all road works of 2000-01 by March, 2003. Bihar and Jammu & Kashmir are expected to complete their works by June, 2003.

The charts shown above reveal that among the major States, States of Bihar, Jharkhand, West Bengal and Karnataka have been relatively slow to pick up.

Release of funds

Since the Programme is being executed in a Project Mode, the release of funds depends on the performance of the State in both physical and financial terms. Funds are now released to the States only when they report completion of at least 80% of the road works of the first year and utilise 60% of funds already released to the State. During 2002-03, so far, Rs. 580.00 crore has been cleared for release to 8 States and proposal to release Rs.370 crore to 4 more States is under examination. Remaining States are likely to become eligible for release of funds in February-March, 2003. Details are given at Annexure-XX.

The Ministry and the National Rural Roads Development Agency (NRRDA) are regularly reviewing the progress of works.

The States, particularly those with large number of Unconnected Habitations such as Uttar Pradesh, Bihar, Madhya Pradesh, Jharkhand, West Bengal, Orissa, Chhattisgarh, Rajasthan and Assam, are being urged to take steps to improve their absorption capacity. It has been impressed upon the States that they need to critically scrutinise administrative procedure, delegate financial and administrative powers, strengthen the Programme Implementation Units at the District level, improve quality consciousness and put in place an effective monitoring mechanism.

Quality of Works

Under the PMGSY, quality is sought to be ensured through a three-tier Quality Control System, in which the Executing Agency is primarily responsible for maintaining the quality through its Executive Engineers, at the Programme Implementation Unit (PIU) level, as well as through an independent State level Quality Control mechanism, independent of the Field Engineers.

In addition, the National Rural Roads Development Agency (NRRDA), as the third-tier, engages National Quality Monitors (NQMs) to verify on a systematic randomised basis, the quality of road works. NQMs are generally senior retired officials with adequate experience in road construction programmes. The reports of the NQMs are sent to the State Government for necessary action. Of the 3378 road works inspected by NQMs between March and December, 2002, 7% have been categorised 'very good', 62% as 'good', 25% as 'average' and 6% as 'poor'. Details are enclosed at Annexure-XXI. Steps are being taken to ensure that any deficiency detected by the Monitors are rectified before the State Authorities can make further payments. A suitable mechanism in this regard has been built into the On-line Management & Monitoring System (OMMS) and have been incorporated in the Revised Guidelines.

In order to have an in-built Quality Control System effectively in place, the NRRDA has developed a Quality Control Handbook and Quality Control Registers which are to be maintained for all road works. These are being printed and supplied to the State Authorities. It has been stipulated in the Revised Guidelines that payment shall not be made to the Contractor unless the tests have been found to be successful. The record of tests shall be computerised on the format prescribed by the NRRDA. The State Governments/UT Administrations are also expected to put in place systems to identify and take appropriate action (including blacklisting of contractors in serious cases) against the Contractors and the Field Engineers who are found negligent in ensuring the quality of road works. Recurrent adverse reports about quality of road works in a given District/State might entail suspension of the Programme in that area till the underlying causes of defective work have been addressed. These measures are expected to lead to construction of good quality roads under the PMGSY.

External Funding Agencies

Keeping in view the resource gap for the Programme, Government of India have been taking steps to arrange additional funds for the Programme. The World Bank and the Asian Development Bank (ADB) have agreed to fund the Programme and we expect ADB funding for a project of $500 million (approximately Rs. 2500 crore) to commence from the year 2003-04. This is likely to be the first in a series of loans for the PMGSY. In the first stage, the States of Madhya Pradesh and Chhattisgarh are being taken up under the ADB Project. Likewise, the World Bank is also likely to begin funding projects from 2003-04 in the States of Uttar Pradesh, Rajasthan, Jharkhand and Himachal Pradesh. Discussions are presently under way regarding the size and nature of loan.

Project proposals for Rs.2500 crore have been invited from the States and are likely to be cleared by February-March, 2003. Proposed States for ADB and World Bank funding have been requested to keep in readiness project proposals so that the projects could be grounded as soon as the Loan negotiations are completed with the ADB and the World Bank.

Accounting System

The Institute of Public Auditors of India (IPAI) submitted their Report on the Accounting and Audit System for the PMGSY and based on the same, the arrangements for Flow of Funds, Procedure for Release and Audit have been suitably amended and incorporated in the Revised Guidelines of the PMGSY.

Training and Research

The NRRDA has drawn up an elaborate strategy for training of Engineers, contractors and all other personnel involved with the execution of the PMGSY at the District, State and National level. These would cover, inter alia, the following aspects:-

- Planning and preparation of Detailed Project Reports (DPRs) including Project Scheduling
- Design of road geometrics, Pavements and Cross-Drainage works
- Construction methods for the road components
- Quality Assurance and Control
- Maintenance of Rural Roads
- On-line Management & Monitoring System
- Management of Social and Environmental Aspect in different stages of Rural Roads Development

It is proposed to involve the Principal Technical Agencies, State Technical Agencies and retired Field Engineers for imparting training.

The NRRDA has also identified seven Principal Technical Agencies (PTAs) to act as the Regional Coordinators of the STAs as well as the extended arms of NRRDA in the pursuit of its objectives. The role and responsibilities of the PTAs include overseeing the activities of the STAs in the region, carry out random checks of the proposals scrutinised by STAs, organise orientation/ refresher programmes to the STA personnel for proper scrutiny of project proposals, evaluate specifications, practices and the use of locally available materials for making the proposals cost effective, formulate design specifications for new and innovative technologies, advise the PIUs on any region specific issues that may have a bearing on the design construction and performance of Rural Roads, study the gaps in the existing practices in Rural Roads construction, to identify area for research and development, to develop course material for different modules of the Training Programmes at Regional level and act as Resource Institutions for the training of Field Engineers and the Trainers where necessary. The PTAs are also to assist the NRRDA in processing the research and development proposals, and identifying and resolving issues arising out of quality monitoring and quality audit of roads in progress as well as completed road works. The identified PTAs are the Central Road Research Institute (CRRI); IIT, Mumbai; Department of Civil Engineering, University of Bangalore; IIT, Kharagpur; IIT Roorkee, Birla Institute of Technology, Pilani and National Institute of Technology, Warangal.

The National Council for Building Materials (NCCBM) has been asked to supervise the construction of 200 km. of cement concrete roads as pilot projects in selected States. It is also proposed to take up pilot projects involving use of Modified Bitumen (including Rubber Modified Bitumen) for wearing courses in all the States under the PMGSY.

ON-LINE MANAGEMENT & MONITORING SYSTEM

The internet-based On-line Management & Monitoring System has been set up for the PMGSY. The Centre for Development of Advanced Computing (C-DAC), Pune have prepared the 9 Application Software Modules and these have been released in November, 2002. The PMGSY website has been launched in November, 2002 and the site can be accessed at www.pmgsy.org . Details of road works including, inter alia, the name of road works, length of road, cost, name of Executing Agency and name of contractor are being made available on the PMGSY web site.

Orientation Training for State IT Nodal Officers has been conducted and the Training of Master Trainers has also been completed in December, 2002. State level Training for personnel from the Programme Implementation Units(PIUs)/ Districts are being organised. Version 2.0 of the User Manual has also been developed and published and copies have been made available to the States. The requisite Hardware has been supplied to the Districts and the States.

THE CONSTITUTION (SEVENTY-THIRD AMENDMENT) ACT, 1992

[20th April, 1993.]

An Act further to amend the Constitution of India.

BE it enacted by Parliament in the Forty-third Year of the Republic of India as follows:-

1. Short title and commencement.-(1) This Act may be called the Constitution (Seventy-third Amendment) Act, 1992.

(2) It shall come into force on such date_680 as the Central Government may, by notification in the Official Gazette, appoint. 2. Insertion of new Part IX.- After Part VIII of the Constitution, the following Part shall be inserted, namely:-

PART IX: THE PANCHAYATS

243. Definitions.- In this Part, unless the context otherwise requires,- (a) "district" means a district in a State;

(b) "Gram Sabha" means a body consisting of persons registered in the electoral rolls relating to a village comprised within the area of Panchayat at the village level;

(c) "Intermediate level" means a level between the village and district levels specified by the Governor of a State by public notification to be the intermediate level for the purposes of this Part;

(d) "Panchayat" means an institution (by whatever name called) of self-government constituted under article 243B, for the rural areas;

(e) "Panchayat area" means the territorial area of a Panchayat;

(f) "population" means the population as ascertained at the last preceding census of which the relevant figures have been published;

(g) "village" means a village specified by the Governor by public notification to be a village for the purposes of this Part and includes a group of villages so specified.

243A. Gram Sabha.- A Gram Sabha may exercise such powers and perform such functions at the village level as the Legislature of a State may, by law, provide.

243B. Constitution of Panchayats.- (1) There shall be constituted in every State, Panchayats at the village, intermediate and district levels in accordance with the provisions of this Part.

(2) Notwithstanding anything in clause (1), Panchayats at the in-termediate level may not be constituted in a State having a population not exceeding twenty lakhs.

243C. Composition of Panchayats.- (1) Subject to the provisions of this Part, the Legislature of a State may, by law, make provisions with respect to the composition of Pancayats:

Provided that the ratio between the population of the territorial area of a Panchayat at any level and the number of seats in such Panchayat to be filled by election shall, so far as practicable, be the same throughout the State.

(2) All the seats in a Panchayat shall be filled by persons chosen by direct election from territorial constituencies in the Panchayat area and; for this purpose, each Panchayat area shall be divided into territorial constituencies in such manner that the ratio between the population of each constituency and the number of seats allotted to it shall, so far as practicable, be the same throughout the Panchayat area.

(3) The Legislature of a State may, by law, provide for the re- presentation-

(a) of the Chairpersons of the Panchayats at the village level, in the Panchayats at the intermediate level or, in the case of a State not having Panchayats at the intermediate level, in the Pancayats at the district level;

(b) of the Chairpersons of the Panchayats at the intermediate level, in the Panchayats at the district level;

(c) of the members of the House of the People and the members of the Legislative Assembly of the State representing constituencies which comprise wholly or partly a Panchayat area at a level other than the village level, in such Panchayat;

(d) of the members of the Council of States and the members of the Legislative Council of the State, where they are registered as electors within-

(i) a Panchayat area at the intermediate level, in Panchayat at the intermediate level;

(ii) a Panchayat area at the district level, in Panchayat at the district level.

(4) The Chairperson of a Panchayat and other members of a Panchayat whether or not chosen by direct election from territorial constituencies in the Panchayat area shall have the right to vote in the meetings of the Panchayats.

(5) The Chairperson of -

(a) a Panchayat at the village level shall be elected in such manner as the Legislature of a State may, by law, provide; and

(b) a Panchayat at the intermediate level or district level shall be elected by, and from amongst, the elected members thereof.

243D. Reservation of seats.- (1) Seats shall be reserved for-

(a) the Scheduled Castes; and

(b) the Scheduled Tribes,

in every Panchayat and the number of seats of reserved shall bear, as nearly as may be, the same proportion to the total number of seats to be filled by direct election in that Panchayat as the population of the Scheduled Castes in that Panchayat area or of the Scheduled Tribes in that Panchayat area bears to the total population of that area and such seats may be allotted by rotation to different constituencies in a Panchayat.

(2) Not less than one-third of the total number of seats reserved under clause (1) shall be reserved for women belonging to the Scheduled Castes or, as the case may be, the Scheduled Tribes.

(3) Not less than one-third (including the number of seats reserved for women belonging to the Scheduled Castes and the Scheduled Tribes) of the total number of seats to be filled by direct election in every Panchayat shall be reserved for women and such seats may be allotted by rotation to different constituencies in a Panchayat.

(4) The offices of the Chairpersons in the Panchayats at the village or any other level shall be reserved for the Scheduled Castes, the Scheduled Tribes and women in such manner as the Legislature of a State may, by law, provide:

Provided that the number of offices of Chairpersons reserved for the Scheduled Castes and the Scheduled Tribes in the Panchayats at each level in any State shall bear, as nearly as may be, the same proportion to the total number of such offices in the Panchayats at each level as the population of the Scheduled Castes in the State or of the Scheduled Tribes in the State bears to the total population of the State:

Provided further that not less than one-third of the total number of offices of Chairpersons in the Panchayats at each level shall be reserved for women: Provided also that the number of offices reserved under this clause shall be allotted by rotation to different Panchayats at each level.

(5) The reservation of seats under clauses (1) and (2) and the reservation of offices of Chairpersons (other than the reservation for women) under clause (4) shall cease to have effect on the expiration of the period specified in article 334.

(6) Nothing in this Part shall prevent the Legislature of a State from making any provision for reservation of seats in any Panchayat or offices of Chairpersons in the Panchayats at any level in favour of backward class of citizens.

243E. Duration of Panchayats, etc.- (1) Every Panchayat, unless sooner dissolved under any law for the time being in force, shall continue for five years from the date appointed for its first meeting and no longer.

(2) No amendment of any law for the time being in force shall have the effect of causing dissolution of a Panchayat at any level, which is functioning immediately before such amendment, till the expiration of its duration specified in clause (1).

(3) An election to constitute a Panchayat shall be completed-

(a) before the expiry of its duration specified in clause (1);

(b) before the expiration of a period of six months from the date of its dissolution:

Provided that where the remainder of the period for which the dissolved Panchayat would have continued is less than six months, it shall not be necessary to hold any election under this clause for constituting the Panchayat for such period.

(4) A Panchayat constituted upon the dissolution of a Panchayat before the expiration of its duration shall continue only for the remainder of the period for which the dissolved Panchayat would have continued under clause (1) had it not been so dissolved.

243F. Disqualifications for membership.-(1) A person shall be disqualified for being chosen as, and for being, a member of a Panchayat-

(a) if he is so disqualified by or under any law for the time being in force for the purposes of elections to the Legislature of the State concerned:

Provided that no person shall be disqualified on the ground that he is less than twenty-five years of age, if he has attained the age of twenty-one years;

(b) if he is so disqualified by or under any law made by the Legislature of the State.

(2) If any question arises as to whether a member of a Panchayat has become subject to any of the disqualifications mentioned in clause (1), the question shall be referred for the decision of such authority and in such manner as the Legislature of a State may, by law, provide.

243G. Powers, authority and responsibilities of Panchayats.- Subject to the provisions of this Constitution, the Legislature of a State may, by law, endow the Panchayats with such powers and authority as may be necessary to enable them to function as institutions of self-government and such law may contain provisions for the devolution of powers and responsibilities upon Panchayats at the appropriate level, subject to such conditions as may be specified therein, with respect to-

(a) the preparation of plans for economic development and social justice;

(b) the implementation of schemes for economic development and social justice as may be entrusted to them including those in relation to the matters listed in the Eleventh Schedule.

243H. Powers to impose taxes by, and Funds of, the Panchayats.-The Legislature of a State may, by law,-

(a) authorise a Panchayat to levy, collect and appropriate such taxes, duties, tolls and fees in accordance with such procedure and subject to such limits;

(b) assign to a Panchayat such taxes, duties, tolls and fees levied and collected by the State Government for such purposes and subject to such conditions and limits;

(c) provide for making such grants-in-aid to the Panchayats from the Consolidated Fund of the State; and

(d) provide for Constitution of such Funds for crediting all moneys received, respectively, by or on behalf of the Panchayats and also for the withdrawal of such moneys therefrom, as may be specified in the law.

243-I. Constitution of Finance Commission to review financial position.-(1) The Governor of a State shall, as soon as may be within one year from the commencement of the Constitution (Seventy-third Amendment) Act, 1992, and thereafter at the expiration of every fifth year, constitute a Finance Commission to review the financial position of the Panchayats and to make recommendations to the Governor as to-

(a) the principles which should govern-

(i) the distribution between the State and the Panchayats of the net proceeds of the taxes, duties, tolls and fees leviable by the State, which may be divided between them under this Part and the allocation between the Panchayats at all levels of their respective shares of such proceeds;

(ii) the determination of the taxes, duties, tolls and fees which may be assigned to, or appropriated by, the Panchayat;

(iii) the grants-in-aid to the Panchayats from the Consolidated Fund of the State;

(b) the measures needed to improve the financial position of the Panchayats;

(c) any other matter referred to the Finance Commission by the Governor in the interests of sound finance of the Panchayats.

(2) The Legislature of a State may, by law, provide for the composition of the commission, the qualifications which shall be requisite for appointment as members thereof and the manner in which they shall be selected.

(3) The Commission shall determine their procedure and shall have such powers in the performance of their functions as the Legislature of the State may, by law, confer on them.

(4) The Governor shall cause every recommendation made by the Commission under this article together with an explanatory memorandum as to the action taken thereon to be laid before the Legislature of the State.

243J. Audit of accounts of Panchayats.- The Legislature of a State may, by law, make provisions with respect to the maintenance of accounts by the Panchayats and the auditing of such accounts.

243K. Elections to the Panchayats.-(1) The superintendence, direction and control of the preparation of electoral rolls for, and the conduct of, all elections to the Panchayats shall be vested in a State Election Commission consisting of a State Election Commissioner to be appointed by the Governor.

(2) Subject to the provisions of any law made by the Legislature of a State, the conditions of service and tenure of office of the State Election Commissioner shall be such as the Governor may by rule de-termine: Provided that the State Election Commissioner shall not be removed from his office except in like manner and on the like grounds as a Judge of a High Court and the conditions of service of the State Election Commissioner shall not be varied to his disadvantage after his appointment.

(3) The Governor of a State shall, when so requested by the State Election Commission, make available to the State Election Commission such staff as may be necessary for the discharge of the functions conferred on the State Election Commission by clause (1).

(4) Subject to the provisions of this Constitution, the Legislature of a State may, by law, make provision with respect to all matters re-lating to, or in connection with, elections to the Panchayats.

243L. Application to Union territories.-The provisions of this Part shall apply to the Union territories and shall, in their application to a Union territory, have effect as if the references to the Governor of a State were references to the Administrator of the Union territory appointed under article 239 and references to the Legislature or the Legislative Assembly of a State were references, in relation to a Union territory having a Legislative Assembly, to that Legislative Assembly:

Provided that the President may, by public notification, direct that the provisions of this Part shall apply to any Union territory or part thereof subject to such exceptions and modifications as he may specify in the notification.

243M. Part not to apply to certain areas.-(1) Nothing in this Part shall apply to the Scheduled Areas referred to in clause (1), and the tribal areas referred to in clause (2), of article 244.

(2) Nothing in this Part shall apply to-

(a) the States of Nagaland, Meghalaya and Mizoram;

(b) the Hill Areas in the State of Manipur for which District Councils exist under any law for the time being in force.

(3) Nothing in this Part-

(a) relating to Panchayats at the district level shall apply to the hill areas of the District of Darjeeling in the State of West Bengal for which Darjeeling Gorkha Hill Council exists under any law for the time being in force;

(b) shall be construed to affect the functions and powers of the Darjeeling Gorkha Hill Council constituted under such law.

(4) Notwithstanding anything in this Constitution,-

(a) the Legislature of a State referred to in sub-clause (a) of clause (2) may, by law, extend this Part to that State, except the areas, if any, referred to in clause (1), if the Legislative Assembly of that State passes a resolution to that effect by a majority of the total membership of that House and by a majority of not less than two-thirds of the members of that House present and voting;

(b) Parliament may, by law, extend the provisions of this Part to the Scheduled Areas and the tribal areas referred to in clause (1) subject to such exceptions and modifications as may be specified in such law, and no such law shall be deemed to be an amendment of this Constitution for the purposes of article 368.

243N. Continuance of existing laws and Panchayats.- Notwithstanding anything in this Part, any provision of any law relating to Panchayats in force in a State immediately before the commencement of the Constitution (Seventy-third Amendment) Act, 1992, which is inconsistent with the provisions of this Part, shall continue to be in force until amended or repealed by a competent Legislature or other competent authority or until the expiration of one year from such commencement, whichever is earlier: Provided that all the Panchayats existing immediately before such commencement shall continue till the expiration of their duration, unless sooner dissolved by a resolution passed to that effect by the Legislative Assembly of that State or, in the case of a State having a Legislative Council, by each House of the Legislature of that State.

243-O. Bar to interference by courts in electoral matters.- Notwithstanding anything in this Constitution,-

(a) the validity of any law relating to the delimitation of constituencies or the allotment of seats to such constituencies, made or purporting to be made under article 243K, shall not be called in question in any court;

(b) no election to any Panchayat shall be called in question except by an election petition presented to such authority and in such manner as is provided for by or under any law made by the Legislature of a State.'.

Constitution, after sub-clause (b), the following sub-clause shall be inserted, namely:-

"(bb) the measures needed to augment the Consolidated Fund of a State to supplement the resources of the Panchayats in the State on the basis of the recommendations made by the Finance Commission of the State;".

Constitution, the following Schedule shall be added, namely:-

ELEVENTH SCHEDULE

(Article 243G)

1. Agriculture, including agricultural extension.
2. Land improvement, implementation land reforms, land consolidation and soil conservation.
3. Minor irrigation, water management and watershed development.
4. Animal husbandry, dairying and poultry.
5. Fisheries.
6. Social forestry and farm forestry.
7. Minor forest produce.
8. Small scale industries, including food processing industries.
9. Khadi, village and cottage industries.
10. Rural housing.

11. Drinking water.

12. Fuel and fodder.

13. Roads, culverts, bridges, ferries, waterways and other means of communication.

14. Rural electrification, including distribution of electricity.

15. Non-conventional energy sources.

16. Poverty alleviation programme.

17. Education, including primary and secondary schools.

18. Technical training and vocational education.

19. Adult and non-formal education.

20. Libraries.

21. Cultural activities.

22. Markets and fairs.

23. Health and sanitation, including hospitals, primary health centres and dispensaries.

24. Family welfare.

25. Women and child development.

26. Social welfare, including welfare of the handicapped and mentally retarded.

27. Welfare of the weaker sections, and in particular, of the Scheduled Castes and the Scheduled Tribes.

28. Public distribution system.

29. Maintenance of community assets.

THE CONSTITUTION (SEVENTY-FOURTH AMENDMENT) ACT, 1992

[20th April, 1993.]

An Act further to amend the Constitution of India.

BE it enacted by Parliament in the Forty-third Year of the Republic of India as follows:-

1. Short title and commencement.-(1) This Act may be called the Constitution (Seventy-fourth Amendment) Act, 1992.

(2) It shall come into force on such date_681 as the Central Government may, by notification in the Official Gazette, appoint.

2. Insertion of new Part IXA.-After Part IX of the Constitution, the following Part shall be inserted, namely:-

PART IXA: THE MUNICIPALITIES

243P. Definitions.-In this Part, unless the context otherwise requires,-

(a) "Committee" means a Committee constituted under article 243S;

(b) "district" means a district in a State;

(c) "Metropolitan area" means an area having a population of ten lakhs or more, comprised in one or more districts and consisting of two or more Municipalities or Panchayats or other contiguous areas, specified by the Governor by public notification to be a Metropolitan area for the purposes of this Part;

(d) "Municipal area" means the territorial area of a Municipality as is notified by the Governor;

(e) "Municipality" means an institution of self-government constituted under article 243Q;

(f) "Panchayat" means a Panchayat constituted under article 243B;

(g) "population" means the population as ascertained at the last preceding census of which the relevant figures have been published.

243Q. Constitution of Municipalities.-(1) There shall be constituted in every State,-

(a) a Nagar Panchayat (by whatever name called) for a transitional area, that is to say, an area in transition from a rural area to an urban area;

(b) a Municipal Council for a smaller urban area; and

(c) a Municipal Corporation for a larger urban area, in accordance with the provisions of this Part:

Provided that a Municipality under this clause may not be constituted in such urban area or part thereof as the Governor may, having regard to the size of the area and the municipal services being provided or proposed to be provided by an industrial establishment in that area and such other factors as he may deem fit, by public notification, specify to be an industrial township.

(2) In this article, "a transitional area", "a smaller urban area" or "a larger urban area" means such area as the Governor may, having regard to the population of the area, the density of the population therein, the revenue generated for local administration, the percentage of employment in non-agricultural activities, the economic importance or such other factors as he may deem fit, specify by public notification for the purposes of this Part.

243R. Composition of Municipalities.- (1) Save as provided in clause (2), all the seats in a Municipality shall be filled by persons chosen by direct election from the territorial constituencies in the Municipal area and for this purpose each Municipal area shall be divided into territorial constituencies to be known as wards.

(2) The Legislature of a State may, by law, provide-

(a) for the representation in a Municipality of-

(i) persons having special knowledge or experience in Municipal administration;

(ii) the members of the House of the People and the members of the Legislative Assembly of the State representing constituencies which comprise wholly or partly the Municipal area;

(iii) the members of the Council of States and the members of the Legislative Council of the State registered as electors within the Municipal area;

(iv) the Chairpersons of the Committees constituted under clause (5) of article 243S:

Provided that the persons referred to in paragraph (i) shall not have the right to vote in the meetings of the Municipality;

(b) the manner of election of the Chairperson of a Municipality.

243S. Constitution and composition of Wards Committees, etc.-(1) There shall be constituted Wards Committees, consisting of one or more wards, within the territorial area of a Municipality having a population of three lakhs or more.

(2) The Legislature of a State may, by law, make provision with respect to-

(a) the composition and the territorial area of a Wards Committee;

(b) the manner in which the seats in a Wards Committee shall be filled.

(3) A member of a Municipality representing a ward within the territorial area of the Wards Committee shall be a member of that Committee.

(4) Where a Wards Committee consists of-

(a) one ward, the member representing that ward in the Municipality; or

(b) two or more wards, one of the members representing such wards in the Municipality elected by the members of the Wards Committee, shall be the Chairperson of that Committee.

(5) Nothing in this article shall be deemed to prevent the Legislature of a State from making any provision for the constitution of Committees in addition to the Wards Committees.

243T. Reservation of seats.-(1) Seats shall be reserved for the Scheduled Castes and the Scheduled Tribes in every Municipally and the number of seats so reserved shall bear, as nearly as may be, the same proportion to the total number of seats to be filled by direct election in that Municipality as the population of the Scheduled Castes in the Municipal area or of the Scheduled Tribes in the Municipal area bears to the total population of that area and such seats may be allotted by rotation to different constituencies in a Municipality.

(2) Not less than one-third of the total number of seats reserved under clause (1) shall be reserved for women belonging to the Sche- duled Castes or, as the case may be, the Scheduled Tribes.

(3) Not less than one-third (including the number of seats reserved for women belonging to the Scheduled Castes and the Scheduled Tribes) of the total number of seats to be filled by direct election in every Municipality shall be reserved for women and such seats may be allotted by rotation to different constituencies in a Municipality.

(4) The officers of Chairpersons in the Municipalities shall be reserved for the Scheduled Castes, the Scheduled Tribes and women in such manner as the Legislature of a State may, by law, provide.

(5) The reservation of seats under clauses (1) and (2) and the reservation of offices of Chairpersons (other than the reservation

for women) under clause (4) shall cease to have effect on the expiration of the period specified in article 334.

(6) Nothing in this Part shall prevent the Legislature of a State from making any provision for reservation of seats in any Municipality or offices of Chairpersons in the Municipalities in favour of backward class of citizens.

243U. Duration of Municipalities, etc.-(1) Every Municipality, unless sooner dissolved under any law for the time being in force, shall continue for five years from the date appointed for its first meeting and no longer:

Provided that a Municipality shall be given a reasonable opportunity of being heard before its dissolution.

(2) No amendment of any law for the time being in force shall have the effect of causing dissolution of a Municipality at any level, which is functioning immediately before such amendment, till the expiration of its duration specified in clause (1).

(3) An election to constitute a Municipality shall be completed,-

(a) before the expiry of its duration specified in clause (1);

(b) before the expiration of a period of six months from the date of its dissolution:

Provided that where the remainder of the period for which the dissolved Municipality would have continued is less than six months, it shall not be necessary to hold any election under this clause for constituting the Municipality for such period.

(4) A Municipality constituted upon the dissolution of a Municipality before the expiration of its duration shall continue only for the remainder of the period for which the dissolved Municipality would have continued under clause (1) had it not been so dissolved.

243V. Disqualifications for membership.-(1) A person shall be disqualified for being chosen as, and for being, a member of a Municipality-

(a) if he is so disqualified by or under any law for the time being in force for the purposes of elections to the Legislature of the State concerned: Provided that no person shall be disqualified on the ground that he is less than twenty-five years of age, if he has attained the age of twenty-one years;

(b) if he is so disqualified by or under any law made by the Legislature of the State.

(2) If any question arises as to whether a member of a Municipality has become subject to any of the disqualifications mentioned in clause (1), the question shall be referred for the decision of such authority and in such manner as the Legislature of a State may, by law, provide.

243W. Powers, authority and responsibilities of Municipalities, etc.- Subject to the provisions of this Constitution, the Legislature of a State may, by law, endow-

(a) the Municipalities with such powers and authority as may be necessary to enable them to function as institutions of self-government and such law may contain provisions for the devolution of powers and responsibilities upon Municipalities, subject to such conditions as may be specified therein, with respect to-

(i) the preparation of plans for economic development and social justice;

(ii) the performance of functions and the implementation of schemes as may be entrusted to them including those in relation to the matters listed in the Twelfth Schedule;

(b) the Committees with such powers and authority as may be necessary to enable them to carry out the responsibilities conferred upon them including those in relation to the matters listed in the Twelfth Schedule.

243X. Power to impose taxes by, and Funds of, the Municipalities.-The Legislature of a State may, by law,-

(a) authorise a Municipality to levy, collect and appropriate such taxes, duties, tolls and fees in accordance with such procedure and subject to such limits;

(b) assign to a Municipality such taxes, duties, tolls and fees levied and collected by the State Government for such purposes and subject to such conditions and limits;

(c) provide for making such grants-in-aid to the Municipalities from the Consolidated Fund of the State; and

(d) provide for constitution of such Funds for crediting all moneys received, respectively, by or on behalf of the Municipalities and also for the withdrawal of such moneys therefrom.

As may be specified in the law.

243Y. Finance Commission.-(1) The Finance Commission constituted under article 243-I shall also review the financial position of the Municipalities and make recommendations to the Governor as to-

(a) the principles which should govern-

(i) the distribution between the State and the Municipalities of the net proceeds of the taxes, duties, tolls and fees leviable by the State, which may be divided between them under this Part and the allocation between the Municipalities at all levels of their respective shares of such proceeds;

(ii) the determination of the taxes, duties, tolls and fees which may be assigned to, or appropriated by, the Municipalities;

(iii) the grants-in-aid to the Municipalities from the Consolidated Fund of the State;

(b) the measures needed to improve the financial position of the Municipalities;

(c) any other matter referred to the Finance Commission by the Governor in the interests of sound finance of the Municipalities.

(2) The Governor shall cause every recommendation made by the Commission under this article together with an explanatory memorandum as to the action taken thereon to be laid before the Legislature of the State.

243Z. Audit of accounts of Municipalities.-The Legislature of a State may, by law, make provisions with respect to the maintenance of accounts by the Municipalities and the auditing of such accounts.

243ZA. Elections to the Municipalities.-(1) The superintendence, direction and control of the preparation of electoral rolls for, and the conduct of, all elections to the Municipalities shall be vested in the State Election Commission referred to in article 243K.

(2) Subject to the provisions of this Constitution, the Legislature of a State may, by law, make provision with respect to all matters relating to, or in connection with, elections to the Municipalities.

243ZB. Application to Union territories.-The provisions of this Part shall apply to the Union territories and shall, in their application to a Union territory, have effect as if the references to the Governor of a State were references to the Administrator of the Union territory appointed under article 239 and references to the Legislature or the Legislative Assembly of a State were references in relation to a Union territory having a Legislative Assembly, to that Legislative Assembly:

Provided that the President may, by public notification, direct that the provisions of this Part shall apply to any Union territory or part thereof subject to such exceptions and modifications as he may specify in the notification.

243ZC. Part not to apply to certain areas.-(1) Nothing in this Part shall apply to the Scheduled Areas referred to in clause (1), and the tribal areas referred to in clause (2), of article 244.

(2) Nothing in this Part shall be construed to affect the functions and powers of the Darjeeling Gorkha Hill Council constituted under any law for the time being in force for the hill areas of the district of Darjeeling in the State of West Bengal.

(3) Notwithstanding anything in this Constitution, Parliament may, by law, extend the provisions of this Part to the Scheduled Areas and the tribal areas referred to in clause (1) subject to such exceptions and modifications as may be specified in such law, and no such law shall be deemed to be an amendment of this Constitution for the purposes of article 368.

243ZD. Committee for district planning.-(1) There shall be constituted in every State at the district level a District Planning Committee to consolidate the plans prepared by the Panchayats and the Municipalitiies in the district and to prepare a draft development plan for the district as a whole.

(2) The Legislature of a State may, by law, make provision with respect to-

(a) the composition of the District Planning Committees;

(b) the manner in which the seats in such Committees shall be filled:

Provided that not less than four-fifths of the total number of members of such Committee shall be elected by, and from amongst,

the elected mambers of the Panchayat at the district level and of the Municipalities in the district in proportion to the ratio between the population of the rural areas and of the urban areas in the district;

(c) the functions relating to district planning which may be assigned to such Committees;

(d) the manner in which the Chairpersons of such Committees shall be chosen.

(3) Every District Planning Committee shall, in preparing the draft development plan,-

(a) have regard to-

(i) matters of common interest between the Panchayats and the Municipalities including spatial planning, sharing of water and other physical and natural resources, the integrated development of infrastructure and environmental conservation;

(ii) the extent and type of available resources whether financial or otherwise;

(b) consult such institutions and organisations as the Governor may, by order, specify.

(4) The Chairperson of every District Planning Committee shall forward the development plan, as recommended by such Committee, to the Government of the State.

243ZE. Committee for Metropolitan planning.-(I) There shall be constituted in every Metropolitan area a Metropolitan Planning Committee to prepare a draft development plan for the Metropolitan area as a whole.

(2) The Legislature of a State may, by law, make provision with respect to-

(a) the composition of the Metropolitan Planning Committees;

(b) the manner in which the seats in such Committees shall be filled: Provided that not less than two-thirds of the members of such Committee shall be elected by, and from amongst, the elected members of the Municipalities and Chairpersons of the Panchayats in the Metropolitan area in proportion to the ratio between the population of the Municipalities and of the Panchayats in that area;

(c) the representation in such Committees of the Government of India and the Government of the State and of such organisations and institutions as may be deemed necessary for carrying out the functions assigned to such Committees;

(d) the functions relating to planning and coordination for the Metropolitan area which may be assigned to such Committees;

(e) the manner in which the Chairpersons of such Committees shall be chosen.

(3) Every Metropolitan Planning Committee shall, in preparing the draft development plan,-

(a) have regard to-

(i) the plans prepared by the Municipalities and the Panchayats in the Metropolitan area;

(ii) matters of common interest between the Municipalities and the Panchayats, including co-ordinated spatial planning of the area, sharing of water and other physical and natural resources, the integrated development of infrastructure and environmental conservation;

(iii) the overall objectives and priorities set by the Government of India and the Government of the State;

(iv) the extent and nature of investments likely to be made in the Metropolitan area by agencies of the Government of India and of the Government of the State and other available resources whether financial or otherwise;

(b) consult such institutions and organisations as the Governor may, by order, specify.

(4) The Chairperson of every Metropolitan Planning Committee shall forward the development plan, as recommended by such Committee, to the Government of the State.

243ZF. Continuance of existing laws and Municipalities.- Notwithstanding anything in this Part, any provision of any law relating to Municipalities in force in a State immediately before the commencement of THE CONSTITUTION (Seventy-fourth Amendment) Act, 1992, which is inconsistent with the provisions of this Part, shall continue to be in force until amended or repealed by a competent Legislature or other competent authority or until the expiration of one year from such commencement, whichever is earlier: Provided that all the Municipalities existing immediately before such commencement shall continue till the expiration of their duration, unless sooner dissolved by a resolution passed to that effect by the Legislative Assembly of that State or, in the case of a State having a Legislative Council, by each House of the Legislature of that State.

243ZG. Bar to interference by courts in electoral matters.- Notwithstanding anything in this Constitution,-

(a) the validity of any law relating to the delimitation of constituencies or the allotment of seats to such constituencies, made or purporting to be made under article 243ZA shall not be called in question in any court;

(b) no election to any Municipality shall be called in question except by an election petition presented to such authority and in such manner as is provided for by or under any law made by the Legislature of a State.'.

3. Amendment of article 280.- In clause (3) of article 280 of the Constitution, sub-clause (c) shall be relettered as sub-clause (d) and before sub-clause (d) as so relettered, the following sub-clause shall be inserted, namely:-

"(c) the measures needed to augment the Consolidated Fund of a State to supplement the resources of the Municipalities in the State on the basis of the recommendations made by the Finance Commission of the State;".

4. Addition of Twelfth Schedule.-After the Eleventh Schedule to the Constitution, the following Schedule shall be added, namely:-

TWELFTH SCHEDULE

(Article 243W)

1. Urban planning including town planning.

2. Regulation of land-use and construction of buildings.

3. Planning for economic and social development.

4. Roads and bridges.

5. Water supply for domestic, industrial and commercial purposes.

6. Public health, sanitation conservancy and solid waste manage- ment.

7. Fire services.

8. Urban forestry, protection of the environment and promotion of ecological aspects.

9. Safeguarding the interests of weaker sections of society, including the handicapped and mentally retarded.

10. Slum improvement and upgradation.

11. Urban poverty alleviation.

12. Provision of urban amenities and facilities such as parks, gardens, playgrounds.

13. Promotion of cultural, educational and aesthetic aspects.

14. Burials and burial grounds; cremations, cremation grounds and electric crematoriums.

15. Cattle pounds; prevention of cruelty to animals.

16. Vital statistics including registration of births and deaths.

17. Public amenities including street lighting, parking lots, bus stops and public conveniences.

18. Regulation of slaughter houses and tanneries.

5

Rural Development and Panchayat Raj Department

THE RIGHT TO INFORMATION ACT-2005 MANUAL

The Government of India have enacted the Right to Information Act-2005 on 15th June 2005 to provide the system of Right to Information for citizens to secure access to information under the control of Public Authorities in order to promote transparency and accountability in the working of every public authority. The Act came into force on 12th October 2005.

DEFINITIONS

a) "Act" means the Right to Information Act – 2005.

b) "Information" means any material in any form, including records, documents, memos, e-mails, opinions, advices, press releases, circulars, orders, log books, contracts, reports, papers, samples, models, data material held in any electronic form and information to check up the Act provision which can be accessed by a public authority under any other law for the time being in force;

c) "Public Authority" means any authority or body or institution of self – government established or constituted-i) by or under the Constitution. ii) by any other law made by Parliament; iii) by any other law made by State Legislature;

iv) by notification issued or order made by the appropriate Government, and includes any.

v) body owned, controlled or substantially financed;

vi) non-Government organization substantially financed, directly or indirectly by funds provided by the appropriate government;

d) "Record" includes-

i. any document, manuscript and file;

ii. by microfilm, microfiche and facsimile copy of a document;

iii. any reproduction of image or images embodied in such microfilm (whether enlarged or not); and

iv. any other material produced by a computer or any other device;

e) "Right to Information : means the right to information accessible under this

Act which is held by or under the control of any public authority and includes the right to :-

i. inspection of work, documents, records;

ii. taking notes, extracts or certified copies of documents or records;

iii. taking certified samples of material'

iv. obtaining information in the form of diskettes, floppies, tapes, video cassettes or in any other electronic mode or through printouts where such information is stored in a computer or in any other device;

f) "State Public Information Officer" means the State Public Information Officer designated under sub-section (1) and includes a State Assistant Public Information Officer designated as such under sub-section (2) of Section 5;

3. OBJECTIVE OF THE MANUAL : The objective of this Manual is to make available information about the Department of Rural Development and Panchayat Raj to the citizens who desire to have information under the Act.

4. INTENDED USERS OF THIS MANUAL : All citizens who desire to obtain any information on the subjects relating to the Rural Development and Panchayat Raj Department.

5. PROCEDURE AND FEE STRUCTURE FOR GETTING INFORMATION : A person, who desires to obtain any information

under this Act, shall make a request in writing or through electronic means in English or Tamil accompanying such fee to the Public Information Officer designated by the department specifying the particulars of the Information sought by him or her.

FEES :

(a) Every application for obtaining information under sub-section (1) of section 6 of the Right to Information Act shall be made in writing either in person or by post to the Public Information Officers mentioned in paragraph 1.4 above and must be accompanied by an application fee of Rs.10/-(Rupees Ten only) in cash or demand draft or banker's cheque payable to the following head of account:-

"0075.00 Miscellaneous General Services – 800. Other receipts – BK. Collection of fees under Tamil Nadu Right to Information (Fees) Rules 2005" (DPC 0075 00 800 BK 0006)

The applicant may also remit the fee under the above head of account through Treasury/Pay and Accounts Office/State Bank of India/Reserve Bank of India and produce the chalan to the Public Information Officer as an evidence for having remitted the fee. The petitioner may also affix Court Fee Stamp for Rs.10.

(b) For providing information as under sub-section (1) of section 7 of the Right to Information Act, the applicant shall pay the fee prescribed below, in any of the modes specified at (a) above:-

i. Rs.2 (Rupees Two only) for each page (in A-4 or A-3 size paper)

Created or copied.

ii. Actual charge or cost price of a copy in larger size paper;

iii. Actual cost or price for samples or models; and

iv. For inspection of records, no fee for the first hour; and a fee of Rs.5/- (Rupees five only) for each fifteen minutes (or fraction thereof) thereafter.

(c) For providing the information as under sub-section(5) of section 7 of the Right to Information Act, the applicant shall pay the fee prescribed below, in any of the modes specified at (a) above.

i. For information provided in diskette or floppy, Rs.50/- (Rupees fifty only) per diskette or floppy; and

ii. For information provided in printed form, the price incurred for such publication.

Persons below the poverty line are exempted from the payment of fee mentioned in paragraph 5(a) and (b) above for seeking information under the Right to Information Act, 2005. The list of persons below poverty line approved by the Gram Panchayat and local bodies will be the basis for claiming this concession. An extract of the list, duly certified, has to be produced to avail this concession.

Particulars of the organization, functions and duties : (under section 4(i) (b) (i) of RTI Act)

ADMINISTRATIVE SET UP :

Secretary to Government Rural Development and Panchayat Raj Department, Chennai – 9.	25670769
Director of Rural Development and Panchayat Raj, Chennai – 15.	044-24323794
Commissioner of Rural Development and Panchayat Raj (Training), Chennai – 15.	044-24344624
Managing Director, Tamil Nadu Corporation for Development of Women Limited, No.100, Anna Salai, Chennai-600 032.	044 - 22200600
Project Director, Vazhndhu Kattuvom Project, 91, St Mary's Road, Abiramapuram, Chennai-18.	044 - 43511104/ 05/ 06/2007
Project Director, Tsunami Implementation Unit, No.4, Rajaji Salai, Chennai – 600 001.	044 - 25243563
Secretary, State Election Commission, 58, Revathi Street, Jawaharlal Nehru Road, Vadapalani, Chennai – 600 026.	(044) 24843000, 24843002

The Director of Rural Development and Panchayat Raj, Commissioner of Rural Development (Training), Tamil Nadu State

Election Commission, Tamil Nadu Corporation for Development of Women Limited, Vazhndhu Kattuvom Project and Tsunami Project Implementation Unit are functioning, under the control of Rural Development and Panchayat Raj Department. This Department also provides administrative support to the State Election Commission.

OBJECTIVE OF THE DEPARTMENT (Rural Development and Panchayat Raj): The Rural Development and Panchayat Raj Department is responsible for the implementation of various Centrally sponsored and State schemes for poverty alleviation, employment generation, sanitation, capacity building, womens' social and economic empowerment, apart from provision of basic amenities and services. The department is also entrusted with the responsibility of enabling the various Panchayat Raj Institutions (PRIs) to function as effective units of Local Self-Government. There are 12,618 Village Panchayats, 385 Panchayat Unions (co-terminous with Blocks) and 29 District Panchayats under the purview of the department.

PANCHAYAT RAJ INSTITUTIONS : In 1992, the 73rd Amendment to the Constitution was enacted and it brought about a number of fundamental changes in the Panchayat Raj system. Consequently, the Tamil Nadu Panchayats Act 1994 came into force with effect from 22.4.1994. Some of the important changes brought about by the 73rd Amendment to the Constitution and the Tamil Nadu Panchayats Act 1994 are listed below:

a) Introduction of a three tier system – at the Village, Intermediate (Block) and District level.

b) Mandatory conduct of Local Body elections every five years.

c) Introduction of reservation of seats (i.e. ward members) and offices (i.e Chairpersons/Presidents) for Scheduled Castes/ Scheduled Tribes in proportion to their population in every Local Body with provision for rotation of the reserved seats and offices.

d) Introduction of reservation of one third of total number of seats and offices for women with provision for rotation.

e) Constitution of a State Election Commission as an

independent body to conduct elections to both rural and urban Local Bodies regularly.

f) Establishment of a quinquennial State Finance Commission to recommend devolution of resources from the State Government to the rural and urban Local Bodies.

g) Constitution of a District Planning Committee to consolidate the plans prepared by the rural and urban Local Bodies in the district with a view to preparing a comprehensive development plan for the district.

h) Introduction of the concept of 'Grama Sabha' comprising all registered voters in a Village Panchayat.

Function of Village Panchayats

The important functions of village panchayats are as follows:

a) Construction, repair and maintenance of all village roads.

b) Extension of Village sites and the regulation of buildings.

c) Lighting of public roads and public places in built-up areas.

d) Construction of drains.

e) Cleaning of streets and improvement of the sanitary condition of the village.

f) Construction and maintenance of public latrines.

g) Sinking and repairing of wells, the excavation, repair and maintenance of ponds or tanks and the construction and maintenance of water-works for the supply of water.

h) Maintenance of burial and burning grounds.

i) Maintenance of parks and reading room,

j) Implementation of schemes such as Indira Awaas Yojana (IAY) and

National Rural Employment Guarantee Scheme (NREGS). k) Such other duties as the Government may, by notification, impose.

Function of Panchayat Union Council

The important function of Panchayat Union Council are as follows:-

a) Construction, repair and maintenance of all Panchayat union roads.

b) Construction of water works for the supply of water for drinking, washing and bathing purposes.

c) Construction and maintenance of elementary and middle schools.

d) Control of fairs and festivals under the control of the Panchayat Union.

e) Opening and maintenance of Panchayat Union public markets.

f) Implementing various centrally sponsored and State schemes.

g) Preventive and remedial measures connected with any epidemic or with malaria.

Function of District Panchayats

The functions of the District Panchayats are mainly advisory in nature such as:

a) Preparation of development plan for the district.

b) Compilation of administration reports of Village Panchayats and Panchayat Union Councils of the district and preparation of Annual Report for the District.

c) Planning and review of Agriculture, Land Development, Animal Husbandry, Dairy, Poultry, Fisheries and Rural Industries etc.

d) Planning and review of rural housing programmes particularly housing for SC/STs.

Identification of major water supply schemes.

Following are the Centrally sponsored Schemes implemented thro' the Rural Development and Panchayat Raj Department

INDIRA AWAAS YOJANA (IAY)

Indira Awaas Yojana, which used to be a component of Jawahar Rozgar Yojana, became an independent scheme from 1997-98 onwards. Its objective is construction of free houses to members of the Scheduled Castes/Scheduled Tribes, freed bonded labourers in rural areas and also to non SC/ST Rural poor people living below the poverty line. Beneficiaries are selected from the Below-the-Poverty-Line (BPL) list approved by the Grama Sabha. At least

60% of the total IAY allocation during a financial year should be utilized for construction/upgradation of dwelling units for SC/ST BPL households. A maximum 40% of allocation is for non-SC/ST BPL rural households. 3% of the above categories should be allocated for physically and mentally challenged persons. Government of India has also asked the States to earmark 15% of the beneficiaries from amongst the minorities. New houses as well as upgradation of kutcha houses are being taken up under the scheme. It is funded by the Centre and the State in the ratio of 75:25.

New houses

From 01.04.2005 onwards, the unit cost of a new house has been fixed at Rs. 25,000 for ordinary soil and Rs.27,500 for difficult soil. Based on the budget announcement of the Union Finance Minister in February, 2008, this amount is likely to be increased by Rs.10, 000/- and the unit cost raised to Rs.35, 000/- for ordinary soil and Rs.37, 500/- for difficult soil. Moreover, the State Government provides an additional amount for RCC roofing cost in addition to its matching share. With effect from 2006-07, the above RCC roofing cost has been raised from Rs.9,000 to Rs.12,000 per house. The minimum plinth area of a house should be 20 square metres. All new houses are provided with the toilets and smokeless chulhas. Beneficiaries undertake the construction with locally available materials employing

low cost technologies. As the cost of construction of new houses has increased substantially, it has been decided to raise the RCC roofing cost from the existing Rs.12, 000 to Rs.20, 000 per house. This, along with the increase in unit cost as announced by the Central Government will raise the total cost of an IAY house from existing Rs.37,000 and Rs.39,500 to Rs.55,000 and Rs.57,500 for ordinary soil and difficult soil respectively. A further subsidy of Rs.1,200 out of Total Sanitation Funds is dovetailed to enable each beneficiary to construct a toilet in the IAY house.

Upgradation of kutcha houses

This can be taken up to a maximum of 20% of IAY allocation. The unit cost is Rs.12,500.

During 2008-09, 69,239 new houses are likely to be constructed and 15,386 kutcha houses upgraded at a financial outlay of Rs.400.00 crores, inclusive of the State Government's additionality of Rs.138.48 crores towards the RCC roofing cost.

National Rural Employment Guarantee Scheme - Tamil Nadu

The National Rural Employment Guarantee Act was enacted in September 2005. The National Rural Employment Guarantee Scheme was launched on 02.02.2006 and is being implemented in ten districts, viz., Cuddalore, Dindigul, Nagapattinam, Sivagangai, Tiruvannamalai and Villupuram from 02.02.2006 onwards and in four more districts viz. Thanjavur, Tiruvarur, Tirunelveli and Karur from 01.04.2007 onwards. From 01.04.2008 onwards, the scheme is being extended to the remaining twenty districts of the State which are; 1. Ariyalur, 2. Dharmapuri, 3. Perambalur, 4. Pudukottai, 5. Ramanathapuram, 6. Namakkal, 7. Vellore, 8. Thoothu kudi, 9. Virudhunar 10. Salem, 11. Erode, 12.

Tiruchirapalli, 13. Kancheepuram 14. Theni, 15. Tiruvallur, 16. Madurai, 17. Nilgiris, 18. Kanniyakumari, 19. Coimbatore and 20. Krishnagiri.

Objectives of the Scheme

The National Rural Employment Guarantee Act, 2005 (NREGA) guarantees 100 days of employment in a financial year to any rural household whose adult members are willing to do unskilled manual work. This Act is an important step towards the realization of the right to work. It is also expected to enhance people's livelihoods on a sustained basis, by developing the economic and social infrastructure in rural areas.

The Village Panchayat will issue job cards to every registered individual. Payment of the statutory minimum wage and equal wages for men and women are the notable features of the scheme.

Funding Pattern

The cost of the scheme is shared between the Centre and the State in the ratio of 90:10. The Central Government will bear the following costs:

a) The entire cost of wages for unskilled manual workers.
b) 75 percent of the cost of material and wages for skilled and semi-skilled workers.
c) Administrative expenses, which will include, inter alia, the salary and allowances of Programme Officers and their support staff and work site facilities.
d) Administrative expenses of the Central Employment Guarantee Council.

The State Government will bear the following costs:

a) 25 percent of the cost of material and wages for skilled and semi-skilled workers.
b) Unemployment allowance payable in case the State Government cannot provide wage employment within 15 days of application.
c) Administrative expenses of the State Employment Guarantee Council.

Priority of works

Taking into account the field conditions in Tamil Nadu, the works are being taken up in Tamil Nadu in the following priority:

a) Formation of new ponds.
b) Renovation of existing Ponds, Kuttais, Kulams, Ooranies, Temple tanks etc.
c) Desilting of channels.
d) Desilting and strengthening of bunds of irrigation tanks.
e) Formation of new roads.
f) Other water conservation/soil conservation measures/flood protection measures.

Swarna Jayanti Gram Swarozgar Yojana (SGSY)

SGSY is being implemented since April 1999 as a major anti-poverty scheme for the rural poor, by organizing them into Self Help Groups (SHGs), providing them with skill development training and helping them to get credit linkage with financial institutions and providing infrastructure and marketing support for the products produced by them. Government of India and the

State Government are sharing the costs in the ratio of 75:25. The SGSY fund is used to provide subsidy for the Revolving fund and Economic assistance to Self Help Groups.

Part of the Scheme component is also utilised for formation of groups and conduct of training for their basic orientation and skill upgradation. Upto 20% of the total allocation can also be spent on putting up of Infrastructure required for promotion of activities of SHGs.

The SHGs, after the first grading, are provided with a revolving fund of Rs.25,000 (bank loan of Rs.15,000 and Rs.10,000 as subsidy). After the second grading, the successful groups are provided with economic assistance, the maximum eligible subsidy being 50% of the project cost with a ceiling of Rs.1.25 lakhs.

Total Sanitation Campaign (TSC)

The Government of India have restructured the Comprehensive Rural Sanitation Programme with effect from 1.4.1999 and launched the Total Sanitation Campaign (TSC). The project envisages a demand-driven approach with increased stress on awareness building and meeting the demand with alternate delivery mechanisms. With effect from 1.4.2006, the sharing pattern between the Centre and the State is as follows:

a) 80:20 for Information, Education and Communication (IEC) activities, administrative costs, and rural sanitary marts.

b) 60:20:20 for individual household toilets and solid and liquid waste management and community sanitary complexes, with 20% contribution from beneficiaries/ Panchayats.

c) 70:30 for School and Anganwadi toilets.

Nirmal Gram Puraskar

To give a fillip to the Total Sanitation Campaign, the Government of India launched an incentive scheme from June 2003 in the form of an award for total sanitation coverage, maintenance of clean environment and open defecation-free Village Panchayats, Blocks and Districts called 'Nirmal Gram Puraskar' as may be seen below.

Table 8: Cash Incentive Criteria for Nirmal Gram Puraskar

Particulars	*Population*	Incentive (Rs in lakhs)
Village Panchayat	Less than 1,000	0.5
	1,000 to 1,999	1
	2,000 to 4,999	2
	5,000 to 9,999	4
	10,000 and above	5
Block	Upto 50,000	10
	50,001 and above	20
District	Upto 10 lakhs	30
	Above 10 lakhs	50

Member of Parliament Local Area Development Scheme (MPLADS)

The objective of this Scheme is to fill the gaps existing in the provision of infrastructure through various Central and State schemes thereby enabling wholesome development. A sum of Rs.2 crore is allotted per Member of Parliament (Lok Sabha and Rajya Sabha) per year for taking up developmental works identified by the concerned M.P. In the case of Lok Sabha, the scheme is implemented in the districts falling within the constituency of the concerned MP. In the case of Rajya Sabha, the MP can suggest works in one or more districts within the State from which he is elected. As far as the nominated MPs are concerned, they can suggest works anywhere in India. The District Collector gives administrative sanction for the works. The guidelines contain a 'negative list' of works not permitted under this scheme and also an illustrative list of works that may be taken up. Under the scheme, all maintenance works of any type are prohibited. Desilting of ponds, rivers, tanks, canals etc. are also treated as maintenance activities and cannot be taken up under MPLADS.

For 2008-09, an amount of Rs.114 crores is likely to be allotted for works under MPLADS.

Pradhan Mantri Gram Sadak Yojana (PMGSY)

The Government of India launched PMGSY on 25th December 2000 to provide all weather roads to all rural habitations with population more than 1000 by the year 2003 and to all habitations with population between 500 and 1000 by the year 2007. This is a 100% Centrally assisted scheme. Now, Government of India have conceived a time bound plan to upgrade rural infrastructure under the Bharat Nirman plan using the PMGSY funds. As part of the Programme, Government of India intends to connect every habitation of over 1000 population or over 500 in hilly and tribal areas with an all weather road by the end of 2008 – 2009.

National Project on Biogas Development

This is a 100% Centrally sponsored scheme envisaging a subsidy of Rs.2,100 for general category and Rs. 2,800 for SC/ST and small farmers and Rs.3, 500 for hilly areas.

FOLLOWING ARE THE STATE SCHEMES IMPLEMENTED THRO' THE RURAL DEVELOPMENT AND PANCHAYAT RAJ DEPARTMENT

Anaithu Grama Anna Marumalarchi Thittam

This Government launched a landmark scheme called the 'Anaithu Grama Anna Marumalarchi Thittam' vide its G.O.Ms.no.115, Rural Development and Panchayat Raj (SGS-2) Department, dated 11.09.2006 and G.O.Ms.no.189, Rural Development and Panchayat Raj (SGS-2) Department, dated 27.12.2006 which aims at substantial injection of resources into the Village Panchayats in the State in five years. In terms of allocation, this is by far the biggest among all the Centrally sponsored and State funded schemes currently under implementation. The scheme was formally inaugurated by the Hon'ble Chief Minister on 21.01.2007 at Tirumathalampakkam Village of Vellore District.

Since many Village Panchayats have very low incomes and are finding it difficult to provide the statutory services or improve infrastructure, this scheme accords priority to the poorest Village

Panchayats in terms of *per capita* income. One fifth of the Village Panchayats in each Block are taken up in each year in the ascending order of per capita income so as to cover all the Village Panchayats in the State over a period of five years. The villages covered under the old Anna Marumalarchi Thittam, which was in vogue during 1997-2002, will be taken up in the fifth year (2010-11).

Under the scheme, the Government had allocated Rs. 508 crores for 2,540 Village Panchayats during 2006-07 and Rs.511.86 crores for 2,534 Village Panchayats during 2007-08 at the rate of Rs. 20 lakhs per Village Panchayat. For 2008-09, the scheme is being taken up in 2,521 villages at an outlay of Rs. 509.64 crores. Further, funds from other schemes of Rural Development and Panchayat Raj department and other departments such as Highways, Public Works, Social Welfare, Health, Education, Agriculture Engineering, and TWAD Board among others will also be dovetailed as far as possible into the Village Panchayats taken up under Anaithu Grama Anna Marumalarchi Thittam. The Government's intention is to ensure the convergence of at least Rs. 1 crore of funds under various Governmental schemes to each AGAMT Village Panchayat.

The following are some of the key guidelines of the scheme:

1. Selection of works to be taken up under AGAMT will be done by a committee consisting of the Block Development Officer (Village Panchayats), Assistant Engineer (RD)/ Block Engineer the Panchayat President concerned and Village Administrative Officer.
2. The works should be got approved by the Grama Sabha.
3. Cement Concrete roads can be taken up for an amount not exceeding Rs.3 lakhs in tied component per village.
4. At least one Pond/Oorani is to be constructed at a cost of Rs.3-5 lakhs in each AGAMT village and it should have Bathing ghat, Baby pond, Retaining wall etc. In case of a Pond or Oorani being unavailable in the village, Temple tank or Minor Irrigation tank can be taken up for desilting in the village. Desilting the pond for a minimum depth of 2 metres from the existing level and the baby pond for further depth of 1 metre has been stipulated.

5. Fish ponds are to be taken up wherever feasible and preference given to the Self Help Groups for getting fishery rights.
6. Burial ground in each AGAMT village will be improved with approach road, Compound wall, Cremation shed, Water facility and Lighting.
7. A School Sports Centre at an outlay of up to Rs.1.5 lakhs or Community Sports Centre at an outlay of up to Rs.1 lakh is to be put up in each AGAMT village.
8. A library will be opened in each AGAMT village. A new building may be constructed or an existing building may be modified suitably and books worth at least Rs.50,000 are to be bought and furniture worth Rs.50,000 procured for the library. An Honorary Librarian is to be appointed for each AGAMT library.
9. Village shandies are to be improved wherever available.
10. An amount of 1% of the total allocation is to be used for IEC activities.

The Village Panchayats have been permitted to incur an expenditure of up to Rs. 10,000 per year for replacement of sports consumables in AGAMT Sports Centres.

Member of Legislative Assembly Constituency Development Scheme (MLACDS)

Member of Legislative Assembly Constituency Development Scheme is fully funded by the State Government. The main objective of the scheme is to take up works to bridge the critical infrastructural gaps in the Assembly constituencies. Under this scheme, each MLA proposes the works that should be executed in his constituency. The District Collector gives administrative sanction for the works. The allocation per constituency was increased from Rs.1 crore to Rs.1.20 crore vide G.O.Ms.No.134, RD & PR (SGS.II) Department, dated 29.9.2006. 50% of the allocation (Rs.60 lakhs) is earmarked for priority works specified by Government. Out of the remaining 50%, MLAs can choose works of their choice not falling within the negative list.

During 2007-08, the following items of works were held as

priority under the earmarked component of Rs.60 lakhs: 1.Upgradation to/renewal of B.T. roads 2. Provision of Cement concrete roads for rural areas and in urban areas along with above works 3. Provision of Cement concrete pavements along with the provision of storm water drain.

The Government have permitted the MLAs to allocate their funds under MLACDS for the construction of individual / Group houses and upgradation of Kutcha Houses (like IAY scheme in rural areas) in Village Panchayats and Town Panchayats for SC/ST/MBC/BC beneficiaries who are below the poverty line. The Government have also permitted the MLAs to allot funds under MLACDS to repair the group houses that have been constructed up to 1997 under Government Schemes in Village Panchayats and Town Panchayats.

Under the untied funds, following works can also be taken up:

i) Construction of buildings, compound walls and purchase of furniture and equipments for all types of Government Hospitals, PHCs and Government Veterinary Hospitals.

ii) Construction of Buildings, Compound walls and purchase of furniture and equipments for Panchayat Union/ Government Schools and Government colleges.

iii) Construction of buildings for Public Distribution Shops, Direct Purchase Centres, Milk Producers' Co-operative Societies and Bulk Chilling Centres.

In Urban areas, repairs to houses constructed (up to 1997) by Tamil Nadu Slum Clearance Board / Tamil Nadu Housing Board/ TAHDCO with the recommendation of concerned MLA subject to a ceiling of Rs.10,000/- per house.

Panchayat Union School Renovation Programme

The programme of Panchayat Union School Renovation introduced in 2007-08 envisages repair and improvement of all Panchayat Union Elementary Schools and Middle Schools in the State in a phased manner. There are around 22,000 Panchayat Union Primary Schools and 4,500 Panchayat Union Middle Schools which are being maintained by Block Panchayats. Due to lack of proper maintenance, most of these School buildings have become dilapidated. Hence, the repair and renovation of such long neglected 10,248 School buildings in AGAMT Village Panchayats of both AGAMT 2006-07 and 2007-08 Villages was initially taken up during 2007-08 at a cost of Rs.135 crores.

During the year 2008-09 around 5500 Elementary and Middle School buildings in AGAMT 2008-09 villages will be taken up for repairs and improvement and Rs. 60 crores will be allocated to carry out works under this scheme.

Namakku Naame Thittam

Namakku Naame Thittam is being implemented as State Sponsored Scheme with a minimum of one-third amount as public contribution and two-third contribution from Government as grants in both Rural and Urban areas. Under this Scheme, the public themselves can select works as they need and execute it as per the provisions in the guidelines of the Scheme.

Construction of Government and Local Body School Buildings (including Compound Walls), Libraries, Hospitals, Primary Health Centres, Veterinary Dispensaries, Noon Meal Centres, Hostels, Creation of Water Supply Sources, Public Distribution Shop Buildings, Bridges and Culverts, Upgradation of Roads and Streets, CC Pavements, Parks, Play Grounds, Traffic Islands, Fountains, Street lights, Purchase of Furniture, Computers and equipments for Government and Local Body Schools and Libraries and construction of class rooms, laboratories and toilets in Government aided schools and colleges can be undertaken under Namakku Naame Thittam.

Periyar Ninaivu Samathuvapuram

To promote social justice and spread Thanthai Periyar's message of social equality, Government of Tamil Nadu established Samathuvapurams since 1997-98 in the districts where all communities live with unity and brotherhood. Accordingly, 145 Samathuvapurams were established in the State. Government have now decided to revive the scheme and construct another 95 Samathuvapurams. In the first phase, 29 Samathuvapurams will be established at the rate of one Samathuvapuram in each district except Nilgiris District during the year 2008-09. Each

Samathuvapuram will have 100 houses at an approximate cost of Rs.1.20 lakhs per house. Roads, street lights, drinking water supply and Public Distribution Shop will also be provided in each of the Samathuvapurams.

Programme for Comprehensive Development of Dharmapuri and Krishnagiri districts

To curb the rise of Naxalite elements in the backward districts of Dharmapuri and Krishnagiri, a Socio-economic Development Programme was launched in the year 2003-04. For 2007-08, a provision of Rs. 7.50 crores has been made. In the year 2007-08, construction of new houses, various infrastructure development works and training programmes for rural youth have been taken up. For the year 2008-09 also, a provision of Rs.7.50 crores has been made.

TAMIL NADU CORPORATION FOR DEVELOPMENT OF WOMEN

Tamil Nadu Corporation for Development of Women Ltd (TNCDW) was established in 1983 with the prime objective of bringing about socio-economic development and empowerment of women. The Department implements its flagship programme Mahalir Thittam, besides implementing the IFAD Assisted Post Tsunami Sustainable Livelihoods Programme.

The Self Help Group (SHG) approach was started in a small way in Dharmapuri district in the year 1989 and has seen steady growth particularly with the introduction of Mahalir Thittam from 1997-98. It has now become a very vibrant movement spread across all districts of the State encompassing in its fold the poor, underprivileged women living on the fringes of society.

This programme has evolved from promoting traditional thrift and credit practices to supporting economic activities, building capacity of women at every stage. TNCDW has progressively introduced a wide range of definitive interventions, which have created a positive impact in the lives of women.

Vision for TNCDW

The SHG movement with nearly 59 lakh women as members

has grown from strength to strength over the years bringing about substantial social change. It would be the endeavour of the Corporation to extend the benefits of the SHG approach to the uncovered areas of the state and uncovered sections of society. The immediate goal of TNCDW is to ensure that all poor women particularly widows, destitutes and marginalised are included in SHGs in the next three years. TNCDW has been very successful in bringing about social empowerment of women which has not fully translated into economic empowerment. The Corporation will strive to promote more economic activities among SHG women by converging Mahalir Thittam and SGSY implementation.

Strengthening the Federations of Self help groups is the key to achieving sustainability in the long run. TNCDW's vision is to build strong and self reliant SHG federations at the Village Panchayat, Block and district levels throughout the State.

Mahalir Thittam

The programme is implemented in partnership with NGOs and community based organizations which are affiliated with TNCDW after due process. Under Mahalir Thittam 3,65,709 SHGs have been formed as of March 2008 with 58,80,875 women members and with total savings of Rs.1,737.81 crores. This includes 25,484 new SHGs formed in 2007-08 of which 9,999 SHGs have been formed in Anaithu Grama Anna Marumalarchi Thittam villages.

The hallmark of the SHGs promoted by Mahalir Thittam is the systematic training provided to the SHG members and the office bearers. This capacity building brings about qualitative changes in the attitude of the women and promotes cohesion and effective functioning of the group.

All the SHG members are imparted training in 4 modules for 4 days to orient them to the SHG concept. The office bearers of the SHGs (Animator and Representative) are given training in 3 modules for 6 days. This training enhances the leadership quality, team building spirit and capacity to maintain books of accounts. In addition, SHG members who are interested in starting economic activities or develop skills to get self employment are provided skill training. The skill training includes a 5 day capsule on entrepreneurial development.

Credit rating and Linkage

Credit rating is a benchmarking exercise to assess the group and ascertain its credit worthiness. SHGs are rated on various parameters to test their financial discipline and effective functioning. It is done by a committee consisting of representatives from Mahalir Thittam, DRDA, PLF, NGO and a Bank. The first credit rating which is done six months after group formation enables the group to access Revolving Fund or direct credit from Banks. The second credit rating is done after a lapse of another 6 months to ascertain the readiness and suitability of the group to undertake economic activity. Out of 3,31,782 SHGs which have passed credit rating, 3,11,798 SHGs have been linked to Banks as of March 2008.

Revolving Fund to Urban SHGs

After the groups in rural areas pass the first credit rating, Revolving Fund (RF) subsidy of Rs.10,000/- is provided under Swarnajayanti Gram Swarozgar Yojana (SGSY) to facilitate credit linkage with the Banks. In addition to the subsidy given by the Government, the Banks provide cash credit upto Rs.30,000/- per group. The RF subsidy was not available to SHGs in urban areas which restricted their access to credit from Banks. Therefore the Government announced a scheme to provide RF subsidy to urban groups from the year 2006-07. Rs.30 crores have already been provided to give RF subsidy to 30,000 urban SHGs. In 2008-09, the Government have decided to provide RF subsidy to all the eligible 1.50 lakh SHGs.

Affiliation of Non-Governmental Organisations

Mahalir Thittam is implemented in partnership with Non-Governmental Organizations (NGOs) who help in formation of SHGs, provide training and monitor them. The NGOs are provided funds for providing the above services. Interested NGOs are affiliated as partners to Mahalir Thittam if they satisfy the norms for affiliation. The affiliation norms for NGOs and the NGO agreement have been revised. The salient features of the new agreement are:

- Emphasis on quality of NGOs and not numbers

- Incentive to NGOs for facilitating credit linkage and economic activities.
- Performance based and linked to outputs.
- Adequate space for growth of community based organisations like Panchayat Level Federations and Village Poverty Reduction Committees. The affiliation process is in progress and the new agreement will come into force from the year 2008-09.

Manimegalai Awards

To encourage well-functioning SHGs and PLFs, the Government had announced Manimegalai awards at State and district levels. Awards are presented to 5 best PLFs and 10 best SHGs at the State level. One PLF selected as best at the district level and 3 SHGs found to be the best at the district level are given Manimegalai awards and the best SHG at the Block level is given a certificate. The awards and have been instrumental in motivating the SHGs and PLFs to strive for better performance.

Panchayat Level Federation

Under Mahalir Thittam, it is envisaged that Federations of SHGs will be formed at the Village Panchayat level called the Panchayat Level Federations (PLF). The PLFs, by pooling in talent and resources and exploiting economies of scale in production and marketing, can benefit member SHGs immensely. Strong federations are a sure way to ensure sustainability and self reliance of SHGs.

Skill Training for Youth

Given the popularity of the State as an industrial investment destination, there is huge demand for skilled manpower in manufacturing and services sector. By providing relevant skill training, unemployed youth can be productively engaged benefiting the society as well as the individual. With this objective in mind, TNCDW has imparted skill training to 11,485 youth through reputed industrial houses and institutions like MRF, NOKIA, Saint Gobain among others.

The Government announced the Youth SHG scheme in 2006-

07 to channelise the energies of youth constructively and productively. As on March 2008, 19,698 youth groups have been formed and 2,640 youth SHGs have been provided RF subsidy of Rs.10,000/- each.

International Fund for Agricultural Development Assisted Post Tsunami Sustainable Livelihoods Programme

TNCDW is the nodal agency for implementing the International Fund for Agricultural Development (IFAD) Assisted Post Tsunami Sustainable Livelihoods Programme (PTSLP).

The objective of PTSLP is to build self reliant, coastal communities which are able to manage their livelihood in a sustainable manner. This would be achieved by developing viable enterprises and resource management systems.

The project will be implemented at a total outlay of Rs. 298.57 crores over a period of 8 years.

The project area for implementation is the coastal Panchayats of six districts of Kancheepuram, Tiruvallur, Villupuram, Cuddalore, Nagapattinam and Kanyakumari benefiting nearly 6 lakh population.

The Cluster Resource Centre (CRC) is the basic implementation unit covering a group of Panchayats and the project area has been divided into 30 clusters. The CRC personnel will give facilitation support to the traditional community institutions in preparing and implementing project activities.

The programme is to be operationalized in collaboration with Non-Government Organizations and involving traditional community institutions and local bodies. The process for recruiting NGOs and other specialists is under way.

The programme envisages the development of community infrastructure, formation of fish marketing societies, support for Self help groups through capacity building, skill training for youth and assistance through micro credit for SHGs.

The project would promote responsible fishing practices to ensure sustainable livelihood to fishermen. The expertise of relevant institutions will be utilized to identify the coastal and fisheries management issues that affect the community and accordingly remedial measures will be taken up on pilot basis.

The Government have released Rs.10 crores for the first year and the initial project activities have commenced. For the year 2008-09, Rs.54.37 Crores have been provided in the budget for this project.

VAZHNDHU KAATTUVOM PROJECT

One of the prime developmental objectives of Government of Tamil Nadu is alleviating poverty and ensuring inclusive growth. An important intervention in this direction is the World Bank funded Vazhndhu Kaattuvom Project which was designed based on a concept note 'Tamil Nadu Poverty Reduction Initiative' developed in 2000–01. The Vazhndhu Kaattuvom Project was launched in November 2005 and will be implemented over a 6 year period with World Bank assistance. The total outlay of this project is Rs. 717 crores. The target population of this project will be poor households, the most vulnerable sections including the physically challenged and the marginalized communities. The project adopts community driven development approach involving Village communities at every stage of project implementation. The target population is identified by Village communities using participatory methodologies.

Project Area

The project will be implemented in 2,480 Village Panchayats in 70 backward Blocks spread over 15 districts.

Institutional Arrangements

The responsibility for implementation of the project vests with the Vazhndhu Kaattuvom State Society at State level and District Vazhndhu Kaattuvom societies in the project districts.

At the cutting edge level, a 5 member project facilitation team covers 10 – 15 Village Panchayats constituted into a cluster. At the Village Panchayat level the implementation agency is an inclusive community organization by name Village Poverty Reduction Committee (VPRC). In addition, a Social Audit Committee (SAC) is constituted by Grama Sabha which plays the role of guardian of the project principles.

Village Poverty Reduction Committee

The Village Poverty Reduction Committee is a community organization formed under the project predominantly with representatives of the target population. Each hamlet of the Panchayat is represented by a woman SHG member from the target population in the VPRC. The PLF Secretary, a representative of the disabled, 2 members representing other Village level committees are also nominated to the VPRC by the Grama Sabha. The Village Panchayat President is the Ex-officio Chairperson of the VPRC.

Details of Project Area

Sl. No.	District	Number of Blocks	Number of Village Panchayats
1	Coimbatore	5	80
2	Cuddalore	4	236
3	Kancheepuram	4	231
4	Nagapattinam	4	182
5	Namakkal	6	121
6	Ramanathapuram	4	164
7	Salem	6	146
8	Theni	4	81
9	Tiruvallur	5	203
10	Tiruvarur	4	159
11	Tirunelveli	6	156
12	Thiruvannamalai	4	160
13	Thoothukudi	4	154
14	Vellore	5	211
15	Villupuram	5	196
	Total	70	2,480

Social Audit Committee

A 5 member Social Audit Committee nominated by the Grama Sabha monitors project activities and ensures adherence of the project principles during implementation. The Committee is accountable to the Grama Sabha and reports to the Grama Sabha on a regular basis.

Project Implementation Cycle

The project activities to start with are aimed at social mobilization of the poor and marginalized. After formation and building capacity of the community organizations, the project focuses on livelihood promotion of the target population. The implementation stages of the project are:

a. Initiation stage:

- Communication campaign to create awareness about the project.
- Release of Panchayat initiation fund to participating Village Panchayats.
- Identification of the target poor by participatory methodology.
- Formation of VPRC and SAC.

b. Capacity Building stage:

- Mobilizing the left out poor, disabled into new SHGs.
- Building the capacity of VPRC, SAC and SHG members.
- Employment oriented skill training for youth.
- Promoting credit linkage to SHGs.

c. Livelihood stage:

- Livelihood resource mapping to identify potential economic activities at Village level.
- Assistance for individual livelihood activities as well as group activities.

d. Consolidation stage:

- Formation and strengthening economic activity federations and SHG federations.
- Establishing partnerships and linkages with corporate sector and other resource institutions.

Progress in project implementation

The project implementation was taken up in 15 Blocks in the first phase from October 2006 and another 15 Blocks in the second phase from April 2007. The project activities are in progress in 1,177 Village Panchayats in the first two phases. The following activities have been accomplished:

- The project staff, both at district and cluster levels are in position in all districts after induction training.
- Village Panchayat initiation fund of Rs.35,000/- per Village Panchayat has been released to all 1,177 Village Panchayats.
- Participatory identification of the poor has been completed in 1,162 Village Panchayats and the list approved by Grama Sabha.
- Village Poverty Reduction Committee and Social Audit Committee have been formed in 1,147 Village Panchayats. In addition, 42 special VPRCs have been formed exclusively in tribal areas.
- The first instalment of VPRC fund of Rs.20.15 crores has been released to 696 VPRCs.
- 2,629 new women SHGs have been formed from among the left out poor. Similarly 1,619 new SHGs have been formed among the disabled.
- 14,294 disabled persons have been given national ID cards through the intervention of the project.
- 2,694 unemployed youth have been imparted job oriented skill training in collaboration with Mahalir Thittam.

TSUNAMI REHABILITATION SCHEMES

The Tsunami which struck the Tamil Nadu Coast on 26th December, 2004 was unprecedented in its suddenness and ferocity, causing huge damages to lives, livelihood and properties in Tamil Nadu. It was widespread in scale affecting villages and towns all along the coastline. It inundated areas ranging from 200 metres to 3000 metres from the High Tide Line (HTL) in the coastal districts.

The Government of Tamil Nadu mobilized its resources to take up rescue and relief works. The Government have further undertaken, in collaboration with Non-Governmental Organisations (NGOs), Multilateral Institutions and the Government of India, various reconstruction programmes to restore livelihood, recreate habitats and rehabilitate damaged public properties and infrastructure. Among these are:-i) Tsunami Emergency Assistance Project (TEAP) of the Asian Development

Bank (ADB) at a cost of about Rs.307 crores with loan and grant components. ii) Rajiv Gandhi Rehabilitation Package (RGRP) of the Government of India for

Tsunami affected areas at a cost of about Rs.740 crores, as grant. iii) Emergency Tsunami Reconstruction Project (ETRP), part-funded by the World Bank at a projected cost of about Rs.672 crores as loan.

Several departments of the Government including Rural Development and Panchayat Raj Department are implementing the Tsunami Reconstruction Projects. The Project Management Unit (PMU) established in the Revenue Department is coordinating these projects. In view of the large financial allocation and physical spread of activities undertaken by the Rural Development and Panchayat Raj Department, a separate Project Implementation Unit (PIU) has been set up since 1.8.2005 for overseeing the implementation of the projects implemented by this department.

Tsunami Emergency Assistance Project (TEAP) funded by the Asian Development Bank (ADB)

The main objective of the Project is to support the efforts of the Government of Tamil Nadu to accelerate economic growth and poverty alleviation in the Tsunami affected areas of the State by assisting in the restoration of livelihoods, especially of the poor and disabled and complementary rehabilitation and reconstruction of damaged public infrastructure.

This project is being implemented at a cost of about Rs.307 crores over a period of three years starting from 06.04.2005. The coastal stretch in the 12 tsunami affected districts of Thiruvallur, Kancheepuram, Villupuram, Cuddalore, Nagapattinam, Thiruvarur, Thanjavur, Pudukottai, Ramanathapuram, Thoothukudi, Tirunelveli and Kanniyakumari are benefited through the project. The Asian Development Bank provides 100% grant towards livelihood, sanitation and incremental operating cost components, and a soft loan towards projects for creation of infrastructure like roads and drains, public buildings, etc.

Livelihood Component

A sum of Rs.190.10 crores has been allocated for the restoration of livelihood of Tsunami affected people in the coastal areas. Under this component the

vulnerable sections of the society are provided with Revolving Fund assistance, Economic Assistance, grant for disabled persons for capacity building, and special assistance etc. Cent percent targets have been achieved in respect of these activities.

a)Revolving Fund: 33,547 Self Help Groups (SHGs) have been assisted with Revolving Fund at a cost of Rs.88.82 crores. Every SHG has been assisted with Rs.30,000/- as Revolving Fund. Many of these groups have also availed of credit linkages with Banks.

This has transformed the lives of poor women by providing them with cheap, reliable and accessible credit for meeting their consumption and working capital needs. Many of them have used this money to improve their livelihood by creating new or improving their existing income generating assets.

b)Economic Assistance: Groups which are stabilized and have the aptitude for taking up micro enterprises have been provided with economic assistance with 50% subsidy, the balance 50% being the credit linkage from the Banks. 2472 SHGs have availed this economic assistance at a cost of Rs.31.55 crores for undertaking a variety of activities including animal husbandry, palm leaf products, fish pickle, brick making, small business enterprises etc. The members of these groups are enabled to earn increased income as a result of this assistance.

An additional 4% interest subsidy will also be given to these groups upto the end of the project period, or for the repayment period, whichever is earlier.

c)Special Assistance for the Disabled: It is well known that the disabled, widows and deserted women are the most vulnerable sections in society, more so in the disaster-affected areas. Their social capital is often meagre and they find it difficult to access schemes meant for the general population. Bank credit is also hard to come by. This Government launched a massive campaign to improve the livelihood of the disabled. Under this, 34,632 persons with disabilities have been assisted with a grant of Rs.10,000/- each, at a cost of Rs.34.63 crores. Many of them have also availed of a loan of Rs.5,000/- each from the Banks. Interest subsidy at 4%

will also be extended to these persons upto the end of the project period, or for the repayment period, whichever is earlier.

This assistance has been provided to the eligible disabled persons in the entire coastal districts, instead of restricting it to the coastal Blocks / Panchayats. The quality of life of these individuals has substantially improved after availing of this assistance. This is one of the single largest initiatives ever undertaken by the Government for the welfare of the disabled.

d) Capacity Building: SHG members are being given Basic Orientation Training and Animator & Representative training to enable them to function as viable groups. Entrepreneurial Development Programme and Skills Upgradation Training are being given to groups which are taking up economic activities. A sum of Rs.4.39 crores has been spent for providing these training. Reputed institutions with good placement records have been selected for imparting vocation skills as follows:-

Capacity Building through Institutions

Sl. No.	Institute	Skills	Number trained	Cost of training Rs.in lakhs
1.	TNOU & TALLY	Accounting	684	37.62
2.	NIIT	Computer 830		49.80

These organisations are assisting the trained persons to get suitable employment.

Rajiv Gandhi Rehabilitation Package(RGRP) funded by Government of India

The Rajiv Gandhi Rehabilitation Package (Reconstruction component) forms part of Tsunami Rehabilitation Programme (TRP) drawn by the Government of India for reconstruction of damaged physical and social infrastructure and for revival of impaired livelihoods due to the Tsunami on 26.12.2004. The programme emphasizes on improving quality of life using replacement and upgradation of assets as means to achieve it.

Schemes which are implemented

a) In sites where NGOs constructed houses, certain basic facilities like cement concrete roads, provision of street lights, sanitation arrangements, land filling, etc. have not been provided by these NGOs and these facilities are being provided under the Project.

b) Houses which have originally been agreed to be constructed by NGOs but subsequently backed out by them are being constructed with necessary basic amenities.

c) Vulnerable houses within 200 meters from High Tide Line (HTL) and also government built houses which are 10 years old as on 01.01.2006, within 1000 meters from the HTL are being reconstructed and required basic amenities in these housing sites are also being provided.

Provision of basic amenities in NGOs built sites

i) Cement Concrete roads to a length of 138 Kms. at a cost of Rs.40.62 crores have been taken up in 128 sites.

ii) Out of 3019 street lights to be provided at a cost of Rs.266.31 lakhs, 2696 street lights have already been erected.

iii) Sanitation arrangement by way of septic tanks and soak pits are being provided to 4262 houses built by NGOs without these facilities and 495 stand alone toilets are also being constructed, at a total cost of Rs.4.54 crores. Out of this,2725 houses have already been provided with sanitation facilities.

iv) In 9 sites in Nagapattinam district where NGOs have constructed houses in low lying areas, land filling has been taken up in order to prevent flooding of the houses during rainy seasons at a cost of Rs.2.76 crores, in order to prevent inundation during rains.

Reconstruction of vulnerable houses

With the object of relocating the people who are living in vulnerable houses within 1000 metres from the HTL, a decision was taken up by the State Government to reconstruct these vulnerable houses as multi hazard resistant structures. As a first step, vulnerable houses located within 200 metres from the HTL and the houses built by the Government under different schemes like Indira Awaaz Yojana and Singaravelar Fishermen Housing Scheme, within 1000 metres from HTL, but 10 years old as on

01.01.2006 have been taken up for reconstruction under the project. About 20,000 such houses have been taken up for reconstruction in coastal districts. All these constructions are programmed to be completed within the financial year 2008-09.

Basic amenities such as Cement Concrete Roads, Street Lights, Burial Ground / Cremation Sheds, Village Ponds, necessary Public Buildings etc. are also proposed for the entire coastal stretch of 1000 metres from the HTL in these coastal Panchayat Villages by utilising funds allocated at the rate of Rs.40,000 per house.

STATE ELECTION COMMISSION:

The main function of the Tamil Nadu State Election Commission is to conduct Ordinary Elections for Village Panchayats, Panchayat Union and District Panchayat once in five years. After the enactment of Tamil Nadu Panchayat Act in 1994, the first ordinary Election was held in 1996. The next two ordinary Elections were held in 2001 and 2006.

Details of seats and offices in Rural Local Bodies

1.	Village Panchayat wards	40,879
2.	Village Panchayat ward members	97,458
3.	Panchayat Union wards	6,570
4.	District Panchayat wards	656
5.	Village Panchayat Presidents	12,618
6.	Panchayat Union Chairpersons	385
7.	District Panchayat Chairpersons	29

The Election to the post of Ward Members of Village Panchayats, Panchayat Unions and District Panchayats and Presidents of Village Panchayats are direct. The Elections to the post of Vice Presidents of Village Panchayats and Chairpersons and Vice Chairpersons of Panchayat Unions and District Panchayats are indirect. The Elections to the Ward Members in the Village Panchayats and Presidents of the Village Panchayats are held on non party basis. Elections to the Ward Members in the Panchayat Unions and the District Panchayats and Panchayat Union Chairpersons and District Panchayat Chairpersons are held on party basis.

POWERS AND DUTIES OF OFFICERS AND EMPLOYEES (Under Section 4(1) (b) (ii) of the Right to Information Act-2005)

This Department is headed by the Secretary to Government of Tamil Nadu.

The Secretary is the administrative head of the Department on all matters of policy and administration relating to this Department. He is assisted by one Joint Secretary, four Deputy Secretaries, nine Under Secretaries besides other staff of this Department to exercise the administrative and financial powers as laid down in the Business Rules and Secretariat Instructions, Tamil Nadu Government Secretariat Office Manual, Tamil Nadu Financial code etc., The powers and duties of the officers in the department are indicated below :-

Secretary to Government

The Secretary is the head of office. He is responsible for the careful observance of the Business Rules and Secretariat Instructions in the transaction of the Business of this department. He exercises general supervision and control over the officers and staff under his control including Joint Secretary, Deputy Secretaries and Under Secretaries and is responsible for ensuring that the members of the staff do the work allotted to them efficiently and expeditiously. Policy matters and all important matters are dealt with in consultation with the Secretary who will be in over all charge of the Department.

Joint Secretary / Deputy Secretary

The Joint Secretary / Deputy Secretary will deal with cases relating to the subjects allotted to them and submit to Secretary such cases as may be specified. The Joint Secretary / Deputy Secretary also exercises control over the sections placed in her/his charge both in regard to dispatch of business and in regard to discipline.

Under Secretaries

The Under Secretaries exercise control over the sections placed in their charge, both in regard to dispatch of business and in regard to discipline.

PROCEDURE FOLLOWED IN DECISION MAKING PROCESS : (Under Section 4(1) (b) (iii) of Right to Information Act, 2005

The Rural Development and Panchayat Raj Department Secretariat, follows the procedures as laid down in the Secretariat Office Manual and the Tamil Nadu Government Business Rules and Secretariat Instructions. Apart from this, the provisions in the Tamil Nadu Financial Code, Tamil Nadu State and Subordinate Services Rules, Tamil Nadu Civil Services (D&A) Rules and the Tamil Nadu Government Servants' Conduct Rules, 1973 are also followed wherever applicable.

The decisions are taken based on the merits of the issues, relative priorities and availability of funds etc. in accordance with the documented procedures/laid down procedures/defined criteria/ rules. The process of examination is initiated by Assistant Section Officer and passes through the Section Officer, Under Secretary and Deputy Secretary/Joint Secretary and to the Secretary. If need be, other departments are consulted. In case of matters involving funds, Finance Department is invariably consulted. In respect of the cases relating to service, rules Personnel and Administrative Department is consulted. In respect of cases involving amendment to Tamil Nadu Panchayats Act/Rules and cases involving legal issues including Court cases, Law Department is consulted. Wherever the Business Rules require circulation of files to the Minister or Chief Minister or Governor, orders are obtained in circulation. Afterwards appropriate orders are issued in the form of G.O/Notification.

NORMS SET FOR THE DISCHARGE OF FUNCTIONS : (Under Section 4(1) (b) (iv) of the Right to Information Act, 2005)

For the discharge of functions allocated to the Rural Development and Panchayat Raj Department, the provisions contained in the "Secretariat Office Manual" are followed. The day-to-day administrative functioning is governed by a set of various Acts, Rules and Instructions issued by the Government from time to time. Some of the commonly used Acts/Rules/Manuals are as follows:-

i) Secretariat Office Manual
ii) The Tamil Nadu Government Business Rules and Secretariat Instructions.
iii) The Tamil Nadu Government Servants Conduct Rules, 1973.
iv) Tamil Nadu State and Subordinate Services Rules.
v) Tamil Nadu Civil Service (D&A) Rules
vi) Fundamental Rules.

RULES, REGULATIONS, INSTRUCTIONS, MANUALS AND RECORDS FOR DISCHARGING FUNCTIONS : (Under Section 4(1) (b) (v) of Right to Information Act-2005

1. The Business in the department is carried out with reference to the provisions contained in the following Rules and Regulations and Manuals.
   i) Tamil Nadu Government Business Rules and Secretariat Instructions.
   ii) The Tamil Nadu Secretariat Office Manual
   iii) Tamil Nadu Budget Manual
   iv) Tamil Nadu State and Subordinate Services Rules
   v) Tamil Nadu Civil Services (Discipline and Appeal) Rules
   vi) Tamil Nadu Government Servants Conduct Rules, 1973
   vii) Tamil Nadu Pension Rules
   viii) Fundamental Rules
   ix) Tamil Nadu Financial Code
   x) Tamil Nadu Accounts Code
   xi) Tamil Nadu Treasures Code
   xii) Tamil Nadu Panchayat Development Service rules.
   xiii) Tamil Nadu Panchayat Development subordinate service rules.
   xiv) Tamil Nadu Panchayats service Rules.

TAMIL NADU PANCHAYATS ACT – 1994 :

Besides the above mentioned rules, the provisions of the Tamil Nadu Panchayats Act – 1994 are followed in the discharge of functions of this Department.

PARTICULARS OF FACILITIES AVAILABLE TO CITIZENS FOR OBTAINING INFORMATION

(Under Section 4(1) (b) (xv) of Right to Information Act-2005)

The Public can obtain information through Notice Boards, Newspapers, Website, Exhibitions and other means of advertising.

Following officers in the Rural Development and Panchayat Raj Department have been designated as Public Information Officers and Assistant Public Information Officers. (Under section 4 (1) (b) (xvi) of RTI Act-2005.

6

Rural Development and Panchayat Raj Department Policy Note 2010-2011

INTRODUCTION

Perarignar Anna's vision is being translated into reality in Tamil Nadu under the dynamic leadership of our Honourable Chief Minister, Kalaignar M. Karunanidhi. Never before in the history of the State has so much been done for the rural poor in so many different ways as in the past four years. By virtue of the Anaithu Grama Anna Marumalarchi Thittam (AGAMT), every Village Panchayat of Tamil Nadu will have its own library, playground, village pond, and burial ground-cum-cremation shed together with drinking water systems, streetlights and cement concrete streets in every hamlet, by 2011. Under the Mahatma Gandhi National Rural Employment Guarantee Scheme (MGNREGS), a sum of Rs.3,352.58 crores has been disbursed as wages till 31.3.2010 to the rural poor, among whom 56% are Scheduled Castes and 76% are women. Tamil Nadu has won accolades as one of the best-performing States in this Scheme from no less an institution than the Honourable Supreme Court of India. As regards rural roads, the total length of black-topped roads has gone up from about 29,280 kilometres in 2006 to about 54,620 kilometres in 2010. The women's Self-Help Groups movement has been given a fillip as may be seen from the fact that the total Bank Credit disbursed to SHGs during the past 4 years was Rs.6,364 crores as against a sum of only Rs.1,765 crores disbursed to SHGs during the 17 years from 1989 to 2006. The Kalaignar Veettu Vasathi Thittam launched by the Honourable Chief Minister on 3.3.2010 is by far the biggest State-funded Scheme and aims at replacing all the huts in rural Tamil Nadu with permanent concrete houses over a six year period from 2010-11 to 2015-16, with 3 lakh huts being taken up for replacement during 2010-11 at a cost of Rs.1,800 crores. In short, there has been a major transformation of the rural landscape in Tamil Nadu during the past four years.

The Rural Development and Panchayat Raj Department is responsible for the implementation of various Centrally sponsored, State-funded, and Externally-aided schemes for poverty alleviation, employment generation, sanitation, capacity building, women's social and economic empowerment, Tsunami rehabilitation, apart from provision of basic amenities and services.

The Department is also entrusted with the responsibility of enabling the various Panchayat Raj Institutions (PRIs) to function as effective units of Local Self-Government. There are 12,620 Village Panchayats, 385 Panchayat Unions (coterminus with Blocks) and 29 District Panchayats under the purview of the Department.

The Directorate of Rural Development and Panchayat Raj including the Training wing, the Tamil Nadu Corporation for Development of Women, the Vazhndhu Kaattuvom Project Society and the Tsunami Project Implementation Unit come under this Department. This Department also provides administrative support to the State Election Commission.

PANCHAYAT RAJ INSTITUTIONS

History of Panchayat Raj Institutions

Tamil Nadu has a long history of local self-governance as is evident from the Uthiramerur stone inscriptions in Kancheepuram district. Tamil Nadu, in those days, was a land of village republics, with community groups undertaking many activities for their area development. This tradition reached its peak during the 10th and 11th centuries under the reign of Cholas when Village Councils used to levy taxes, improve community life and administer justice in their limited area. These Village Councils had effective links with the Chola rulers. "Kuda Olai Murai" was the name of the secret ballot method exercised to elect members to the Village Councils. With the downfall of Cholas, the State experienced a decline of the Village autonomy and rise of the centralized feudal administrative system. This continued till British rulers introduced local self-governance primarily as an administrative convenience for the imperial Government.

In the post independence era, the first enactment in democratic decentralization in the State was the Madras Village Panchayats Act, 1950. Pursuant to the White Paper on the "Reform of Local Administration" in 1957, the Madras Panchayats Act, 1958 and Madras District Development Council Act, 1958 were enacted with the following salient features:

a) A two-tier system of Village Panchayats and Panchayat Unions.

b) Creation of Panchayat Unions co-terminus with the Community Development Blocks.

c) Village Panchayat Presidents to become ex-officio members of the Panchayat Union Councils with the Chairperson of the Panchayat Union Council directly/indirectly elected.

d) Entrusting the Panchayat Unions and Village Panchayats with a large number of developmental and welfare functions.

e) Abolition of District Boards.

f) Creation of District Development Council as an advisory body.

This two-tier system operated very well till 1975 and elections were held regularly. Subsequently, the tenures of the Panchayat Unions and Village Panchayats were extended up to 1.2.1977 and 12.9.1979 respectively.

Thereafter, Special Officers (Block Development Officer for all the Village Panchayats in a Block and Divisional Development Officer for all the Panchayat Unions in a Division) managed the rural Local Bodies till the next elections in 1986. The elected rural Local Bodies continued in office till March 1991. Again, no elections were held till October 1996 and the Special Officers managed the rural Local Bodies.

Constitution (73rd Amendment) Act, 1992.

Though the Panchayat Raj Institutions were in existence in various forms in various States, these institutions did not acquire the status and dignity of viable and responsive people's bodies due to a number of reasons including absence of regular elections, prolonged supersession, insufficient representation of weaker sections like Scheduled Castes, Scheduled Tribes and Women, inadequate devolution of powers and lack of financial resources. In the light of the experience gained and the short-comings that had been rd observed, the 73 amendment of the Constitution was enacted in 1992, to enshrine in the Constitution certain basic and essential features of Panchayat Raj Institutions to impart certainty, continuity and strength to them. A number of fundamental changes were brought about in the Panchayat Raj System by virtue of this Act. Pursuant to this, the Tamil Nadu Panchayats Act 1994 was enacted and it came into force with effect from 22.04.1994.

Some of the important changes brought about by the 73rd Amendment to the Constitution and the Tamil Nadu Panchayats Act 1994 are listed below:

a) Introduction of a three tier system – at the Village, Intermediate (Block) and District levels. [There are 12,620 Village Panchayats, 385 Panchayat Unions (coterminous with Blocks) and 29 District Panchayats in Tamil Nadu].

b) Mandatory conduct of Local Body elections every five years and conduct of elections before the expiry of the duration of the Local Body or before the expiry of a period of 6 months from the date of its dissolution.

c) Introduction of reservation of seats (i.e. ward members) and offices (i.e. Chairpersons/ Presidents) for Scheduled Castes/Scheduled Tribes in proportion to their population in every Local Body with provision for rotation of the reserved seats and offices.

d) Introduction of reservation of one-third of total number of seats and offices for women with provision for rotation.

e) Constitution of a State Election Commission as an independent body to conduct elections to both rural and urban Local Bodies regularly.

f) Establishment of a quinquennial State Finance Commission to recommend devolution of resources from the State Government to the rural and urban Local Bodies.

g) Constitution of a District Planning Committee to consolidate the plans prepared by the rural and urban Local Bodies in the district with a view to prepare a comprehensive development plan for the district.

h) Introduction of the concept of 'Grama Sabha' comprising all registered voters in a Village Panchayat.

TAMIL NADU'S STAND ON THE 73RD CONSTITUTIONAL AMENDMENT

The Government of Tamil Nadu has had rd reservations regarding certain aspects of the 73 Constitutional amendment and our experience of working under the new system for the past 12 years has only confirmed the same. The system prevailing under the old Tamil Nadu Panchayats Act of 1958 wherein the Presidents of Village Panchayats were ex-officio members of the Panchayat Union Council at the Block level ensured organic linkage between the two tiers. Hence, the name 'Panchayat Union' and it genuinely functioned as a 'union' of Village Panchayats. Since the Village Panchayat Presidents themselves 'doubled up' as ex-officio members of the Panchayat Union Council, there were no separate ward members for the Council. Having separate ward members for Panchayat Unions (6,570 for the State as a whole) and District Panchayats (656) has vastly increased the number of 'members' and has paved the way for inter-tier friction and disharmony. Although Article 243 C (3) of the Constitution states that a State may, by law, provide for the representation of Village Panchayat Presidents on the Panchayat Union Council and Panchayat Union Chairpersons on the District Panchayat, this arrangement is not satisfactory because it can render the Panchayat Union Councils and District Panchayats too unwieldy with too many members and can create disharmony between the two distinct power blocs within each Council. Hence, Tamil Nadu has not invoked Article 243 C (3). The lack of organic linkages between the three tiers results in a scenario where each tier is unaware of what the other two tiers are doing. It often leads to duplication in the selection of works and avoidable paperwork and loss of time in reworking the choices. Tamil Nadu has been pressing for the reversion to the 1958 model where the Presidents of Village Panchayats were ex-officio members of the Panchayat Union Council at the Block level.

Under the 1958 Act, the Chairpersons of the Panchayat Union Council could be either directly or indirectly elected. Most of the time, Tamil Nadu had direct elections for the posts of Chairpersons of Panchayat Unions and this arrangement was found to be working well as the Chairperson commanded respect and there was no scope for vexatious no-rd confidence motions. But after the 73 amendment, the Constitution itself stipulates that Chairpersons of Panchayat Unions and District Panchayats should be elected indirectly. Only in the case of elections of Village Panchayat Presidents, the States have the freedom to opt for either direct election or indirect election. The State Government has been pressing that the States should have similar freedom in respect of elections of Chairpersons of Panchayat Unions and District Panchayats.

The Government of Tamil Nadu have, for long held the view that there should have been a single consolidated Amendment to the Constitution covering both rural and urban Local Bodies instead of two Amendments–one covering rural Local rd Bodies (73) and the other urban Local Bodies th (74). This 'compartmentalization' has resulted in a scenario whereby the District Panchayat – instead of being a nodal body responsible for coordinating and monitoring all the rural and urban Local Bodies in the district – finds that its jurisdiction is confined only to the rural areas. In a State like Tamil Nadu with about 42% urban population, and with several highly urbanised districts such as Coimbatore (69.1%), Kanniyakumari (66%), The Nilgiris (58%), Theni (54%) and Madurai (52%), the argument that the District Panchayat should become a nodal body responsible for coordinating and monitoring the development activities *in the entire district* becomes weak. A system whereby all the Chairpersons of Panchayat Unions, Municipalities and Town Panchayats are ex-officio members of the District Panchayats, with the Chairman of the District Panchayat being either directly or indirectly elected would have been more meaningful and credible. This weakness has been sought to be overcome through the District

Planning Committee which has members drawn from both rural and urban Local Bodies, but its composition is flawed because there is no representation for Panchayat Union and Village Panchayat members on it.

A mention was made in His Excellency the Governor's Address in the Tamil Nadu Legislative Assembly in 2006 that the Tamil Nadu would press for the amendment of the Constitution seeking a two tier system of Panchayats and the abolition of District Panchayats. Tamil Nadu did have powerful elected District Boards till they were abolished in 1961. In their place, the District Development Council, an advisory-cum-planning body, comprising all the MPs, MLAs, Chairpersons of Panchayat Unions, Town Panchayats, Municipalities and Corporations in the district with the District Collector as Chairman were set up.

The Government of Tamil Nadu believes that Village Panchayats and Panchayat Unions are the two tiers closest to the people, qualifying for the appellation 'local' and represent the 'cutting edge' of Local Self-Government. These two tiers need to be strong and vibrant and strengthened further.

This Government is of the opinion that the reasons which led to the abolition of the old District Boards are still valid and applicable to the third tier of District Panchayat, which at present has only an advisory-cum-planning role. At the same time, this Government is aware that other States may have different views on this topic based on their own past legacy. For example, some States want Village and District Panchayats but do not want the intermediate tier (Block or Taluk Panchayat). But there is a general consensus that there is one tier too many under the present system.

It may be noted that with regard to the States, the Legislative Assembly is mandatory while the Legislative Council is optional as per the Constitution. Similarly, in order to accommodate divergent needs, the Constitution may be so amended so as to make the Village Panchayats mandatory for all the States and leaving it to the discretion of the concerned State Legislatures whether to have the intermediate Panchayats only or District Panchayats only or both. The State Government would press for such an amendment to the Constitution.

PANCHAYAT ELECTIONS

Conduct of 2006 Local Body Elections

Though the Tamil Nadu Panchayats Act was enacted in April 1994, only after the change of Government in May 1996, the first ordinary elections were held to all the rural and urban Local Bodies in October 1996. The second ordinary elections to the Local Bodies were conducted during October 2001. The third ordinary elections to the Local Bodies were conducted in October 2006.

Table 1 furnishes the number of seats and offices in the three tiers of Panchayats for which the elections in October 2006 were held.

Table-1: Details of seats and offices in Rural Local Bodies

1.	Village Panchayat wards	40,879
2.	Village Panchayat ward members	97,458
3.	Panchayat Union wards	6,570
4.	District Panchayat wards	656
5.	Village Panchayat Presidents	12,618
6.	Panchayat Union Chairpersons	385
7.	District Panchayat Chairpersons	29

Reservation of Seats and Offices and Rotation

Article 243 D of the Constitution relates to reservation and rotation of seats for Scheduled Castes, Scheduled Tribes and Women in rural Local Bodies. The relevant provisions of Tamil Nadu Panchayats Act, 1994 are Sections 11, 20, 32 & 57. These are supplemented by the Tamil Nadu Panchayats (Reservation of Seats and Rotation of Reserved Seats) Rules, 1995. The Rules provide for the reservation of seats by adopting a list of wards or Panchayats arranged in the descending order of the percentage of SCs, STs and Women and applying a 'cut off' at the point where the number of reserved seats and offices is equal to the prescribed ratio. The periodicity of rotation is also fixed under the Rules. The Government amended Rule 7 of the Tamil Nadu Panchayats (Reservation of Seats and Rotation of Reserved Seats) Rules, 1995 vide G.O.Ms. No. 105, RD & PR (C4) Department, dated 1.9.2006 by virtue of which the posts of Presidents of Village Panchayats and Chairpersons of Panchayat Unions and District Panchayats reserved for SCs, STs and Women were rotated - after 10 years - for the October 2006 elections. While the posts of ward members of all the 3 tiers reserved for Women were rotated - after 10 years – those reserved for SCs and STs were not rotated; in other words, they would continue to be reserved as such until the Government direct otherwise.

Table 2 shows the details of reservation of seats and offices to Women, Scheduled Castes and Scheduled Tribes in rural Local Bodies:

Table- 2: Reservation of Offices and Seats for Women SCs and STs

Sl No	Category of Reser	Total no.	Reserved for Women		Reserved for SCs		Reserve d for	
			No.	%	No.	%	No	%
1	District Panchayat Chair persons	29	10	34%	7	24%	0	0%
2	Panchayat Union Council Chair persons	385	140	36%	87	23%	4	1%
3	Village Panchayat Presi dents	12,61 8	4,275	34%	3,143	25%	156	1%
4	District Panchayat Ward Members	656	226	34%	154	23%	8	1%
5	Panchayat Union Ward Members	6,570	2,302	35%	1,534	23%	64	1%
6	Village Panchayat Ward Members	97,45 8	32,638	33%	24,630	25%	983	1%

However, the Government took a conscious decision not to rotate the posts of Presidents of Pappapatti, Keeripatti and Nattarmangalam Village Panchayats in Madurai district and Kottakachiyendal Village Panchayat in Virudhunagar district reserved for SCs where elections could not take place for a prolonged period due to local opposition to reservation. This Government solved, what appeared to be an intractable problem, by successfully conducting elections to the posts of Presidents and ward members in all the four Panchayats during the ordinary elections held in October 2006. It is gratifying to note that the various communities of these Panchayats have overcome their past differences and have wholeheartedly accepted the newly elected Scheduled Caste Presidents.

CONVERSION OF MULTI-MEMBER WARDS TO SINGLE MEMBER WARDS

The system of Multi-Member Wards is in existence only in Village Panchayats and not in any other rural or urban Local Body. It has posed difficulties at the time of voting and also during the counting process. There has also been lack of clear demarcation of responsibility amongst the multiple members. The Third High Level Committee headed by the Hon'ble Deputy Chief Minister has recommended for the conversion of Multi-Member Village Panchayat Wards into Single Member Wards. On the basis of this recommendation, Section 12 of Tamil Nadu Panchayats Act, 1994, has been amended by abolishing the Multi Member Ward System in Village Panchayats and replacing it with Single Member Wards - vide Tamil Nadu Act No. 20 of 2009. The above system of single member wards in Village Panchayats will be brought into effect in 2011 Local Body elections.

Devolution of Powers

Local Government is a State subject figuring as item 5 in List II of the Seventh Schedule to the Constitution of India. Article 243 G of the Indian Constitution enshrines the basic principle for devolution of power to the rural Local Bodies. As per this article, subject to the provisions of this Constitution, the Legislature of a State may, by law, endow the Panchayats with such powers and authority as may be necessary to enable them to function as institutions of self-Government and such law may contain provisions for the devolution of powers and responsibilities upon Panchayats at the appropriate level, subject to such conditions as may be specified therein, with respect to the preparation of plans for economic development and social justice; the implementation of schemes for economic development and social justice as may be entrusted to them including those in relation to the 29 matters listed in the Eleventh Schedule.

The Government of Tamil Nadu is committed to ensuring that the Panchayat Raj Institutions function as effective institutions of Local Self-Government. At the same time, since State autonomy is a firm and abiding principle of the Government of Tamil Nadu, it has opposed certain proposals of the Ministry of Panchayati Raj at the Centre which appeared to transgress into the Constitutional space earmarked for States, as for example, by trying to constitute an 'Advisory Committee' for each State for monitoring the devolution of powers and functions from State Governments to Local Governments; by seeking a 'MOU' between the State Chief Minister and the Union Minister for Panchayati Raj; by trying to get a resolution passed for the transfer of the subject of 'Local Government' from the State List to the Concurrent List at a National Convention of Chairpersons of District Panchayats and Block Panchayats in April 2008; and so on.

It is a matter of pride that all the three High Level Committees for recommending the devolution of greater powers and functions to rural and urban Local Bodies were constituted only during Kalaignar's tenure as Hon'ble Chief Minister of Tamil Nadu. In 1996, soon after the conclusion of the first ordinary elections to the three tiers of Panchayats, the Government of Tamil Nadu constituted the First High Level Committee under the Chairmanship of Thiru L.C. Jain, the then full-time Member of the State Planning Commission to give recommendations on the entrustment of powers and functions to the three tiers of Panchayats. The Committee submitted its report to the Government in April, 1997.

Many of the recommendations of the L.C. Jain Committee have been crystallized into action towards empowering the Panchayats. Apart from the Rural Development Department, other departments such as Agriculture, Animal Husbandry, Forests, Social Welfare, Revenue, Khadi and Village Industries, Education, Health and Family Welfare, Adi-Dravidar Welfare, Co-operation, Food and Consumer Protection, have issued Government Orders for devolution of powers and functions in their respective spheres to the three tiers of Panchayats.

Again, the Government in G.O. Ms. No. 320, Rural Development (C1) Department, dated 11.11.1997 constituted the Second High Level Committee under the Chairmanship of Thiru.Ko.Si.Mani, the then Hon'ble Rural Development and Local Administration Minister with experienced persons including sitting MLAs of various political parties as members of the Committee to recommend more devolution of powers and functions to the Panchayats. This High Level Committee submitted its report on 11.1.1999 with 1209 recommendations to the Government. The Government accepted 718 recommendations and issued orders for their implementation.

This Government, in continuance of its commitment to devolve greater powers and responsibilities to rural and urban Local Bodies, constituted the Third High Level Committee under the Chairmanship of the Hon'ble Deputy Chief Minister, Thiru. M.K. Stalin vide G.O. Ms. No.6 RD & PR (C1) Department, dated 22.1.2007 and with select District Panchayat Chairpersons, Panchayat Union Chairpersons and Village Panchayat Presidents besides certain subject experts as members. The Committee was required to study the duties, functions and powers already entrusted to the rural and urban Local Bodies and make recommendations for further devolution of the same in order to make them more effective.

High Level Committee under the Chairmanship of Thiru M.K.Stalin

The Third High Level Committee was formed under the Chairmanship of Hon'ble Deputy Chief Minister to devolve more powers and functions to the Local bodies. The first meeting of the Committee was held on 7.3.2007. In continuation of this, a conference of Local Body representatives was held in the presence of Hon'ble Chief Minister on 18.3.2007, following which Regional

Conferences of local body representatives were held in Erode (24.7.2007), Trichy (25.7.2007), Tiruvannamalai (03.8.2007), and Virudhunagar (23.8.2007) under the Chairmanship of Hon'ble Deputy Chief Minister.

The second meeting of High Level Committee was conducted on 19.9.2007. Further, Hon'ble Deputy Chief Minister conducted discussions on 11.10.2007 and 12.10.2007 with the Secretaries of other departments in order to devolve more powers to the rural Local Bodies. The Committee presented its report to the Hon'ble Chief Minister of Tamil Nadu on 10.12.2007 and submitted a total of 99 recommendations categorized under 39 subjects.

Recommendations of the M.K. Stalin Committee

The important recommendations of the third High Level Committee are highlighted below:

- Grama Sabha to act as a forum of Social Audit for all the schemes implemented by various Departments.
- Approval of the list of all individual beneficiary schemes to be done by Grama Sabha.
- Conversion of multi-member wards into single member wards in all the Village Panchayats as is there in the case of the Panchayat Unions and District Panchayats.
- Stability of tenure of rural and urban Local Body representatives by making the moving and passing of No Confidence Motions more stringent.
- Designating November 1st of every year as the 'Local Bodies Day'.
- Empowering weaker Village Panchayats by enhancing their State Finance Commission grants and allocating the entire Central Finance Commission grants to Village Panchayats so as to enable them to meet the expenditure relating to water supply, electricity charges and sanitation.
- Pooling of assigned revenues of Local Cess, Local Cess Surcharge, and Surcharge on Stamp Duty and Entertainment tax at State Level and apportioning it to the districts thereafter.
- Giving Panchayat Raj Institutions greater operational

independence by enhancing administrative sanction powers of Village Panchayats, Panchayat Unions and District Panchayats for works taken out of their General Funds.

- Rationalisation of Village Panchayat Accounts.
- Issue of Identity Cards to the Heads of three tiers of Panchayat and for the Members of Panchayat Unions and District Panchayats.
- Making BDOs (Village Panchayats) as separate Pay Drawing Officers.
- Provision of Telephone facility to all Village Panchayats.
- Provision of Wireless to Panchayat Unions.
- Vehicles for Panchayat Raj Institutions and key functionaries of Rural Development Department.
- Revival of Namakku Naame Thittam.
- Formulation of Panchayat Union School Renovation Programme.
- Setting up of Libraries and Sports Centres in all Panchayats under AGAMT.
- Designating Village Panchayats as 'Village Level Committee' for selecting the beneficiaries and implementing the schemes of various other departments at Village level.

It is important to note that most of the recommendations have already been accepted by the Government and necessary orders issued.

It may be noted that as per the rankings of various States in India done by the Ministry of Panchayat Raj, Government of India based on the devolution of powers, functions and funds to the Panchayat Raj Institutions, Tamil Nadu stood fourth in 2006-07; first in 2007-08; third in 2008-09 and second in 2009-10.

Delimitation of Local Bodies

A large number of requests for upgradation, downgradation, bifurcation and amalgamation of rural and urban Local Bodies have been received by Government. Government have issued orders vide G.O.Ms No. 131, RD & PR (C1) Department, dated 16.3.2007 prescribing the procedure for the conduct of public hearings by Collectors/Heads of Departments before making their final recommendations to Government in response to such requests. It has been clarified to all the rural and urban Local Bodies that the terms of office of the present office bearers will not, in anyway, be affected.

The District Collectors have already conducted public hearings pertaining to the requests from various rural and urban Local Bodies and the proposals are under the consideration of the Government. So far, decision has been taken by the Government only in respect of Village Panchayats lying in the vicinity of a few Municipal Corporations. In 2011, it has been proposed to merge 25 Village Panchayats of Kancheepuram and Tiruvallur Districts with Chennai Corporation, 61 Village Panchayats of Vellore District with Vellore Corporation, 7 Village Panchayats of Erode District with Erode Corporation, 10 Village Panchayats of Thoothukudi District with Thoothukudi Corporation and 8 Village Panchayats of Tiruppur District with Tiruppur Corporation.

Before the recent delimitation of Assembly Constituencies, 278 Panchayat Unions were coming fully within the boundary of an Assembly Constituency; after delimitation, this number has come down to 213. At present, 172 Panchayat Unions are coming under 2 or more Assembly Constituencies. Hence, the Government have taken up steps to study the reorganization of Panchayat Union boundaries in order to ensure that an Assembly Constituency comprises only full Panchayat Unions. However, the alteration of Panchayat Union boundaries will not, in anyway, affect the present term of office of the elected representatives. This work has been temporarily kept in abeyance due to the ban on changing jurisdictions of administrative units with effect from 1.1.2010 in view of the forthcoming Census operations.

DISQUALIFICATION OF MEMBERS OF PANCHAYATS

In order to bring the procedure for disqualification of elected members of Panchayat Raj Institutions in line with that relating to disqualification of MPs and MLAs under the Representation of the People Act, 1951 certain amendments to Sections 34, 35, 37, 38, 39 and 41 of the Tamil Nadu Panchayats Act, 1994 have been introduced. As per the amended provisions, the Government will decide the question of disqualification of members of Panchayats in consultation with the Tamil Nadu State Election Commission. New sections 41-A, 41-B, 41-C and 41-D, have been added to the Act enabling the Tamil Nadu State Election Commission to conduct enquiries relating to disqualification of members of the Panchayats.

Grama Sabha

The Grama Sabha is the grass root level democratic institution in each Village Panchayat. A vibrant Grama Sabha is essential for the effective functioning of Village Panchayats by promoting transparency and accountability in administration, enhancing public participation in the planning and implementation of schemes and in the choice of beneficiaries, and paving the way for social audit.

The Government have ordered the conduct of Grama Sabha meetings a minimum of four times a year i.e. on 26th January, 1st May, 15th August and 2nd October.

In order to streamline the procedure for the conduct of Grama Sabha, this Government brought out suitable amendments to the Tamil Nadu Grama Sabha (Quorum and Procedure for convening and conducting of meetings) Rules, 1998 vide G.O.Ms No. 130 RD & PR (C4) Department dated 25.9.2006 and specified that the Grama Sabha shall meet in each of the Village Panchayat wards by rotation.

Since a quorum of 10% of the voters was unattainable and unwieldy for the bigger Village Panchayats, a reduced quorum based on the population of Village Panchayats has been prescribed as shown in Table 3.

Table-3 Revised Quorum for Grama Sabhas

Sl. No.	Population of a Village Panchayat	Quorum for the meeting
1	Upto 500	50
2	501-3,000	100
3	3,001-10,000	200
4	Above 10,000	300

It has also been specified that out of the quorum, at least 1/3rd shall be women and the number of SC/ST participants shall bear the same proportion to the quorum as the population of SCs / STs bears to the total population of the Village Panchayat. Recording of Grama Sabha attendance and proceedings through proper registers and keeping photographic record have been made mandatory for the conduct of Grama Sabhas.

The Third High Level Committee constituted under the Chairmanship of Hon'ble Deputy Chief Minister had recommended that the expenditure limit for conducting Grama Sabha may be increased from Rs.500 to Rs.1,000. The Government have accepted the above recommendation and ordered that the Village Panchayat Presidents can incur the expenditure for conducting Grama Sabha to a maximum limit of Rs.1,000 with the approval of the Village Panchayat, vide G.O.Ms.No.160 RD & PR (PR.1) department dated 30.09.2008.

VILLAGE PANCHAYATS

There are 12,620 Village Panchayats in the State spread across the 31 districts, including two new Village Panchayats, viz., Perumathur and Indira Nagar in Kurinjipadi Panchayat Union of Cuddalore District that were notified on 16.8.2008.

Table- 4: Classification of Village Panchayats on the basis of Population (2001 Census

Sl.No.	Population	No. of Village Panchayats
1	Below 500	66
2	501-1,000	1,177
3	1,001-3,000	7,243*
4	3,001-5,000	2,569
5	5001-10,000	1,379
6	Above 10,000	186
	Total	12,620*

Including the two newly formed Villages Panchayats in Cuddalore district.

There are 385 Blocks. The average number of Village Panchayats per district is 421 and per Block is 32. The Nilgiris (35), Kanniyakumari (99), Theni (130) and Karur (158) are some of the districts with fewer Village Panchayats while Villupuram (1104), Tiruvannamalai (860), Vellore (753), Cuddalore (683) and Kancheepuram (648) are some of the districts with a large number of Village Panchayats. As can be seen from Table 4, the population of Village Panchayats in Tamil Nadu is widely varying with some Village Panchayats having populations even below 500 while others have populations exceeding 25,000.

Among the three tiers, Village Panchayats assume a pre-eminent role in view of the wide variety of civic duties and other functions entrusted to them under Sections 110 and 111 of the Tamil Nadu Panchayats Act, 1994. This Government have always taken efforts to empower the Village Panchayats further in order to enable them to perform their functions in an effective manner. Various efforts have been taken by this Government to improve the finances of the Village Panchayats.

Since the Village Panchayats in Tamil Nadu vary widely in population from below 500 to above 25,000 and as the devolution of State Finance Commission grant is mostly linked to population, the smaller Village Panchayats got less grant and the bigger Village Panchayats got more.

While the needs of the bigger Village Panchayats are also greater, it is a fact that there are certain fixed costs associated with the running of a Village Panchayat irrespective of the size and the SFC grant to a Village Panchayat should be sufficient to cover at least the fixed costs, if not the variable costs. There were cases where some Village Panchayats found it difficult to pay their electricity bills on time; a few couldn't pay the salaries and wages of their employees on time. The State Finance Commission recommended the earmarking of certain percentage of the SFC grant as 'Equalisation Fund' to assist such weaker Village Panchayats. But past experience showed that the allocation of the Equalisation Fund by Collectors was by discretion which introduced a certain element of arbitrariness.

The Government have thus passed G.O.Ms.No.199 Finance (Finance Commission – IV) Department dated 25.5.2007 wherein a floor amount of Rs.3 lakhs has been earmarked for each Village Panchayat irrespective of the population and only after the apportionment of this amount, the remaining amount is distributed among the Village Panchayats in proportion to population. By virtue of this decision of the Government, the huge disparity in the income of the Village Panchayats has been reduced and at the same time weaker Village Panchayats have been empowered further towards self-sustainable.

The Government have also vide G.O.Ms.No.119 R.D. & P.R.(C2) Dept. dated 26.02.2007 decided to allocate the entire Twelfth Finance Commission grant to the Village Panchayats alone as can be seen in Table 5 given underneath:

Table- 5: Income-wise Classification of Village Panchayats

Sl. No.	**Income Range**	**No. of Village Panchayats before release of Minimum SFC Grant. (Based on average income of 3 years from 2003-04 to**	**No. of Village Panchayats after release of Minimum SFC Grant. (Based on income in 2009-10)**
1.	Upto Rs.50,000	10	0
2.	Rs.50,000 to Rs.1 lakh	178	0
3.	Rs.1 lakh to Rs. 5 lakhs	7,422	1,021
4.	Rs. 5 lakhs to Rs 10 lakhs	3,181	7,146
5.	Rs. 10 lakhs to Rs. 25 lakhs	1,489	3,902
6.	Rs.25 lakhs to Rs.50 lakhs	252	393
7.	Rs.50 lakhs to Rs. 1 crore	60	121
8.	Rs.1 crore to Rs.3 crores	24	32
9.	Above Rs.3 crores	2	3
	Total	**12,618**	**12,618**

It is, hence, seen that the average income levels have not only increased for majority of the Village Panchayats, but also the inequity of the income levels amongst various Village Panchayats has decreased due to the steps taken by the Government.

Functions

Sections 110 & 111 of the Tamil Nadu Panchayats Act, 1994 prescribe the duties and functions of Village Panchayats. Some of the important functions of a Village Panchayat are:

a) Construction, repair and maintenance of all village roads.

b) Extension of village sites and the regulation of buildings.

c) Lighting of public roads and public places in built-up areas.

d) Construction of drains.

e) Cleaning of streets and improvement of the sanitary condition of the village.

f) Construction and maintenance of public latrines.

g) Sinking and repairing of wells, the excavation, repair and maintenance of ponds or tanks and the construction and maintenance of water-works for the supply of water.

h) Maintenance of burial and burning grounds.

i) Maintenance of parks and reading rooms.

j) Implementation of schemes such as Indira Awaas Yojana (IAY) and National Rural Employment Guarantee Scheme (NREGS).

k) Such other duties as the Government may, by notification, impose.

Resources

The important sources of revenue for the Village Panchayat are:

a) Tax revenue

Among the three tiers, the Village Panchayat alone has the power to levy taxes. House tax, Profession tax and Advertisement tax are the commonly levied taxes.

b) Non Tax revenue

Licensing fees for building plan and layout approval, fees and charges on Dangerous & Offensive trades, water charges, fees on cart-stands, fishery rentals, 2C patta fees, income from markets and fairs, ferries, fines and penalties and so on.

c) Assigned and shared revenues

These revenues include the items pooled at the State level (Surcharge on Stamp duty and Entertainment Tax) which are released by the Director of Rural Development and Panchayat Raj to all the three tiers of the Panchayats including the Village Panchayats. Other items of Assigned and shared revenues for the Village Panchayats include the seigniorage fees (100%) and lease amount (50% share) on minor minerals and social forestry auctions amount.

d) Grants:

Central Finance Commission Grant, State Finance Commission Grant, development grants under Centrally-sponsored and State schemes.

Administrative Powers

The Village Panchayat President himself has been designated as the Executive Authority. Cheques for payment have to be signed jointly by the President and Vice-President. Where the relationship between the two is not cordial, the Collector, in his capacity as Inspector of Panchayats, can designate any other member of the Village Panchayat as joint cheque signing authority along with the President.

The Government have brought out Tamil Nadu Panchayats (Preparation of Plan and Estimates for works and Mode and Conditions of works) Rules, 2007 vide G.O.Ms.No.203 R.D. & P.R. (PR.1) Department, dated 20.12.2007, wherein the Village Panchayats have been empowered to give administrative sanction and execute individual works up to Rs.2 lakhs from their General Funds.

Previously the Village Panchayats were empowered to give administrative sanction for works up to Rs.1 lakh only. For all works costing more than Rs.2 lakhs but not more than Rs.50 lakhs, the District Collector is the competent authority to give the administrative sanction and for works costing more than Rs.50 lakhs, the Director of Rural Development and Panchayat Raj will be competent to accord administrative sanction.

However, the Collector's prior administrative sanction is necessary in respect of all Centrally sponsored and State funded schemes. Village Panchayats have also been given freedom to execute urgent works up to Rs. 2,000 at a time and up to Rs. 5,000 for a year without any technical approval. The President can draw self cheque up to Rs. 500 to meet contingent expenditures.

The Village Panchayats have been given necessary delegation of powers to enable them to attend to repairs and maintenance of hand pumps, power pumps and street lights promptly. They can spend Rs.600 per hand pump per year and up to Rs.7,500 per power pump per year without reference to engineers for preparation of estimates or passing of bills. They can buy street light materials meeting the prescribed quality norms on their own.

Uthamar Gandhi Village Panchayat Award

Uthamar Gandhi Village Panchayat Award was instituted vide G.O.Ms No. 111, RD & PR (C2) Department dated 5.9.2006. This award is being given each year from 2006-07 onwards for those Village Panchayats which have undertaken outstanding works, special initiatives and innovative efforts during the preceding 5 years.

Table-6: Uthamar Gandhi Village Panchayat Award-Winning Panchayats for 2008-09

Sl. No.	Name of the Village Panchayat
1.	Kottavaradampatty, Salem.
2.	Thirupanichettikulam, Thoothukudi.
3.	Vachchakaranpatty, Virudhunagar.
4.	Reddipatty, Namakkal.
5.	Pechiparai, Kanniyakumari.
6.	Bommanaickanpalayam, Erode.
7.	Orathur, Cuddalore.
8.	Kunnathur, Coimbatore.
9.	S. Kuppam, Viluppuram.
10.	Bearhatty, The Nilgiris.
11.	Mela Perumalai, Thiruvarur.
12.	Athiyur, Perambalur.
13.	Ariyanendal, Ramanathapuram.
14.	Kalikkampatti, Dindigul.
15.	Poonappalli, Krishnagiri.

The chosen Panchayats are given a certificate, shield and a cash prize of Rs.5 lakhs each while their Presidents are given a certificate and a medal.

Awards can also be given posthumously. For 2006-07 and 2007-08, 15 Village Panchayats each were conferred with Uthamar Gandhi Village Panchayat Awards by the Hon'ble Chief Minister of Tamil Nadu on 10.10.2007 and 19.12.2008 respectively. For 2008-09, orders have been issued selecting 15

Village Panchayats for Uthamar Gandhi Village Panchayat Award for the year 2008-09. The details of Uthamar Gandhi Village Panchayat Award-winning Panchayats for the year 2008-09 are given in Table 6.

Corporate Social Responsibility Award

Table-7: Corporate Social Responsibility Award winning Organisations

Government instituted an Award to honour the Industrial, Service and Business Organisations that are actively involved in various social and economic upliftment activities as part of their Corporate Social Responsibility, from the year 2007-08 onwards vide G.O. Ms. No.117, Rural Development (SS.2) Department, dated 2.7.2007. The Award consists of Rs. 5 lakhs cash each and a Certificate. This Award will be given to 5 such commercial and industrial establishments every year.

The Government have issued orders selecting 5 organisations for the Corporate Social Responsibility Award for the year 2007-08 and 4 organisations for the year 2008-09. The Awards were given by the Hon'ble Deputy Chief Minister on 19.10.2009. Five organisations have been selected for the year 2009-10. The details of Corporate Social Responsibility Award-winning organisations for the years 2007-08, 2008-09 and 2009-10 are given in Table 7.

Rationalisation of Village Panchayat Accounts

The Government had vide G.O.Ms.No.92 Rural Development Department dated 26.3.1997 issued orders for rationalization of Village Panchayat Accounts and the procedure for operation of the Accounts.

Sl. No.	2007-08	2008-09	2009-10
1.	Tamil Nadu Newsprint and Papers Limited, Karur District.	Chennai Petroleum Corporation Ltd., Chennai.	Neyveli Lignite Corporation Ltd., Neyveli, Cuddalore District.
2.	Oil and Natural Gas Corporation Ltd., Karaikal, Pondichery.	Steel Authority of India Ltd., Salem.	Hyundai Motor India Ltd., Sriperumbudur, Kancheepuram District.
3.	Srinivasan Services Trust, Chennai.	Orchid Chemicals & Pharmaceuticals Ltd., Chennai.	Bannari Amman Sugars Ltd., Sathyamangalam, Erode District.
4.	Saint-Gobain Glass India Ltd., Sriperumbudur, Kancheepuram District.	Sri Ramalinga Mills Ltd., Aruppukottai, Virudhunagar District.	TITAN Industries Ltd.,Hosur, Krishnagiri District.
5.	Sakthi Masala Private Ltd., Erode District.		C.R.I Pumps Private Ltd., Saravanampatti, Coimbatore District.

This was a great step forward in empowering Village Panchayats since it gave freedom to the President and Vice President to operate the various Accounts of a Village Panchayat free from pre-scrutiny by Block officials as was the earlier practice in which the Village Panchayat Consolidated Fund was maintained and operated in the Block office. However, certain weaknesses were noticed in this new system of maintenance of Village Panchayat Accounts. Several instances of the State Finance Commission Grant and Central Finance Commission Grant released to the Village Panchayats' Earmarked Grants Accounts being used for less important purposes and not for payment of dues relating to electricity and water charges came to the notice of the Government. Due to this practice, in order to avoid diversion of funds meant for current consumption charges and water supply maintenance, the District Collectors were directed to deduct the charges payable to TNEB and TWAD Board at the district level before releasing money to the Village Panchayats. However this resulted in the following two anomalies:

a. TNEB issued wrong/duplicate bills in some instances which did not get deducted since payment was made at district level without proper check by the Village Panchayat Presidents concerned.

b. The Panchayat Presidents did not evince interest in ways and means of reducing power consumption as they never paid the electricity/water bills of their own.

Several instances also came to notice, wherein Village Panchayat Presidents and Vice-Presidents issued cheques for Scheme funds works/National Rural Employment Guarantee Scheme works without the works same being measured and check-measured and bills being passed by the Block Development Officer (Village Panchayats) concerned.

The number of instances of unauthorized drawals was greater on the eve of Local Body elections. Therefore, the Government issued G.O. Ms.No.146 Rural Development and Panchayat Raj Department dt.17.8.2007 for further rationalizing the Village Panchayat Accounts and streamlining the procedures for operation of the Accounts so as to:

a. Empower the Village Panchayat Presidents to pay the TNEB and TWAD Board dues from the funds at their disposal and at the same time prevent them from diverting these funds for less important purposes.

b. Prevent unauthorized drawals of money from scheme fund/ NREGS fund Accounts without authorization of Block Development Officer(VP) concerned.

The Government have further streamlined the above accounting procedure through issuance of G.O. Ms.No.178, RD & PR Department dated: 25.11.2008 and G.O. Ms.No.180 RD & PR Department dated: 01.12.2008.

The Government of Tamil Nadu have also taken a stand opposing the imposition of a uniform Accounting System for Village Panchayats across all the States as proposed by the Ministry of Panchayat Raj, Government of India.

The Accounting structure suggested by Ministry of Panchayat Raj was found to be extremely complicated and difficult to comprehend except by officials with accounting background. It was felt that the accounting system proposed did take into account the field realities viz. the level of education and competence of the staff in Panchyat Raj Institutons, especially at Village Panchayat level.

In Tamil Nadu, there are 12,618 Village Panchayat Presidents, who are the Executive Authoriy of the Village Panchayats concerned and each President is assisted by a Panchayat Assistant and a Makkal Nala Paniyalar, both of whom have generally only SSLC qualification. The suggested Accounting system is too complicated for them and there are no commensurate benefits of adopting the Ministry of Panchayat Raj proposed system.

Government of Tamil Nadu has firmly stated that its own Accounting System is much simpler and easier to maintain and has been working well and is suited to the State which has a large number of State funded schemes. Hence, while welcoming any 'Models and Best Examples', Government of Tamil Nadu has opposed the imposition of a uniform Accounting System.

Abolition of Jamabandhi

The Annual Settlement of Panchayat Accounts was introduced in 1992 at a time when there were no elected Local Bodies and the Panchayat Administration was managed by the Special Officers. However, consequent to the Constitution (73rd Amendment) Act, 1992 and the enactment of Tamil Nadu Panchayats Act, 1994, elected representatives assumed office in the rural Local Bodies in the year 1996 and the elected Local Bodies have an inbuilt system of checks and balances on the expenditure of the Local body funds.

Further, the system of Audit of Village Panchayat Accounts has also been introduced and Deputy Block Development Officers have been designated as the Audit Officers. The post of Assistant

Director (Audit) has been created for monitoring the progress of audit and the settlement of audit objections. Grama Sabha has also been strongly propagated as a forum of Social Audit of Village Panchayat accounts. In view of the above, it was viewed that the Annual Settlement of Panchayat Accounts by the Jamabandhi Officers did not contribute any value addition for the betterment of Panchayat Administration and that Jamabandhi had merely degenerated into a ritual. Thus, the Government issued orders vide G.O.Ms.No.175 RD & PR (PR2) Department, dated 14.11.2008 dispensing the Annual Settlement of Panchayat Accounts.

Telephones for Village Panchayats

Given the need for Block officials as well as Presidents to communicate with each other frequently, lack of land-line telephone in most of the Village Panchayats was a major hurdle in the implementation of schemes and in the administration of Panchayats. Hence, the Government vide G.O.Ms.No.118 RD & PR Department, dated 02.07.2007 issued orders permitting each Village Panchayat to have a telephone connection and prescribing a monthly ceiling of Rs.750/- towards telephones charges. So far, a total of 12,572 Village Panchayats out of 12,620 Village Panchayats of Tamil Nadu have been provided with Telephone connections and the remaining 48 Village Panchayats could not be provided with the telephones due to terrain related problems. Once a telephone connection is made available, the Village Panchayat can also have access to the Internet through a dial-up connection.

TNEB Issues

Maintenance of street lights and water supply are the two major functions of the Village Panchayats. Approximately, 70% of the income of the Village Panchayats used to be spent on payment of electricity charges. It was brought to the notice of the Government that in many cases, TNEB raised the bills on Village Panchayats on commercial rates without proper meter reading and levied 12% interest on the dues pending for more than 45 days. Undue delays were also noticed in obtaining estimation for installation of new street lights from TNEB authorities. The Government implemented a series of measures to settle some of these long term problems persisting between TNEB and the Village Panchayats.

The Government have, vide G.O.Ms.No.95 Energy (D2) Department, dated 12.10.2007 reduced the tariff of the EB service connection utilized for public lighting and water supply connection by Village Panchayats from Rs.3.40 per unit to Rs.3 per unit.

The Government have also vide G.O.Ms.No.111 RD & PR Dept. dt.26.6.2007 announced a uniform rate per pole of Rs.9,500/- for installation of new street lights by Village Panchayats.

The period of payment for EB charges has been raised from 20 days to 60 days for the Village Panchayats, and the interest rate payable by the Village Panchayats for payments beyond 60 days has been reduced from 12% to 6%. The surcharge of Rs.18.46 crores prior to 13.3.2007 has been written off.

Based on the Government's direction, TNEB has taken steps to provide electricity meters to all those service connections of Village Panchayats which didn't have meters, besides replacing defective meters.

Meter cards have been provided to all service connections in rural areas and TNEB has been asked to raise bills based only on the initial and final readings of the meters.

Steps have also been taken to pay up all the arrears due from Village Panchayats to TNEB. Where the arrears have been cleared, an entry that "No arrears are due pertaining to this service connection as onhas been directed to be made on the meter cards in order to enable the Village Panchayats to start with a clean slate in future.

Duty of the President to mandatorily implement Schemes entrusted to the Village Panchayat

Village Panchayats implement various Centrally Sponsored schemes and State funded schemes besides undertaking works out of general funds. However, there was no specific provision in the Tamil Nadu Panchayats Act, 1994, to require the President of the Village Panchayat to mandatorily execute or implement the schemes entrusted to the Village Panchayats. Hence, necessary amendment to Section 46 of the Act has been issued making it mandatory for the Presidents of Village Panchayats to execute or implement the schemes entrusted to the Village Panchayats.

Enhancement of Penalties

Tamil Nadu Panchayats Act, 1994, contemplates imposition of penalties on persons who contravene any of the provisions of the Act specified in Schedule-II or who fail to comply with any directions lawfully given to them or requisition lawfully made upon them. Schedule-III of the Act prescribes penalties for the continuing breaches. Since the penalty amounts provided in the above Schedules were prescribed 50 years back and had lost their deterrent effect, amendments were issued to Schedule II and Schedule III enhancing the penalty amounts leviable under the Act. This amendment will aid the rural Local Bodies in the strict enforcement of provisions of the Tamil Nadu Panchayats Act 1994.

Restriction of exemptions granted to Educational Institutions from House Tax

The Third State Finance Commission had recommended that all fee collecting institutions like nursery, Matriculation schools, tutorial colleges, self financed engineering, medical/dental colleges, para medical institutions, teacher training institutions, coaching centres etc should be subjected to House tax. The Government accepted the recommendation of the Third State Finance Commission and suitably amended rule 15 (c) of the Tamil Nadu Panchayats (Assessments and Collection of Taxes) Rules, 1999 vide G.O. Ms. No.38 RD & PR (PR.1) Department, dated 5.3.2008 and the amended provision now enables the Village Panchayats to levy and collect House Tax on the buildings used by Self financing educational institutions and also from the Government-aided institutions which are conducting self-financing unaided courses.

Empowering the District Collectors to levy and collect Advertisement Tax

As per the earlier provisions of the Tamil Nadu Panchayats Act, 1994, and the Tamil Nadu Panchayats (Licensing of Hoardings and Levy and Collection of Advertisement Tax) Rules, 1999, the Executive authority of the Village Panchayat concerned (the Village Panchayat President) was empowered to grant license for erecting hoardings in the rural areas and to levy and collect tax on advertisements on such hoardings, whereas, the District Collector is the licensing authority in the urban area. Further, the Village Panchayats were not able to strongly enforce and monitor the erection of hoardings as per the provisions of the Act.

In order to bring parity with Urban Act and to strengthen the licensing procedure and improve the monitoring of erection of hoardings in rural areas, the Government have suitably amended Sections 172-A, 172-B and sub-sections (2), (3) and (5) of Section 220 of Tamil Nadu Panchayats Act, 1994 by empowering the District Collector to grant license for hoarding and levy of Advertisement tax.

Consequent to the above amendment to the Act, the Government have issued the Tamil Nadu Panchayats (Licensing of Hoardings and Levy and Collection of Advertisement Tax) Rules, 2009 in supersession of the earlier rules.

Exemptions under the Building Rules

In order to bring about parity between Tamil Nadu Panchayats Building Rules, 1997 and urban Rules in grant of exemptions for certain buildings belonging to the Central and Sate Governments, Government have issued necessary amendment to the Tamil Nadu Panchayats Building Rules, 1997. Exemption from the purview of Tamil Nadu Panchayats Building Rules, 1997 has been incorporated in select cases, such as the buildings which are the property of the State or Central Governments or constructed in pursuance of any statutory provisions.

Dispensing with the levy of Local Cess and Local Cess Surcharge

The Government have announced during the Budget Speech 2009-2010 that the existing system of land revenue collection would be simplified and farmers shall not be burdened with any other levy such as Local Cess and Local Cess Surcharge. Consequent upon the above decision of the Government, levy of Local Cess and Local Cess Surcharge needed to be dispensed with. To implement this, Sections 167, 168, 169, 176, 186 (b) and 188 (d) of Tamil Nadu Panchayats Act, 1994 were amended vide Tamil Nadu Act No. 12 of 2009, and the levy of Local Cess and Local Cess Surcharge was dispensed with.

Maintenance of Tanks and Ponds

Traditionally, ponds have been maintained by the Village Panchayats and Minor Irrigation (M.I) tanks (i.e. tanks with ayacut less than 100 acres) have been maintained by the Panchayat Unions. However, the statutory duty of repair and maintenance of both ponds and tanks was vested only with Village Panchayats as per Section 110 (g) of the Tamil Nadu Panchayats Act, 1994. In order to remove this anomaly and to statutorily entrust the maintenance of ponds to Village Panchayats and of M.I tanks to Panchayat Unions, Sections 110 (g) and Section 112 (aa) of the Tamil Nadu Panchayats Act, 1994 have been amended vide Tamil Nadu Act No. 28 of 2009.

PANCHAYAT UNION COUNCIL

At the intermediate level, there are 385 Panchayat Unions (Blocks) in the State. The average number of Panchayat Unions per district is 13. The Nilgiris (4) has the lowest number of Panchayat Unions while Villupuram (22) has the highest.

Functions and Powers

Section 112 of the Tamil Nadu Panchayats Act, 1994 prescribes various powers and functions of Panchayat Union Councils. Some of the important functions of a Panchayat Union Council are:

a) Construction, repair and maintenance of all Panchayat union roads.

b) Construction of water works for the supply of water for drinking, washing and bathing purposes.

c) Construction and maintenance of elementary and middle schools.

d) Control of fairs and festivals under the control of the Panchayat Union.

e) Opening and maintenance of Panchayat Union public markets.

f) Implementing various Centrally sponsored and State schemes.

g) Preventive and remedial measures connected with any epidemic or with malaria.

Resources

Panchayat Unions cannot levy any tax. The revenues of a Panchayat Union consist of the following:

a) Non tax revenues

License fees, market fees, receipt from rentals and properties, fines and penalties.

b) Assigned and shared revenues

The Pooled Assigned Revenue component of Surcharge, Surcharge on Stamp Duty and Entertainment Tax is proportionately distributed to the Panchayat Unions based on the State Finance Commission Grants formula. Lease amount of mines and minerals (50% share) comes individually to the Panchayat Unions concerned and is adjusted at the district level itself.

c) Grants

State Finance Commission Grants, development grants under Centrally sponsored schemes and State schemes, grants for maternity centres, rural dispensaries.

By virtue of enactment of the Tamil Nadu Panchayats (Preparation of Plan and Estimates for works and Mode and Conditions of works) Rules, 2007 vide G.O.Ms.No.203 R.D. & P.R. Dept. dt. 20.12.2007, the Panchayat Union Councils have been empowered to give administrative sanction and execute individual works up to Rs.10 lakhs from their General Funds without any external approval. Earlier the Panchayat Unions were empowered to sanction funds up to Rs.5 lakhs only. For all works costing more than Rs.10 lakhs but not

more than Rs.50 lakhs, the District Collector is the competent authority to give the administrative sanction and for works costing more than Rs.50 lakhs, the Director of Rural Development and Panchayat Raj will be competent to accord administrative sanction. However for Centrally sponsored and State funded schemes, prior administrative sanction of the District Collector is necessary.

Wireless to Panchayat Unions

The Government have, vide G.O. Ms.No. 134 R.D. & P.R. (SGS.4) Department, dated 02.08.2007, issued orders for provision of wireless communication equipment to vehicles and Block offices in 24 districts of Tamil Nadu during 2007-08 and earmarked an amount of Rs.3.76 crores for this purpose. The wireless communication facility has been extended to the remaining 6 districts at the cost of Rs.116.55 lakhs during 2008-09 vide G.O.Ms.No.177 RD & PR (SGS.4) Department, dated 21.11.2008.

Vehicles to Panchayat Union Chairpersons

The Third High Level Committee constituted under the Chairmanship of Hon'ble Deputy Chief Minister recommended that the Panchayat Union Chairpersons should be given an independent vehicle like District Panchayat Chairpersons to facilitate better supervision of schemes.

It was, thus, announced on the floor of the Tamil Nadu Legislative Assembly on 16.4.2008 that new vehicles will be provided for 385 Panchayat Union Chairpersons during 2008-09 and 385 Driver posts would be newly created for this purpose. Accordingly, 385 vehicles were purchased and handed over to 385 Panchayat Union Chairpersons on 28.07.2008 by the Hon'ble Chief Minister. The Government also ordered for the creation of 385 drivers for Panchayat Union Chairpersons' vehicles vide G.O.Ms.No.67 RD & PR (E5) Department dated 12.05.2008.

Reconstitution of Appointment Committee of Panchayat Unions

The earlier system of conduct of annual elections to elect a member of Appointment Committee was not conducive to the smooth functioning of the Panchayat Union administration. Hence in order to provide continuity to the Committee and avoid changing the composition every year with one new member, the Government have issued amendment to Section 96(1)(a) of Tamil Nadu Panchayats Act, 1994 by making the Vice-Chairman of the Panchayat Union as one of the members of the Appointment Committee.

Consequent to the amendment, the three members Appointment Committee will consist of the Chairman of the Panchayat Union Council, the Vice-Chairman of the Panchayat Union Council and the Commissioner of Panchayat Union.

District Panchayats

There are 29 District Panchayats in the State.

Functions

The functions of the District Panchayats are mainly advisory in nature such as:

a) Preparation of development plan for the district.

b) Compilation of administration reports of Village Panchayats and Panchayat Union Councils of the district and preparation of Annual Report for the District.

c) Planning and review of Agriculture, Land Development, Animal Husbandry, Dairy, Poultry, Fisheries and Rural Industries etc.

d) Planning and review of rural housing programmes particularly housing for SC/STs.

e) Identification of major water supply schemes.

Resources

The District Panchayat has no taxation powers. Its only source of revenue is from statutory grants like State Finance Commission Grant and development grants under Centrally sponsored schemes.

By virtue of enactment of the Tamil Nadu Panchayats (Preparation of Plan and Estimates for works and Mode and Conditions of works) Rules, 2007 vide G.O.Ms.No.203 RD & PR Dept. dated 20.12.2007, the District Panchayats have been empowered to give administrative sanction and execute individual works up to Rs.20 lakhs from their General Funds without any external approval.

Earlier the District Panchayats were empowered to sanction funds up to Rs.10 lakhs only. For all works costing more than Rs.20 lakhs but not more than Rs.50 lakhs, the District Collector is the competent authority to give the administrative sanction and for works costing more than Rs.50 lakhs, the Director of Rural Development and Panchayat Raj will be competent to accord administrative sanction. However for Centrally sponsored and State funded schemes, prior administrative sanction of the District Collector is necessary.

Pooling of Assigned Revenues

The major sources of assigned/shared revenues to the rural Local Bodies are Surcharge on Stamp duty, Entertainment tax, seigniorage fee and lease amount of mines and minerals, and sale proceeds of Social Forestry plantations. The total receipts to rural Local Bodies under these heads in a year is about Rs.250-350 crores. The surcharge on stamp duty is pooled at the Block level and apportioned among the Village Panchayats in the Block in proportion to their land revenue collection. The entertainment tax is shared between the Village Panchayats and Panchayat Union in the ratio 70:30, after deducting 10% towards collection expenses. The seigniorage fee on minor minerals is credited to the Village Panchayats concerned while in the case of the lease amount, 50% is credited to the Panchayat Union and 50% to the Village Panchayats concerned. In the case of social forestry auction amounts, 60% of the gross proceeds will go to the Village Panchayats concerned and 40% will be retained by Forest department.

It was observed that there is considerable delay in adjusting the various assigned/shared revenues to the Village Panchayats and Panchayat Unions and the paper work involved is disproportionate to the amounts involved. There was considerable inequity in the distribution of what are essentially Government revenues.

In order to overcome the delays in adjusting the various assigned/shared revenues to the Village Panchayats and Panchayat Unions and reduce the disproportionate paper work involved and inequities in the distribution, the Government have vide G.O.Ms.No.168 RD & PR Dept. dt.4.10.2007 ordered for the pooling of the Assigned Revenues due to the rural Local Bodies from the proceedings of the Local Cess, Local Cess Surcharge, Surcharge on Stamp Duty, and Entertainment Tax at the State level and apportionment of the above revenues to the rural Local Bodies thereafter. The above Pooling of Assigned Revenue has facilitated quick and easy disbursement of these revenues and is also equitable.

State Finance Commission Grant

To augment the resources of the Local Bodies, financial devolution to the Local Bodies is made on the basis of recommendations of the State Finance Commission (SFC). Based on the recommendations of the State Finance Commission, a higher share of State's own tax revenues for the rural and urban Local Bodies beginning with 9% (it being 8% till 2006-07) has been allocated for the year 2007-08 and 2008-09. For 2009-10, the Government have increased the allocation to 9.5% of the State's own tax revenues to the rural and urban Local Bodies. The percentage of devolution will be progressively increased to 10% within the award period of the Third State Finance Commission (2007-08 to 2011-12). The ratio of the shares of rural and urban Local Bodies will be 58:42 as before. Since Village Panchayats are entrusted with most of the basic functions such as maintenance of village roads and streets, drinking water supply, street lights, sanitation and solid waste management and they are also the largest in number (12,620), the allocation for the rural Local Bodies is shared in the ratio 60:32:8 among Village Panchayats, Panchayat Union Councils and the District Panchayats from the year 2007-08 onwards. These policy changes are expected to greatly improve the delivery of services at the grass roots level. The quantum of increase in SFC Grants to rural Local Bodies from2006-07 to 2009-10 is given in Table 8.

Table-8: State Finance Commission Grants to Rural Local Bodies

Year	SFC Grants (Rs.in crores)	Increase over previous year	
		Amount (Rs.in crores)	% of increase
2006-07	1,224.76	230.00	23.1
2007-08	1,583.58	358.82	29.3
2008-09	1,716.44	132.86	8.4
2009-10	1926.57	210.13	12.2

Streamlining the modalities of release of State Finance Commission Grant

The State Finance Commission Grant is released from the Directorate of Rural Development and Panchayat Raj to the District

Collectors electronically through the Core Banking System (CBS). The District Collectors, in turn, had earlier been sending the funds to the Village Panchayats by adopting various methods like Core Banking System, Real Time Gross Settlement (RTGS), Demand draft system etc. There was lack of uniformity in the procedure and a lot of delays in the adjustment of funds in this process. In order to overcome the above drawbacks, a uniform procedure of transferring the funds through 4 Nodal Banks in each of the Districts to the bank accounts of the Village Panchayats has been prescribed with effect from December 2008. This procedure has significantly speeded up the adjustments of Grants to the accounts of rural Local Bodies.

Central Finance Commission Grant

On the basis of the recommendations of the Twelfth Finance Commission (TFC), the Government of India have allotted a sum of Rs.870 crores for the 5-year period from2005-06 to 2009-10.

For 2007-08, this Government decided that the entire Twelfth Finance Commission Grant should be allocated only to Village Panchayats on the basis of population. The grants should be tilized by the Village Panchayats entirely for the operation and maintenance cost of water supply, street lighting and sanitation. This system of allocating entire State Finance Commission grant to Village Panchayats continued in the year 2008-09 also. A sum of Rs.174 crores will be provided for the year 2009-10 under the Twenfth Finance Commission Grant.

Increase in the allowances of Rural Local Body representatives

Fixed Travelling Allowance (FTA) was initially sanctioned by the Government to the Presidents of Village Panchayats and Chairpersons and Members of the Panchayat Unions and District Panchayats vide G.O.Ms.No.262 Rural Development Department dated 20.12.1997. This amount was enhanced by 10% in the year 1999 and was not revised thereafter. The Government have, vide G.O. (D) No.569 RD & PR(C1) Department, dated 28.09.2007, enhanced the FTA of the rural Local Body representatives and the Table 9 below indicates the FTA rates prevalent previously and enhanced now.

Table-9 Monthly FTA for Rural Local Bod representatives

Sl. No.	Name of the office/seat	Previously Monthly FTA (Rs.)	Revised Monthly FTA (Rs.)
1	President, Village Panchayat	330	500
2	Chairperson, Panchayat Union	550	750
3	Member, Panchayat Union	220	400
4	Chairperson, District Panchayat	1,100	1,500
5	Member, District Panchayat	330	500

Issue of Identity Cards to Heads of Panchayat Raj Institutions

Based on the representations given by the Village Panchayat Presidents during the Regional Conferences of Village Panchayat Presidents at Erode and Tiruchirapalli, the Hon'ble Deputy Chief Minister announced to give Identity Cards to all the 12,618 Village Panchayat Presidents which were immediately issued thereafter. Identity Cards were also given to the Chairpersons and members of the Panchayat Unions and District Panchayats.

Local Bodies' Day

The rural and urban Local Bodies are perhaps the agencies

with the maximum public interface. There is need to further strengthen this interface and bring about greater transparency and openness in the functioning of Local Bodies. At the same time, it is also necessary to highlight their achievements and carry out the various information, education and communication campaigns relating to civic administration or implementation of schemes. One method of doing this is to designate a particular day in a calendar year as "Local Bodies' Day" The Government have issued G.O.No.632,RD & PR(C1) Department, dated 26.10.2007 earmarking November 1 as "Local Bodies' Day" to be celebrated by all rural and urban Local Bodies in Tamil Nadu every year. Tamil Nadu is the first State in the country to do this.

Electrification of buildings used by other Departments

The Rural Development and Panchayat Raj (RD & PR) Department constructs various categories of buildings not only for the usage of rural Local Bodies but also for the usage of a number of other departments. Based on the 'user pays' principle, it is for the occupying departments to pay the electricity consumption charges. Since the buildings were owned by RD&PR Department, the user departments were unable to apply for electricity connections in their name. In order to overcome this problem, the Government have, vide G.O.Ms.No.206, RD & PR (SGS.1) Department, dated 31.12.2007 given a blanket 'No Objection Certificate' to the other user departments for which the RD & PR Department has built buildings through its schemes, to enable them to apply to TNEB for electricity connections and pay the recurring current consumption charges to TNEB, without any financial commitment to the rural Local Bodies.

Stability in tenure of Local Body representatives

The Government felt that frequent moving of no-confidence motions on trivial and unjustifiable grounds affected the continuity in planning and implementation of works in rural Local Bodies and are detrimental to public interest. In order to make the provisions for moving and passing the no-confidence motion more stringent, the Government have amended relevant provisions of the Tamil Nadu Panchayats Act, 1994, wherein the minimum strength required for issuance of motion of no confidence against the Vice-President of the Village Panchayat or the Chairperson or the Vice-Chairperson of the Panchayat Union or the District Panchayat concerned has been increased from the existing half of the sanctioned strength to three-fifth and the minimum strength required for carrying the motion has been increased from the existing two-third to four-fifth of the strength of the local body concerned.

Also it has been stipulated that no motion of any confidence can be brought within one year of the assumption of the office or during the last year of the term of office of the Vice-President of the Village Panchayat or the Chairperson, Vice-Chairperson of the Panchayat Union or the District Panchayat concerned.

Annual Report on the functioning of Panchayats

As per the original Section 165 of Tamil Nadu Panchayats Act, 1994, each District Panchayat had to prepare an Annual Report giving a full account of its activities during the previous year and forward it to the Government.

The Government used to lay all such reports on the table of the Legislative Assembly. However, as the reports of the District Panchayats did not give a comprehensive view of the functioning of Panchayat Raj Institutions, Section 165(2) was deleted and a new Section 166A was introduced replacing the old system with a single Annual Report for the State as a whole.

'Annual Reports on the Functioning of Panchayats in Tamil Nadu' for 2006-07, 2007-08, and 2008-09 have already been placed before the Legislative Assembly, and that for the year 2009-10 will be placed in April 2010.

Guidelines for dismantling of old buildings under the control of Village Panchayats and Panchayat Unions

Village Panchayats and Panchayat Unions are maintaining various kinds of buildings such as School Buildings, Kitchen sheds, Library Buildings, Sanitary Complexes, Panchayat Union Offices, Village Panchayat Offices, Over Head Tanks etc. With the passage of time and due to various circumstances, certain buildings become dilapidated and need to be dismantled for safety considerations. In such cases, there were no specific guidelines and clear delegation of powers, for issuing orders for dismantling the dilapidated buildings of Rural Development and Panchayat Raj Department.

Hence, the Government vide G.O. Ms. No.56, RD & PR (SGS-IV) Department, dated 3.4.2008 have issued detailed guidelines to be followed for dismantling of old buildings under the control of Village Panchayats and Panchayat Unions.

Constitution of Fourth State Finance Commission

The Government have, vide G.O.Ms.No.549, Finance (Finance Commission-IV) Department, dated 01.12.2009, constituted Fourth State Finance Commission to review the financial position of the rural and urban local bodies namely Village Panchayats, Panchayat Union Councils, District Panchayats, Town Panchayats, Municipalities and Municipal Corporations. The Commission has the mandate to make recommendations as to –

(a) the principles which should govern –

   (i) the distribution between the State and the said local bodies of the net proceeds of the taxes, duties, tolls and fees leviable by the Government which may be divided between them and the allocation between the said local bodies of their respective shares of such proceeds;

   (ii) the determination of taxes, duties, tolls and fees which may be assigned to or appropriated by the said local bodies;

   (iii) the grants-in-aid to the said local bodies from the Consolidated Fund of the State.

(b) the measures needed to improve the financial position of the local bodies and to suggest possible new avenues for tapping resources in rural and urban local bodies keeping in mind the local body tax structure in other States.

In reviewing the financial position of the local bodies, the Commission has been asked to assess the financial position of the local bodies as on 31st March, 2010. The Commission has been asked to make its report available by 31st May, 2011 covering the period of five years commencing on 1st April 2012.

ESTABLISHMENT

Sanction of Time Scale to the post of Makkal Nala Paniyalars

The Makkal Nala Paniyalars working in the Village Panchayats were getting a consolidated pay of Rs. 950 and a conveyance allowance of Rs.50/- per month. The Government vide G.O.Ms.No.234, Finance (Pay Cell) Department, dated 1.6.2009, have brought the salary of the Makkal Nala Paniyalarkal to the special time scale of pay of Rs. 2,500-5,000 and a grade pay of Rs. 500 per month with effect from 1.6.2009.

Upgradation of posts of PanchayatAssistants Gr.II as Panchayat Assistants

Prior to 2006-07, Panchayat Assistants were categorized into two categories viz. (i) Full-time Panchayat Assistants (also called Panchayat Assistants Grade I) and (ii) Part-time Panchayat .

Clerks (also called as Panchayat Assistants Grade II). The Panchayat Assistants Grade II were about 11,000 in number out of the total 12,618 Panchayat Assistants. Till 1.9.2006, both these two categories of Panchayats Assistants were getting consolidated pay.

With effect from 1.9.2006, the pay of the full-time Panchayat Assistants was fixed in the time scale Rs.1,300-20-1,500-25-2,000, and the pay of the part-time Panchayat Clerks was fixed in the time scale Rs.625-10-725-20-925. The Government revised the scale of Pay of Panchayat Assistants Grade –I to the Pay band of Rs.2,500-5,000 plus Grade Pay of Rs.500/- with effect from 1.6.2009 vide G.O.(Ms.)

No. 234 Finance (PC) Dept. dated 1.6.2009,. However, the pay of Panchayat Assistants Grade II was revised to the pay band of Rs. 1,300-3000 with a Grade pay of Rs 300. Since the nature of work of Panchayat Assistants Grade I and Grade II was the same, the Government ordered the upgradation of all the posts of Panchayat Assistants Grade II on par with Panchayat Assistants Grade I and brought them also to the revised scale of pay of Rs.2,500-5,000 with Grade Pay of Rs.500/-, vide G.O.Ms.No.91 RD & PR (E5) Dept., dated 12.8.2009.

Restructuring of District Rural Development Agencies

The restructuring of the District Rural Development Agencies (DRDAs) was long overdue for various reasons. First, the staffing pattern of DRDAs reflected the needs of yesteryear schemes, which were no longer in vogue. Secondly, the APO level posts that were diverted during bifurcation of Districts in the past few years had resulted in a highly non-uniform staffing pattern in the DRDAs which necessitated the restructuring. Thirdly, there was also a highly non-uniform staffing pattern across districts in respect of subordinate posts resulting in administrative difficulties with the old DRDA pattern. Fourthly, there was a mismatch of deputationists in the DRDAs and a perennial difficulty in getting officers on deputation from other Departments. Fifthly, there was also a steep increase in the outlay of State-funded RD schemes after the introduction of Schemes such as Anaithu Grama Anna Marumalarchi Thittam (AGAMT), Rural Infrastructure Scheme (RIS), MLA Constituency Development Scheme (MLACDS), Samathuvapuram etc. which necessitated the creation of posts of additional supervisory officers of Rural Development and Panchayat Raj Department. Sixthly, there were cuts in DRDA Administration Scheme grants by Government of India due to the deputationist posts lying vacant for long spans of time and consequently the DRDAs not being able to adequately spend the salary component of the DRDA Administration Scheme Grants that they were supposed to as per the allocation.

Hence, the State Government issued orders restructuring DRDAs in accordance with Government of India guidelines issued under DRDA Administration Scheme vide G.O.Ms.No.53, RD & PR (CGS-2) Department dated 19.06.2009. The posts of APO (R), APO (EAS), APO (DWCRA), APO (Industries), APO (Animal Husbandry), APO (Cooperation) and APO (Monitoring) were abolished and among other posts created, the posts of APO (Wage employment), APO (Infrastructure), APO (Self employment), APO (Housing and Sanitation) were created. At present, there are 36 posts of APO (Wage employment), 60 posts of APO (Infrastructure), 31 posts of APO (Self employment), and 31 posts of APO (Housing and Sanitation) in DRDAs.

Tamil Nadu's views on the status of DRDAs

The views of the State Government were sought for by the

Government of India regarding a proposal to abolish the District Rural Development Agencies (DRDAs) and entrust District Panchayats with the responsibility of implementing various Centrally Sponsored Schemes that are being presently implemented by the DRDAs. In this regard, the Hon'ble Chief Minister of Tamil Nadu in his D.O. Letter No.17098/ CGS II/2009 dated 19.9.2009, addressed to the Hon'ble Prime Minister has stated that "according to Article 243G of the Constitution of India, it is up to the State Legislature to decide which powers and functions should be devolved to which tier of Panchayats. Historically, Tamil Nadu had strong Village Panchayats and Block Panchayats and only a Planning-cum-Advisory body called the District Development Council at the district level ever since the erstwhile District Boards were abolished in 1961.

After the enactment of the Constitution 73rd Amendment, Tamil Nadu –while strengthening Village Panchayats and Block Panchayats further – chose to maintain the status quo at the district level by conferring only planning-cum-advisory functions – and no implementation functions – upon District Panchayats vide Section 163 of the Tamil Nadu Panchayats Act, 1994. If DRDAs are brought under the control of district Panchayats or merged with District Panchayats, it would change the very legal character of District Panchayats in Tamil Nadu and confer implementation powers and functions upon them. It would also be contrary to the intent of the Tamil Nadu Legislature....Moreover, abolition of the DRDA, an institution which has been working very well – both in terms of speed and quality of execution – for nearly three decades now, can be detrimental to the effective implementation of development schemes. District Panchayats are political bodies and there is a lot of scope for this tier to become dysfunctional due to political differences. In Tamil Nadu, DRDAs are insulated from such politics because the District Collector is the Chairman of the DRDA. This is one of the reasons why Tamil Nadu is a top performer in the implementation of development programmes".

Thus the Government of Tamil Nadu have strongly represented against any executive order being issued by Government of India to abolish the DRDAs or bring them under the control of the District Panchayats in as much as 'Local Government' is a State subject under the Constitution of India.

Staffing under NREGS

National Rural Employment Guarantee Scheme (NREGS) was introduced in Phase-I in six districts of Tamil Nadu viz. Cuddalore, Villupuram, Tiruvannamalai, Nagapattinam, Dindigul and Sivaganga with effect from 02.02.2006. The Scheme was extended to four more districts of Thanjavur, Tiruvarur, Karur and Tirunelveli in Phase-II with effect from 01.04.2007 and has been extended to the remaining 20 Districts of the State with effect from 01.04.2008. In order to facilitate proper implementation of the Scheme, the Government have sanctioned several technical and supporting staff. During the year 2009-10, Government also created 572 additional posts of Computer Assistants, vide G.O.Ms.No.84, RD&PR(CGS-1) Department, dated 4.8.2009, in order to ensure MIS entries. Government also created 32 posts of Assistant Executive Engineers for the newly formed NREGS sub divisions. The details of post-wise sanction are shown in Table 10 below.

Table-10: Posts sanctioned to supervise NREGS works in Districts

Sl. No.	Category of Post	No.of Posts
A. Administration wing		
1	Superintendents in the level of Block Development Officer	31
2	Deputy Block Development Officers	385
3	Assistants	416
4	Computer Assistants	1,373
5	Drivers	32
6	Office Assistants	32
B. Technical Wing		
1	Assistant Executive Engineers (RD)	32
2	Assistant Engineers (RD)	244
3	Overseers	673
4	Junior Draughting Officers	32
	Total	3,250

The Government have also, vide G.O.Ms.No.164 RD&PR (CGS1) Department, dated 21.10.2008, created a State NREGA Cell, the composition of which is indicated in Table 11 below.

Table-11 Posts sanctioned to State NREGS Cell

Sl. No.	Category of Post	No.of Posts
A. Technical Wing:		
1	Executive Engineer	1
2	Assistant Executive Engineer	1
3	Assistant Engineers	4
4	Junior Draughting Officer	1
B. Social Audit wing:		
1	Assistant Directors	2
C. MIS and Documentation wing:		
1.	MIS specialists	2*

* 2 or more MIS Specialists within overall financial limit of Rs.50,000 per month on outsourcing basis.

Revamping of Engineering Establishment

In 1960, the Highways Department was reorganised and redesignated as "Highways & Rural Works Department" (H&RW) and was required to attend to RD Department works in addition to Highways works by an executive order. Till December 1996, there were among others, 53 posts of Assistant Divisional Engineers and 384 posts of Union Engineers sanctioned by the Government in RD Department and these posts were manned by the Highways & Rural Works Department and their salaries were paid from heads of account of RD Department's budget.

There was a situation of 'dual control' of the engineering staff with their postings and transfers by the Chief Engineer (H&RW)/ Divisional Engineers (H&RW) while the responsibility for implementation of RD Schemes lay with the Director of Rural Development and Collectors. Such an arrangement was unsatisfactory. Further, the allocation of funds under various Centrally-sponsored and State-funded schemes had increased enormously during the 1980s and 1990s, making RD Department one of the biggest spending departments – bigger than even

Highways Department – and warranting the sanction of additional technical posts and the creation of a separate, full-fledged Engineering wing for RD Department.

As a first step toward creating a full-fledged Engineering Wing for RD Department, the Government in RD Department sanctioned 384 additional posts of Assistant Engineers (AEs), 15 additional posts of Assistant Executive Engineers (AEEs), 28 posts of Executive Engineers(EEs) at district level and one post of Superintending Engineer (SE) with the powers of Chief Engineer vide G.O.Ms.No. 263, RD Dept., dated. 27.12.1996.

The next step was to bring the technical control of all the engineering posts in RD Department – original as well as new - under the purview of the SE (RD). Toward this end, the Madras Panchayats, Panchayat Unions (Preparation of Plans and Estimates) Rules, 1963 by which the 'technical control' was vested with engineers of H&RW Department, was superseded by the Tamil Nadu Panchayats, Panchayat Unions and District Panchayats (Preparation of Plans and Estimates) Rules, 1997 framed in G.O.Ms.No. 79, RD (CSS-1) Dept., dt. 20.3.1997.

Subsequently, adhoc Service Rules were framed for the posts of SE, EE, AEE and AE in G.O.Ms.No. 15, RD Dept., dt. 25.1.2000 with retrospective effect from 25.5.1998 for SE, EE, AEE and from 26.9.1997 for AE. Adhoc Service Rules for the posts of Senior Draughting Officer (SDO) and Junior Engineer (JE) categories were framed in G.O.Ms.No. 71, RD (E4) Dept., dt. 20.3.2000 and Adhoc Service Rules for the posts of Overseers/Junior Draughting Officers (JDOs) and Road Iinspectors (RIs) were framed in G.O.Ms.No. 70, RD (E4) Dept., dt. 20.3.2000. The final and complete separation of the Engineering wings between RD and Highways and Rural Works Departments was ordered in G.O.Ms.No. 253, RD Dept., dt. 28.9.2001.

In the meantime, RD Department notified 200 vacancies of AEs to be filled up through TNPSC in September 1997 and the first batch was recruited in 1998. The second batch of 223 AEs was recruited in 2006-07 and the third batch of 253 AEs was recruited in 2007-08. . For the years 2008-09 and 2009-10, the TNPSC has been requested to recruit 71 and 106 (totally 177) Assistant Engineers(RD) respectively. Based on the Service Rules, qualified

245 Assistant Engineers(RD)/JEs were promoted as AEEs(RD) and qualified 46 AEEs(RD) were also promoted as EEs(RD). 146 Overseers/JDOs were also promoted as AEs(RD)/JEs(RD). The RD & PR Department has also been recruiting Overseers/JDOs through Employment Exchanges based on the Service Rules. 1,398 Overseers/Junior Draughting Officers have been recruited, including the 709 newly created posts.

The Technical wing of the RD & PR Department has been entirely revamped between 2006-07 & 2009-10. The number of posts of Executive Engineer (RD), which was 28 earlier, has been increased to 46. The number of Technical sub-divisions which was 68 earlier, has been increased to 100 in the year 2007-08 and the total number of AEE posts has been increased from 125 in 2006-07 to 228 in 2009-10. Earlier there were only 2 Assistant Engineers (RD)/Junior Engineers per Block. The pattern of two AEs (RD) / JEs for every Block was rationalised with the revised norm of having an average of one AE(RD)/JE for every 17 Village Panchayats during the year 2007-08. Thus, the present strength of AEs(RD)/ JEs per Block ranges from 2 to 4. The total strength of AEs(RD)/ JEs has increased from 896 in 2006-07 to 1,253 in 2009-10. Earlier, there were only 2 Union Overseers per Block in the Districts. In view of the increased workload, this strength was rationalised in the year 2007-08 with the revised norm of one Union Overseer for every 9 Village Panchayats. Thus, presently there are 2 to 8 Overseers per Block and the net strength has been increased from 768 in 2006-07 to 1,441 in 2009-10.

A series of writ petitions filed by engineers of other Departments who had been taken on deputation into RD & PR Department and who had sought permanent absorption were disposed off in favour of RD & PR Department and against the writ petitioners by the Honourable High Court of Madras during the past three years. The Hon'ble High Court of Madras, in its judgment dated 29.1.2007 in W.P.No. 19401 to 19410 of 2004 and batch cases, struck down the request of TWAD Board engineers to absorb them in the RD & PR Department and dismissed the Writ petitions as devoid of merits by quoting various Hon'ble Supreme Court Judgments. Similarly, the prayer of the engineers from other technical departments viz. Public Works, Highways and

Agricultural Engineering Departments to absorb them permanently in RD & PR Department in W.P.Nos. 23072, 28434, 24453 of 2004 and batch cases were also struck down and dismissed by the Hon'ble High Court of Madras, vide its judgment dated 13.2.2009, as devoid of merits citing legal reasons and various Hon'ble Supreme Court Judgments.

Several Writ Petitions filed by NREGS Technical Assistants who had been formerly engaged on outsourcing basis seeking absorption as Overseers were dismissed by the Hon'ble High Court of Madras by its judgement dated 8.7.2008. This was upheld by the Division Bench of the Hon'ble High Court of Madras which ruled that persons engaged on outsourcing basis had no rights of absorption.

Re-designation of AEE (RD-PMGSY) and AEE (RD-Water Supply) as AEE (RD-Roads and Bridges)

In order to strengthen technical supervision of roads and bridges and the technical support system in the offices of Executive Engineer (RD) and Superintending Engineer (RD), the Government, vide G.O.Ms.No.67, RD & PR (SGS3) Department dated 20.07.2009, have re-designated the posts of AEE (RD-PMGSY) and AEE (RD-Water Supply) as AEE (RD-Roads and Bridges) and also attached one post of AE(RD) to the office of EE(RD).

Filling up of posts of various categories in the Rural Development Department

This Government had to face a large number of vacancies in all categories of staff when it assumed office in May, 2006, which affected the implementation of schemes adversely. The Government had ordered filling up of the vacancies in all categories from the level of Assistant Director downwards. Out of a total of 17,819 vacant posts, so far 17,503 posts in 13 categories, including those of Assistant Directors, Assistant Engineers, Junior Draughting Officers, Overseers, Road Inspectors, Junior Assistants, Typists, Steno-typists, Drivers, Office Assistants and Night Watchmen have been filled up through various methods of recruitment and the remaining posts will be filled up shortly. At present, among others, there are 17 Additional Director cadre posts, 77 Joint Director cadre posts and 399 Nos. of Assistant Director cadre posts sanctioned for the RD & PR Department. Further, on the technical side, among others, there is one post of SE(RD), 46 posts of EEs(RD), 228 posts of AEEs(RD), 1,253 posts of AEs/JEs(RD), 29 posts of SDOs, 1,438 posts of Overseers, 161 posts of JDOs and 1,128 posts of RIs sanctioned for the RD & PR Department.

CENTRALLY – SPONSORED SCHEMES

Indira Awaas Yojana(IAY)

Indira Awaas Yojana, which used to be a component of Jawahar Rozgar Yojana became an independent Scheme from 1997-1998 onwards. Its objective is construction of free houses to members of the Scheduled Castes/ Scheduled Tribes, freed bonded labourers in rural areas and also to non SC/ST Rural poor people living below poverty line.

Beneficiaries are selected from the Below - the Poverty-line (BPL) list approved by the Grama Sabha. Atleast 60% of the total IAY allocation during a financial year should be utilized for construction/ upgradation of dwelling units for SC/ST BPL households.

A maximum 40% of allocation is for non- SC/ST BPL rural households. 3% of the above categories should be allocated for physically and mentally challenged persons. Government of India have also asked the States to earmark 15% of the beneficiaries from amongst to minorities. New houses as well as upgradation of kutcha houses are being taken up under the Scheme. It is funded by the Centre and State in the ratio of 75:25.

New Houses

From 1.4.2005 onwards, the unit cost of a new house was fixed at Rs.25,000/- for ordinary soil and 27,500/- for difficult soil.

Based on the budget announcement of the Union Finance Minister in February 2008, this amount was increased by Rs.10,000/- and Rs. 11,000/- respectively and the unit cost raised to Rs.35,000/- for ordinary soil and Rs.38,500/- for difficult soil. Moreover, the State Government provides an additional amount for RCC roofing cost in addition to its matching share. With effect from 2006-07, the above RCC roofing cost was raised from Rs.9,000/- to Rs.12,000/- per house. However, as the cost of construction of new house has increased substantially, the State Government, vide G.O.No. 91, RD & PR (CGS.1) Dept. dated 6.6.2008, further raised the RCC roofing cost from Rs.12,000/- to Rs.20,000/- per house with effect from 1.4.2008. This, along with the increase in unit cost as announced by the Central Government, has increased the total cost of an IAY house from existing Rs.37,000/- and Rs.39,500/- to Rs.55,000/- and Rs.58,500/- for ordinary soil and difficult soil respectively.

Based on the announcement of the Union Finance Minister in the Union Budget speech during February 2010, a further increase of Rs.10,000/-has been made to the IAY unit cost. The State Government now proposes to increase the overall unit cost of IAY houses to Rs. 60,000 per house from 2010-11 onwards.

A further subsidy of Rs. 2,200/- out of Total Sanitation Funds is dovetailed to enable each beneficiary to construct a toilet in the IAY house. The minimum plinth area of a house should be 20 square metres.

All new houses are provided with the toilets and smokeless chulahs. Beneficiaries undertake the construction with locally available materials employing low cost technologies.

During 2010-11, approximately 1.02 lakh New IAY Houses will be constructed at a financial outlay of approximately Rs. 617 crores, inclusive of the State Government's additionality towards the RCC roofing cost.

Mahatma Gandhi National Rural Employment Guarantee Scheme -Tamil Nadu

The Mahatma Gandhi National Rural Employment Guarantee Act was enacted in September 2005. The Mahatma Gandhi Rural Employment Guarantee Scheme was initially implemented with effect from 2.2.2006 onwards in six notified districts of Tamil Nadu (in Phase I). It was extended to 4 districts (in Phase II) from 1.4.2007 onwards and to the remaining 20 districts (in Phase III) with effect from 1.4.2008 onwards. The details are as furnished below in Table 12.

Table-12: Coverage of Districts in Phases under MGNREGS

Phase – 1 (2.2.2006 onwards)	Phase – II (1.4.2007 onwards)	Phase – III (1.4.2008 onwards)	
1. Cuddalore	1.Thanjavur	1. Kancheepuram	11. Trichy
2. Villupuram	2.Tiruvarur	2. Tiruvallur	12. Perambalur
3. Tiruvannamalai	3.Karur	3. Vellore	13. Ariyalur
4. Nagapattinam	4.Tirunelveli	4. Salem	14. Pudukottai
5. Dindigul		5. Namakkal	15. Madurai
6. Sivagangai		6. Dharmapuri	16. Theni
		7. Krishnagiri	17. Ramanathapuram
		8. Erode	18. Virdhunagar
		9. Coimbatore	19. Thoothukudi
		10.Nilgiris	20. Kanniyakumari

Objectives of the Scheme

The Mahatma Gandhi National Rural Employment Guarantee Act, 2005 (MGNREGA) guarantees 100 days of employment in a financial year to any rural household whose adult members volunteer to do unskilled manual work. This Act is an important step towards the realization of the "right to work". It is also expected to enhance people's livelihood on a sustained basis, by developing the economic and social infrastructure in rural areas.

The Village Panchayat issues job card to every registered individual. Payment of the statutory minimum wage and equal wages for men and women are the notable features of the scheme.

Funding Pattern

The cost of the Scheme is shared between the Centre and the State in the ratio of 90:10. The Central Government bears the following costs:

(a) The entire cost of wages for unskilled manual workers.

(b) 75% of the cost of material and wages for skilled and semi-skilled workers.

(c) Administrative expenses, which will include, inter alia, the salary and allowances of Programme Officers and their support staff, work site facilities and the State MGNREGA Cell.

(d) Administrative expenses of the Central Employment guarantee Council.

The State Government bears the following costs:

(a) 25 percent of the cost of material and wages for skilled and semi-skilled workers.

(b) Unemployment allowance payable in case, the State Government cannot provide wage employment within 15 days of application.

(c) Administrative expenses of the State Employment Guarantee Council.

Priority of works

Taking into account the field conditions in Tamil Nadu, the works are being taken up in the following priority:

(a) Formation of new ponds.

(b) Renovation of existing Ponds, Kuttais, Kulams, Ooranies, Temple tanks etc.

(c) Desilting of channels.

(d) Desilting and strengthening of bunds of irrigation tanks.

(e) Formation of new roads.

(f) Other water conservation/soil conservation measures / flood protection measures.

Special steps taken to ensure successfulimplementation of MGNREGS

On assumption of office in the month of May 2006, this Government noticed that the Scheme had not taken off properly. This was evident from the fact that the expenditure made up to 31.03.2006 was only Rs. 3 crores and that works had been taken up only in 924 Village Panchayats out of a total of 3,830 Village Panchayats in the six Districts.

This Government was quick to identify the issues and bottlenecks that were responsible for the poor progress in the implementation of the programme and came out with a series of initiatives to address those issues and to remove the implementation bottlenecks.

The following special steps were initiated to streamline and expedite the implementation of the Scheme:

1. Intensive IEC Efforts have been taken to ensure that there is extensive registration of rural househods in each Village Panchayat under this Scheme. The average percentage of registration in Phase-I & II districts has crossed 72%, in Phase III districts it has crossed 54% and overall, in the State, it is 61%, which indicates that there is widespread awareness about the Scheme.
2. A separate Rural Schedule of Rates has been sanctioned exclusively for this Scheme every year since 2006-07. To ensure that the workers earn the minimum wage for a day's work, the Rural Schedule of Rates ensured that there was a mark-up of 60% over and above the PWD Schedule of rates till December 2009. Consequent upon the increase in the minimum wages from Rs.80/- to Rs.100/- vide G.O.2(D) No.88, Labour and Employment (J1) Department, dated 1.10.2009, the Rural Schedule of Rates has also been increased correspondingly under MGNREGS, vide G.O.(Ms)No.146, RD&PR (CGS-1) Department, Dt.23.12.2009, with effect from 1.1.2010 and with an increased mark-up of 100% for earthwork components and 150% for jungle clearance components over and above the PWD Schedule of Rates.
3. The existing formats of Job Cards and Nominal Muster Rolls have been revised to make these documents more transparent, informative and difficult to manipulate in the process of Scheme implementation.
4. Payments to the workers are made on a weekly basis on designated days.
5. Since the Scheme requires intensive touring, the Government have sanctioned additional fuel of 50 litres per month for each of the vehicles in the Panchayat Unions. The Government have also sanctioned additional fuel of 75 litres for the vehicles of the Assistant Executive Engineers (RD) vide G.O.Ms.No.27 RD&PR (CGS-I) Department dated 20.02.2008.

6. The Scheme is implemented by Village Panchayats exclusively as they are closest to the people and hence best suited to implement this Scheme. Makkal Nala Paniyalars (MNPs), who are available in each Village Panchayat have also been made responsible for the implementation of the Scheme at the field level.
7. Additional ministerial, technical and computer staff have been sanctioned at District, Division, Block and Village levels in order to ensure proper implementation and close supervision of the Scheme. A State MGNREGA Cell has also been formed vide G.O.Ms.No.164, RD & PR (CGS-1) Department, dated 21.10.2008 to augment the State Capacity in ensuring quality, efficiency and transparency in the implementation of the Scheme.
8. Only 100% labour intensive works have been taken up in order to prevent the entry of contractors who are strictly banned as per the MGNREG Act.
9. Only bigger works not less than Rs. 3 lakhs in value have been taken up in order to ensure that i) adequate numbers of workers get sustained employment at a work site for at least 30 days, ii) the assets created are visible, durable and genuinely beneficial to the community, iii) resources are not wasted by being spread too thinly, iv) the works are monitored closely and leakages are minimised.
10. In order to create awareness among the beneficiaries about the volume of work to be done to get the minimum wages, the system of pre- marking of the expected weekly quantum of work has been initiated in all the districts with effect from 2008-09.
11. In order to ensure greater transparency and fair play, it has been ordered to disburse the wages to the workers in the presence of at least four members of the following Committee:
    a) President of the Village Panchayat.
    b) Vice–President of the Village Panchayat.
    c) Ward Member of the area where the work is executed.
    d) An SC/ST Ward Member, if none of the persons in Sl. Nos. a, b and c above belongs to SC/ST Community.

e) Two animators of graded Self Help Groups.

f) A representative of the Panchayat Level federation.

12. Savings Bank Accounts have been opened for the MGNREGS workers to enable payment of their wages directly to their bank accounts in case they are not available to personally receive the wages on the fixed day of the payment.

13. A 25-member Tamil Nadu State Employment Guarantee council has been constituted vide the G.O Ms No. 117, RD & PR (CGS-I) Department, dated 14.09.2006 to monitor and review the implementation of the Scheme. Consequent upon the implementation of the Scheme in all the 31 Districts of the State, a revised Council was constituted with representatives from all phases vide G.O. (MS) NO.118 RD & PR (CGS-1) Department, dated 11.07.08, G.O.Ms.No.51, RD & PR (CGS-1) Department,, Dated 18.6.2009. The first, second, third, fourth, fifth and sixth meetings of this Council were held on 25.11.2006, 11.06.2007, 03.03.2008, 08.08.2008, 16.9.2009 and 9.4.2010 respectively.

14. In order to ensure efficient monitoring of the Scheme through Management Information System (MIS), three computers and a printer have been sanctioned to each of the 385 block offices of Phase-I, II and III MGNREGS districts. Apart from this, all the existing 68 Sub-Divisions and the newly created 32 Sub-Divisions have been provided with one Computer and a Printer each.

15. In order to ensure a total transparency in the implementation of the Scheme, the Government ordered for the conduct of Social Audit of the Scheme every year in all Village Panchayats of NREGS districts along with the conduct of Grama Sabha meeting on 1st May, 15th August, 2nd October and 26th January. Like wise the conduct of the Social Audit of the Scheme will be conducted along with Grama Sabha meeting in the year 2010-11 also. An exclusive six member Social Audit Committee (consisting of NREGS workers of the Village Panchayat itself) has been constituted in every Village Panchayat for the purpose of conducting

the Social Audit. The members of the Social Audit Committee are being trained through master trainers (Community Resource Persons and Community Professionals) about the conduct a meaningful Social Audit.

16. In order to enable receipt of MGNREGS funds at the State level itself and distribute these alongwith the State share of MGNREGS funds to the districts, the Government have formed a Society for the administration of Tamil Nadu State Employment Guarantee Fund. The Tamil Nadu State Employment Guarantee Fund Rules, 2008 have also been framed vide G.O. (Ms) No. 92 RD & PR (CGS.1) Department, dated 6.6.2008.
17. An exclusive Telephone with a toll free number of "1299" has been installed in all District Headquarters to redress the grievances of the MGNREGS workers.
18. Exclusive telephone and Fax facility has been provided to all 385 BDOs (Village Panchayats) to enable them monitor the NREGS works closely and efficiently.
19. A web-based monitoring software has been developed by the State Government in order to monitor the day-to-day Habitation-wise and Village Panchayat-wise participation of workers under NREGS in all the districts of the State.

As a result of the concerted efforts taken by this Government, a sum of Rs.3,352.58 crores has been utilized generating 4,091 lakh persondays of employment up to 31.03.2010. About 76% of the work force comprises of women and 56% are Scheduled Castes. A notable feature of the Scheme is that it has had a buoyant effect on rural wages.

Tamil Nadu is amongst the leading States in the country in the implementation of National Rural Employment Guarantee Scheme (NREGS) and 3 districts, namely Cuddalore, Dindigul and Sivaganga had been awarded National Awards for excellance under NREGS in February 2009. Likewise, 2 districts- Villupuram and Nagapattinam have won the National Awards for Excellence under NREGS in February, 2010. The Honourable Supreme Court of India itself has commended the implementation of MGNREGS in Tamil Nadu and has exhorted other States in the country to follow the Tamil Nadu model

Total Sanitation Campaign (TSC)

Government of India restructured the Comprehensive Rural Sanitation Programme with effect from 01.04.1999 and launched the Total Sanitation Campaign (TSC). The project envisages a demand – driven approach with increased stress on awareness building and meeting the demand with alternate delivery mechanisms. With effect from 01.04.2006, the sharing pattern between the Centre and the State is as follows:-

a) 80:20 for Information, Education and Communication (IEC) activities, administrative costs and rural sanitary marts

b) 60:28:12 for individual household toilets with effect from 01.08.2008 with 12% contribution from beneficiaries and 60:20:20 for solid and liquid waste management and community sanitary complexes, with 20% contribution from beneficiaries/ Panchayats

c) 70:30 for School and Anganwadi toilets.

The maintenance of Sanitation and hygiene in the Villages are the mandatory duties of Village Panchayats as envisaged under Sec.110 (d) of the Tamil Nadu Panchayats Act, 1994. The disposal of solid waste and sewage water is becoming a major problem for many Village Panchayats especially those situated in the vicinity of the Corporation and bigger Municipalities and individual Village Panchayats may not be a viable unit for contracting out solid waste management and sewage disposal. Hence it is proposed to group several suburban Village Panchayats into clusters so as to form a viable unit for contracting out or allow Village Panchayats to enter into partnership with the neighbouring Corporations or Municipalities in this regard. It is also proposed to launch a State level Multi-Media campaign in order to change the mind-set of the rural public regarding sanitation practices and generate demand for individual household toilets.

Nirmal Gram Puraskar

To give a fillip to the Total Sanitation Campaign, the Government of India launched an incentive Scheme in June, 2003 in the form of an award for total sanitation coverage, maintenance of clean environment and open defecation – free Village Panchayats,

Blocks and Districts called 'Nirmal Gram puraskar'. The Village Panchayats are given a cash incentive ranging from Rs.0.5 lakhs to Rs. 5 lakhs depending upon the population of the Village Panchayats concerned. The year-wise break-up of 'Nirmal Gram Puraskar Awards' won by the Village Panchayats and Block Panchayats is furnished below in Table 13.

Table -13 Year- wise break –up of Nirmal Gram Puraskar Awards won by TamilNadu

Year	No. of Village Panchayats	No.of Block Panchayats
2004 - 05	12	1
2005- 06	119	-
2006- 07	296	-
2007- 08	1,474	5
2008- 09	196	-

Member of Parliament Local Area Development Scheme(MPLADS)

The objective of this Scheme is to fill the gaps existing in the provision of infrastructure through various Central and State schemes thereby enabling wholesome development. A sum of Rs.2 crores is allotted per Member of Parliament (Lok Sabha and Rajya Sabha) per year for taking up developmental works identified by the concerned M.P. In the case of Lok Sabha, the Scheme is implemented in the district falling within the constituency of the M.P. concerned. In the case of Rajya Sabha , the M.P can suggest works in one or more districts within the State from which he is elected. As far as the nominated MPs are concerned, they can suggest works anywhere in India. The District Collector gives administrative sanction for the works. The guidelines contain a 'negative list' of works not permitted under this Scheme and also an illustrative list of works that may be taken up. Under the scheme all maintenance works of any type are prohibited. Desilting of ponds, rivers, tanks, canals, etc, are also treated as maintenance activities and cannot be taken up under MPLADS.

As per Government of India (Ministry of Statistics and Programme Implementation) website, Tamil Nadu stands first at All India level, in cumulative utilization of funds under MPLADS with 97.14% fund utilization since 1993. For 2010-11, an amount of Rs.114.00 crores is likely to be allotted for works under MPLADS.

Pradhan Mantri Gram Sadak Yojana (PMGSY)

The Government of India launched PMGSY on 25th December 2000 to provide all-weather roads, to all rural habitations with population more than 1000, by the year 2003 and to all rural habitations with population between 500 and 1,000 by the year 2007. This is a 100% centrally assisted Scheme. The details of yearwise allocation and no. of works taken up under the Scheme are furnished below in Table 14.

Table-14 Year wise allocation and works taken u under PMGSY.

Phase	Allocation (Rs. in Crores)	No. of Roa	Length (in KM)
Phase I (2000 – 01)	152.91	862	1,442.12
Phase II (2001 – 02)	115.29	446	803.70
Phase III (2003 – 04)	160.88	492	1097.50
Phase IV (2004 – 05)	112.65	396	787.97
Phase V (2005 – 06)	170.84	365	799.69
Phase VI/ Bharat Nirman Phase - I (2008 – 09)	465.64	818	2,082.54
Phase VII/ Bharat Nirman Phase - II (2008 – 09)	858.99	1,591	3,031.09
Total	**2,037.20**	**4,970**	**10,044.61**

In the year 2008-09, PMGSY road works at an outlay of Rs.1, 324.63 crores have been sanctioned under Bharat Nirman (Phase

I & II) to Tamil Nadu which is a record achievement for the

State which had been allocated PMGSY road works only to the tune of Rs.142 crores per year in the previous phases.

Funding under the next phase (PMGSY Phase VIII) is going to be sought for upgradation of roads under PMGSY during 2010-11 and for this, the Detailed Project Reports (DPRs) are under advanced stage of preparation.

National Project on Biogas Development

This is a 100% Centrally sponsored Scheme envisaging a subsidy of Rs.8000/- for installation of Biogas plants for all categories and Rs.10,000/- in the hilly areas for the installation of Biogas. The tentative allocation for 2010 – 11 under this Scheme is Rs. 139 lakhs.

Backward Region Grants Fund (BRGF)

The erstwhile Rashtriya Sam Vikas Yojana (RSVY) has been transferred from Union Planning Commission to Ministry of Pancfhayat Raj at Government of India level with effect from 2006-07. The Ministry of Panchayat Raj have modified the Scheme of RSVY into a Backward Regions Grant Fund (BRGF). The main focus of the Scheme is to strengthen and provide professional support to the Local Bodies to improve their performance and delivery of critical functions assigned to them besides redressing regional imbalances in development. This Scheme is being implemented in six districts in Taminadu viz., Cuddalore, Vilupuram, Tiruvannamalai, Nagapattinam, Dindigul and Sivagangai.

The BRGF Scheme consists of two funding windows viz., the 'Capacity Building Fund' and 'Development Grant'. The Government, as per G.O.Ms.No.161, RD & PR (CGS-1) Department, dated 13.10.2006 have released a sum of Rs.16.31 crores to SIRD, Maraimalai Nagar as Central assistance for Capacity Building of Local Bodies under BRGF.

The Government of India have sanctioned Development Grants under BRGF to the six BRGF districts for the year 2007-08 and 2009-10 as detailed in Table 15.

Table-15: Funds Sanctioned under BRGF for 2007-08 and 2009-10

Sl.No.	**Name of the District**	**2007-08 Amount (Rs.in crores)**	**2009-10 Amount (Rs.in Crores)**
1.	Cuddalore	17.76	17.76
2.	Vilupuram	21.73	21.73
3.	Tiruvannamalai	19.27	19.27
4.	Dindigul	18.70	18.70
5.	Nagapattinam	15.06	15.06
6.	Sivagangai	15.52	15.52
	Total	**108.04**	**108.04**

STATE SCHEMES

Kalaignar Veettu Vasathi Thittam

In Tamil Nadu about 33% of the rural houses are 'huts', as per the 2001 Census. In order to convert all these huts into permanent concrete houses, 'Kalaignar Veettu Vasathi Thittam', which is so far the biggest State-funded Scheme, was announced by Government of Tamil Nadu during the Governor's Address in Tamil Nadu Legislative Assembly on 6.1.2010.

The Scheme aims at replacing all the huts in Tamil Nadu with permanent houses over a 6-year period between 2010-11 and 2015-16. Tamil Nadu will, thus, earn the distinction of being the first 'hut free State' of the country by 2016. The following are the salient features of Kalaignar Veettu Vasathi Thittam (KVVT):

1. All huts with thatched roof will be taken up for conversion of permanent houses under KVVT, irrespective of the type of wall (mud, unburnt bricks, burnt bricks, etc.,) of the huts.
2. Only huts that have been built prior to 1.1.2010 will be taken up under this Scheme. Huts built after 1.1.2010, if any will be considered only at the end of the 6-year period (i.e. after 2016 subject to eligibility).

3. Like IAY houses, the Kalaignar Veettu Vasathi Thittam houses will be built with RCC roofing and separate toilet. The minimum stipulated area of the house will be 200 sq.ft. and the unit cost of each houses will be Rs.60,000 per house. Low cost technology and fast track system will also be permitted under the Scheme.
4. Like IAY, the houses will be constructed by the beneficiaries themselves (or by their Agents) and there will be no tendering.
5. The enumeration of all the huts in the State will be taken in 2 phases
   (i) In Phase I, a quick assessment of the number of huts to be replaced by permanent houses under KVVT will be made;
   (ii) In Phase II, the photographs of all the enumerated huts (with the beneficiaries standing in front of their respective huts) will be taken and copies of pattas and other relevant documents will be collected.

The enumeration will be done through a 3-member team comprising the Village Administrative Officer, Makkal Nala Paniyalar and Village Panchayat Assistant. It will be super-checked by officers of both RD & Revenue Departments.

6. The Scheme will be implemented simultaneously in all the 12,618 Village Panchayats across the State.
7. The permanent houses will be allocated among various communities (ST, SC, MBC, BC and OC) in proportion to the total number of huts of the beneficiaries of each community in the Village Panchayat as per the enumeration survey.
8. Within the communities, the beneficiaries will be selected door number-wise, which is a simple, fair and transparent method which will be intelligible to all beneficiaries.
9. The huts of the following types will not be eligible for conversion into a permanent KVVT houses:
   - Huts occupied by tenants.
   - Huts used for commercial purposes or for animals.

- Huts that have part thatched roof and part RCC/Tiled/AC sheet/Tin/GI sheet roof.
- Huts whose occupants also own a Pucca house elsewhere.
- Huts, if any, owned by retired or serving Government servants (full-time, part-time, contract appointment, daily wage appointment) including employees of Local Bodies, PSUs, Government Aided Institutions, Boards and other quasi-Government undertakings or their spouses
- Huts, if any, owned by MPs, MLAs and Local Body functionaries or their spouses.

Anaithu Grama Anna Marumalarchi Thittam (AGAMT)

This Government launched the landmark scheme called the 'Anaithu Grama Anna Marumalarchi Thittam' vide its G.O.Ms.No.115, Rural Development and Panchayat Raj (SGS-2) Department dated 11.09.2006 and G.O.Ms.No.189, Rural Development and Panchayat Raj (SGS-2) Department, dated 27.12.2006 which aims at substantial injection of resources into the Village Panchayats in the State in five years.

The Scheme was formally inaugurated by the Hon'ble Chief Minister on 21.01.2007 at Tirumathalampakkam Village of Vellore District.

Since many Village Panchayats have very low income and are finding it difficult to provide the statutory services or improve infrastructure, this Scheme accords priority to the poorest Village Panchayats in terms of *per capita* income.

One-fifth of the Village Panchayats in each Block are taken up in each year in the ascending order of per capita income so as to cover all the Village Panchayats in the State over a period of five years. The villages covered under the old Anna Marumalarchi Thittam, which was in vogue during 1997-2001, will be taken up during 2010-11.

Under the Scheme, the Government had allocated a sum of Rs.2041.01 crores for the last 4 years as detailed below in Table 16.

Table-16: Year wise allocation for AGAMT

S.No.	Year	No.ofVillagePanchayats	Allocation (in crores)
1.	2006-07	2,540	513.08
2.	2007-08	2,534	511.87
3.	2008-09	2,520	509.04
4.	2009-10	2,510	507.02
	Total	10,104	2,041.01

For 2010-11, this Scheme will be taken up in 2,514 villages at an outlay of Rs.507.82 crores.

The Centrally sponsored schemes usually have tight guidelines and do not offer the flexibility to take up works that may be locally desirable nor do they provide funds enabling Village Panchayats to carry out their statutory functions under the Tamil Nadu Panchayats Act, 1994. The Anaithu Grama Anna Marumalarchi Thittam endeavours to plug both these gaps in the Centrally sponsored schemes by providing untied funds of Rs.5 lakhs

(out of Rs.20 lakhs allocation per Village Panchayat), with the remaining funds to be spent on stipulated items. Further, funds from other schemes of Rural Development and Panchayat Raj department and other departments such as Highways, public works, Social welfare, Health, Education, Agricultural Engineering and TWAD among others will also be dovetailed as far as possible into the Village Panchayats taken up under Anaithu Grama Anna Marumalarchi Thittam. The Government's intention is to ensure the convergence of atleast Rs.1 crore of funds under various Governmental schemes to each AGAMT Village Panchayat.

The following are some of the key guidelines of the Scheme:

1) Selection of works to be taken up under AGAMT will be done by a committee consisting of the Block Development Officer (Village Panchayats), Assistant Engineer (RD) / Block Engineer, the Panchayat President concerned and the Village Administrative Officer.
2) The works should be got approved by the Grama Sabha.
3) Cement Concrete roads can be taken up for an amount not exceeding Rs.3 lakhs in tied component per Village.

4) At least one Pond / Oorani is to be constructed at a cost of Rs.3 - 5 lakhs in each AGAMT village and it should have Bathing ghat, Baby pond, Retaining wall, etc. In case of a Pond or Oorani being unavailable in the village, Temple Tank or Minor Irrigation tank can be taken up for desilting in the village. Desilting the pond for a minimum depth of 2 metre from the existing level and the baby pond for further depth of 1 metre has been stipulated.
5) Fish ponds are to be taken up wherever feasible and preference given to the Self Help Groups for getting fishery rights.
6) Burial ground in each AGAMT village will be improved with approach road, Compound wall, Cremation shed, Water facility and Lighting.
7) A School Sports Centre at an outlay of upto Rs.1.5 lakhs or Community Sports Centre at an outlay of upto Rs.1 lakh is to be put up in each AGAMT village.
8) A library will be opened in each AGAMT village. A new building may be constructed or an existing building may be modified suitably and books worth at least Rs.50,000 are to be bought and furniture worth Rs.50,000 procured for the library. An Honorary Librarian is to be appointed for each AGAMT Library
9) Village shandies are to be improved wherever available.
10) An amount of 1% of the total allocation is to be used for IEC activities.

BDO (Village Panchayats) is designated as the tender inviting authority for all works other than the purchases of sports materials, library books and library furniture. The Government have, vide G.O. (Ms).No.186, RD & PR (SGS-2) Department, dated 16.11.2007 stipulated that the works for which tenders are not received for three consecutive calls or where the quoted rates are exorbitant or where the works are left mid-way by the contractor, can be entrusted to the Village Panchayat for execution departmentally in case the value of the work is below Rs.5 lakh and through tendering in case the value of the work is above Rs.5 lakh each.

The Village Panchayats have been permitted to incur an expenditure of upto Rs.10,000/- per year for replacement of sports consumables in the AGAMT Sports Centers. To encourage the rural youth who are talented in sports and to make proper usage of the Sports Centres established under AGAMT on a regular basis, the Government have ordered vide G.O.Ms.No.73 RD & PR (SGS-I) Department dated 28.7.09 and G.O.(Ms) No.131, RD & PR (SGS-1) Department, dated 27.11.20009, for the conduct of Rural Sports Competitions twice a year on the occasion of Perarignar Anna's birthday on September 15th and during Pongal holidays. Approximately 70,000 teams participated in the team events of Volley ball and Tennikoit and 9.97 lakh individuals participated in the individual events of 100 m sprint, Long jump, High jump, Chess and Carrom on September 15th, 2009. Likewise approximately 74,000 teams participated in the team events of Volley ball and Tennikoit and 11.75 lakh individuals participated in the individual events of 100 m sprint, Long jump,

High jump, Chess and Carrom in the Rural Sports Competitions held during Pongal holidays of 2010.

In order to popularise the usage of libraries and to bring out the literary talent of the children and the youth living in rural areas, the Government issued guidelines vide G.O.Ms.No.132 RD & PR (SGS-1) Dept., dt.1.12.2009 for the conduct of Rural Library Competitions among three categories of students such as Primary & Middle Schools, High Schools & Higher Secondary Schools and others, including school dropouts. Approximately 6.08 lakhs individuals participated in the Rural Library Competitions held during the second fortnight of December, 2009.

Member of Legislative Assembly Constituency Development Scheme (MLACDS)

Member of LegislativeAssembly Constituency Development Scheme (MLACDS) is fully funded by the State Government. The main objective of the Scheme is to take up works to bridge the critical infrastructural gaps in the Assembly constituencies. Under this Scheme, each MLA proposes the works that should be executed in his constituency. The District Collector gives administrative sanction for the works. The allocation per Constituency was increased from Rs.1.50 crores to Rs.1.70 crores vide G.O.Ms.No.90 RD&PR(SGS-1) Department, dated 11.8.09. 50% of the allocation

(Rs.85 lakhs) is earmarked for priority works specified by Government. Out of the remaining 50%, MLAs can choose works of their choice not falling within the negative list prescribed in the MLACDS guidelines.

MLACDS-Works to be taken up under Tied Component:

Since a large number of Anganwadi Buildings, Noon Meal Centres, Noon Meal Kitchen Sheds, especially in urban areas and to a lesser extent in rural areas are functioning in dilapidated buildings, a phased program of construction of new buildings for such cases is to be taken up. Hence in 2009-10, each MLA was requested to allocate Rs.20 lakhs for construction of Anganwadi Buildings, Noon Meal Centres and Noon Meal Kitchen Sheds.

From the remaining amount of Rs.65 lakhs of Tied Component, the MLA can choose one or more of the following works for any amount according to his choice, subject to the overall ceiling of Rs.65 lakhs.

a) In rural areas:

1. Upgradation of gravel/WBM Roads to B.T. standard.
2. Renewal of badly worn out B.T.roads (laying of B.T. layer only with filling up of potholes if necessary).
3. Laying of Cement Concrete Roads.
4. Provision of buildings and/or compound walls for Government and Local body Hospitals, Primary Health Centres, Government Veterinary Hospitals and also for Government Schools, Panchayat Union Schools, Adi Dravida Schools, Kallar reclamation Schools, Government Colleges and Government hostels.
5. Provision of infrastructural facilities to Government Special Schools for the disabled and Government Orphanages.
6. Provision of additional Burial Grounds/Cremation Grounds as per AGAMT pattern in uncovered habitations in AGAMT Village Panchayats of 2006-07, 2007-08, 2008-09 and 2009-10.
7. Construction of new houses and upgradation of kutcha houses as per IAY norms.

8. Construction of bridges.

b) In urban areas:

1. 1-5: Same as in Sl.No.1-5 for rural areas above.
2. Provision of infrastructure facilities to Burial Grounds/ Cremation Grounds.
3. Provision of Concrete Pavements, with storm water drains if so required.
4. Formation of new public parks.
5. Construction of public Toilets.
6. Construction of bridges.
7. Purchase of Jetrodding and Hydraulically perated desilting machines.

MLACDS-Works to be taken up under Untied Component

Certain category of negative works have been prescribed under MLACDS. Any work not falling within the negative list/prohibited works can be taken up under the untied component of MLACDS. Works falling under the tied component also can be taken up under the untied component.

As in the case of Member of Parliament Local Area Development Scheme (MPLADS), works involving desilting of ponds, rivers, ooranies and channels have been banned under MLACDS. Also the works mentioned in the negative list (prohibited works) cannot be taken up under the MLACDS unless specifically included in the exceptions of the guidelines of MLACDS.

An allocation of 19% of the total allocation under MLACDS should be made for areas predominantly inhabited by SC/ST people or benefiting people living in Slums in Urban areas.

The total allocation for MLACDS for 2010-11 is likely to be Rs.399.50 crores.

Panchayat Union School Renovation Programme.

The programme of Panchayat Union School Renovation introduced in 2007-08 envisages repair and improvement of all Panchayat Union Elementary Schools and Middle Schools in the State in a phased manner. There are around 22,000 Panchayat Union Primary Schools and 4,500 Panchayat Union Middle Schools which are being maintained by Block Panchayats. Due to lack of proper maintenance, most of these School buildings have become dilapidated. Hence, the repair and renovation of such long neglected School buildings in AGAMT Village Panchayats were taken up in this Scheme. The repair works include replacement of old and damaged tiled or asbestos roofs with new tiled roofs; replacement of damaged weathering course in RCC-roofed buildings with new ones; attending to cracks in roofs, walls and flooring; replacement of broken doors and windows; and whitewashing and colour-washing of the buildings giving a complete facelift to the Panchayat Union School buildings.

The details are given below in Table 17

Table -17: Year wise allocation for Panchayat Union School Renovation Programme

Sl.No	Year	No.of school Buildings in AGAMT Panchayats	Allocation (in crores)
1	2006-07 & 2007-08	9,547	104.25
2	2008-09	4,430	69.30
3	2009-10	4,124	67.56

During the year 2008-09, 495 Panchayat Union Elementary and Middle Schools located in Town Panchayats and Third Grade Municipalities have been taken up for renovation at an estimated cost of Rs.14.31 crores and all works have been completed. During 2009-10, 450 Panchayat Union and Middle Schools located in Town Panchayats and Third Grade Municipalities have been taken at an estimated cost of Rs.10.60 crores.

During the year 2010-11, around 5,000 Panchayat Union Elementary and Middle School buildings in 2010-11 AGAMT Village Panchayats and in Town Panchayats and Third Grade Municipalities will be taken up for repairs and improvements at an outlay of approximately Rs. 85 crores.

Namakku Naame Thittam

Namakku Naame Thittam is being implemented as a State Sponsored Scheme with a minimum of one-third amount as public contribution and two-third contribution from Government as grants in both Rural and Urban areas. Under this Scheme, the public themselves can select works as they need and execute it as per the provisions in the guidelines of the Scheme. Construction of Government and Local Body School Buildings (including Compound Wall) Libraries, Hospitals, Primary Health Centres, Veterinary Dispensaries, Noon Meal Centres, Hostels, Creation of Water Supply Sources, Public Distribution Shop Buildings, Bridges and Culverts, Upgradation of Roads and Streets, CC Pavements, Parks, Play Grounds, Traffic Islands, Fountains, Street Lights, Purchase of Furniture, Computers and Equipments for Government and Local Body Schools and Libraries and construction of class rooms, Laboratories and toilets in Government aided schools and colleges can be undertaken under Namakku Naame Thittam. A sum of Rs.50.00 crores was allotted by Government of Tamil Nadu for the year 2009-10. Likewise, a sum of Rs.50.00 crores will be allotted by Government of Tamil Nadu for the implementation of this Scheme in 2010-11.

Periyar Ninaivu Samathuvapuram

To Promote social justice and spread Thanthai Periyar's message of social equality, Government of Tamil Nadu, established Samathuvapurams since 1997-98 in the districts where all communities live with unity and brotherhood. Accordingly, 145 Samathuvapurams were established in the State. In the Governor's Address, 2008 made in the Assembly on 23.1.2008, among others, it was announced that "considering the fact that an even better way of spreading Thanthai Periyar's message of social equality would be to establish another 95 Samathuvapurams in his name".

Government have, accordingly, decided to revive the Scheme and construct another 95 Samathuvapurams between 2008-09 and 2010-11. In the first phase in 2008-09 a sum of Rs. 75 crores was allotted and 29 Samathuvapurams were established. In the Second phase, a sum of Rs. 75 Crores was allotted for 2009-10 vide G.O.Ms. No. 59, Rural Development and Panchayat Raj, (SGS-1) Department, dated 14.7.2009 and 30 Samathuvapurams are being established at the rate of one Samathuvapuram in each district except Nilgiris District. In each Samathuvapuram, 100 houses are being constructed at an approximate cost of Rs.1.94 lakhs per house. Roads, street lights, drinking water supply and Public Distribution shop (if so required) are also being provided in each Samathuvapuram to make it a self-sufficient community. A statue of Thanthai Periyar is installed in each Samathuvapuram. For 2010-11, 36 Samathuvapurams will be taken up at an approximate cost of Rs. 75 crores in the State.

Rural Infrastructure Scheme

Since the National Rural Employment Guarantee Scheme has been extended to all the districts from 1.4.2008 onwards, the Central Government has discontinued the Sampoorna Grameen Rozgar Yojana (SGRY). Consequent to this, there was no proper scheme to create basic infrastructure facilities like Cement Concrete Roads and Buildings. Further, it had become essential to make the assets created under National Rural Employment Guarantee Scheme durable by stabilizing them. Taking into consideration the representations received in this regard, a new Scheme called 'Rural Infrastructure Scheme' was introduced during 2008-09 with an allocation of Rs.350 crores for the year 2008-09. The above Scheme was continued for the year 2009-10 with an allocation of Rs.380 crores. In 2009-10, funds to the tune of Rs.200 crores were earmarked for Village Panchayats, Rs.120 crores for Panchayat Unions and Rs.60 crores for District Panchayats. Maintenance of Minor Irrigation Tanks have also been taken during 2009-10 as a priority basis component for Panchayat Unions and District Panchayats under this Scheme. The Rural Infrastructure Scheme will be implemented in 2010-11 also and an amount of Rs.380 crores will be provided for this purpose.

NABARD's Rural Infrastructure Development Fund (RIDF)

RIDF XIV– 2008 -2009

For the year 2008-2009, an amount of Rs.414.58 crores have been sanctioned by NABARD based on the proposal of the State

Government to upgrade the Panchayat and Panchayat Union roads to the length of 2691.73 Kms connecting and passing through AGAMT 2007 – 2008 Village Panchayats. So far, 2,320.68 km of road works have been completed at an expenditure of Rs.296.36 crores and all other roads are in advanced stage of completion.

RIDF XV – 2009 -2010

A proposal for strengthening of Panchayat and Panchayat Union roads for a length of 2,822 km at an estimated cost of Rs.400.73 crores has been forwarded to NABARD by the Government for sanction. In first Phase, NABARD has sanctioned 1495.57 km of road works at an estimate cost of Rs. 200.09 crores, and these road works are under execution in all the districts.

Twelfth Finance Commission Road Works – 2009-2010 and 2010-11

For the year 2009 – 2010, 1727.40 km of road works at an estimated cost of Rs.103.60 Crores were taken up under Twelfth Finance Commission funds. Priority is given to upgrade Panchayat and Panchayat Union roads which are connecting and passing through AGAMT 2009-10 Village Panchayats. So far 1194.37 Km of road works have been completed with an expenditure of Rs.62.25 crores.

During 2010-11, a further allocation of Rs.103.60 crores will be made for the maintenance of Panchayat and Panchayat Union roads under this component.

Programme for Comprehensive Development of Dharmapuri and Krishnagiri Districts.

To curb the rise of Naxalite elements in the backward districts of Dharmapuri and Krishnagiri, a Socio-economic Development Programme was launched in the year 2003-04. For 2009-10 a provision of Rs.7.50 crores has been made. In the year 2009-10, construction of new houses, Group House repairs, tool kits and implements for youth, individual assistance to physically handicapped/widow and destitutes have been taken up. For 2010-11 also, a provision of Rs.7.50 crores will be made for this Programme.

PART - II SCHEMES

The Government have, vide G.O. Ms.No. 81 RD & PR(SGS - IV) Department dated 3.8.2009, sanctioned Renovation of the Conference Hall, Meeting Hall and the provision of invertors in the Directorate of Rural Development and Panchayat Raj, Panagal Building a total cost of Rs. 50 lakhs. For the year 2010 - 11, it is proposed to take up Modernisation of 5th Floor in the Commissionarate of Rural Development and Panchayat Raj, Panagal Building at a cost of Rs. 30 lakhs.

Construction of Office Buildings

During 2010-11, it is proposed to take up construction of Office Buildings to the Development Wing of Collectorate of Coimbatore District and Project Director, District Rural Development Agency, Nilgiris District at a total cost of Rs. 125 lakhs.

Construction of Residential Quarters

It is proposed to construct Residential Quarters for the Project Director, District Rural Development Agency, Pudukottai District at a cost of Rs. 28.50 lakhs.

Provision of Vehicles for Tamil Nadu State Election Commission

The Government have, vide G.O. Ms.No. 83 RD & PR(SGS - IV) Department dated 3. 8.2009, sanctioned Computers at a cost of Rs.8 lakhs for and Fax Machines at a cost of Rs.0.30 lakhs to Tamil Nadu State Election Commission. For the year 2010 -11, it is proposed to provide 2 Vehicles to Tamil Nadu State Election Commission at a cost of Rs. 10 lakhs. During 2010-11, it is proposed to provide Desktop computers and accessories, Laser Printers, Scanners and Fax Machines to the officers of Rural Development and Panchayat Raj Department, Secretariat at a total cost of Rs. 6.50 lakhs.

TAMIL NADU CORPORATION FOR DEVELOPMENT OF WOMEN

The Government of Tamil Nadu is committed to promoting

inclusive growth by ensuring equal rights, equal opportunity and progress for all women with a special focus on the poor and marginalised sections of the society. The Tamil Nadu Corporation for Development of women (TNCDW) was established in 1983 with these objectives in mind. The Corporation implements Mahalir Thittam, IFAD assisted Post Tsunami Sustainable Livelihoods Programme and also Swarnajayanti Gram Swarozgar Yojana (SGSY), a major anti-poverty programme meant for self employment of rural poor.

The Self Help Group movement which was started in a small way in Dharmapuri District in the year 1989 has now grown into a mammoth movement covering all districts of the State targeting poor families and marginalised sections of the society. TNCDW has been spearheading the SHG movement in the State.

Restructuring and strengthening of TNCDW

In order to bring about greater synergy and better coordination in implementing various schemes for Self Help Groups, Tamil Nadu Corporation for Development of Women was brought under the control of Rural Development and Panchayat Raj Department from July 2006.

Further the Board of TNCDW was broad based and reconstituted vide G.O.Ms.No:148,Rural

Development and Panchayat Raj(CGS-II) Department, dated 12.10.2006 to include representatives from Industry, NGO sector, Banks and Specialists who can positively guide the Corporation with their valuable inputs.

In order to strengthen the monitoring arrangements at Block level, Government have issued orders vide G.O.Ms.No:106 Rural Development and Panchayat Raj (CGS-I) Department, dated 20.6.2007 to involve Block Development Officer (VP) and other Block staff for monitoring and supervising Mahalir Thittam Programme.

Additionally 30 Assistant Project Officer posts were sanctioned vide G.O.Ms.No:177, Rural Development and Panchayat Raj (CGS-II) Department, dated.5.12.2006 supplementing the existing strength of the Project Implementation Units.

Recruitment of Assistant Project Officers from open market was done to further strengthen the Project Implementation Units at the districts for effective implementation of the schemes as per G.O.Ms.No:30, Rural Development and Panchayat Raj (CGS-II) Department, dated 8.3.2007. In addition, 3 posts of Additional Director have been created in the head office to facilitate better monitoring vide G.O.Ms.No:108, Rural Development and Panchayat Raj (CGS-I) Department, dated 21.6.2007.

The Government vide G.O.Ms.No:14, Rural Development and Panchayat Raj (CGS-III) Department, dated 4.02.2010 have brought Tamil Nadu Welfare Society for Self Help Groups, the specialized agency to undertake initiatives to market SHG products, under the control of TNCDW.

Mahalir Thittam

The programme is implemented in partnership with NGOs and community- based organizations such as PLFs which are affiliated to TNCDW after due process. So far 4,41,311 SHGs have been formed as of March 2010 with 69.91 lakh women members and with total savings of Rs. 2,568 crores. Out of this 1,25,493 new SHGs with 18.92 lakh women members have been formed over the last four years.

The members and office bearers of the SHGs promoted by Mahalir Thittam are provided systematic training to bring about qualitative changes in their attitude and to promote cohesion and effective functioning of the group.

All the SHG members are imparted training in 4 modules for 4 days to orient them to the SHG concept. The office bearers of the SHGs (Animator and Representative) are given training in 3 modules for 6 days to enhance leadership quality, team building and book keeping.

Group Formation

In order to enable all women living below poverty line to join and benefit from the Self Help Group movement, it has been estimated that one lakh new SHGs have to be formed in the State. To achieve this, 50,000 SHGs were formed in 2009-10 and another 50,000 new SHGs will be formed during 2010 -11.

Though the project was very successful with respect to the number of SHGs formed in the State, the coverage was not universal and inclusive. For example, at the beginning of 2007-08, there were still 3,644 Village Panchayats in the State where the coverage of women in the SHG movement was less than 25% and in 5,014 Village Panchayats the coverage was between 25% to 50%. Similarly the coverage of MGNREGS women workers in SHG movement was also less than 50%. Hence from 2008-09, new SHG formation in rural areas has been taken up with a special focus on the above categories and during the last two years 25,304 SHGs have been formed with MGNREGS women workers and 19,696 SHGs have been formed in Village Panchayats with inadequate coverage.

Similarly in urban areas the number of SHGs formed from among the poorest of the poor such as women residing in slums was less than 1,000 groups at the beginning of 2006-07. A special thrust has been given in the last four years to the formation of new women SHGs in urban slums. Over 38,000 SHGs have been formed in urban slums as on 31.3.2010.

During 2010-11 also, new SHG formation will be undertaken with a special focus on MGNREGS women workers, urban slum dwellers and in Village Panchayats where SHG coverage is still inadequate. Table 18 gives the details of SHGs as on 31.03.2010.

Table -18 Details of SHGs

No. of SHGs	4,41,311
No. of SHG Members	69.91 lakhs
No. of Rural SHGs	3,02,092
No. of Members in Rural SHGs	48,33,472
No. of Urban SHGs	1,39,219
No. of Members in Urban SHGs	21,57,894
Total Savings	Rs.2,568 crores
No. of SHGs credit linked	4,02,046
Total credit	Rs.8,129.61 crores

Non-Governmental Organisations

Mahalir Thittam is implemented in partnership with NGOs who undertake formation of SHGs, organise training support and monitor their activities. For rendering these services, NGOs are paid formation cost, monitoring cost and also incentive for enabling SHGs to access bank credit.

As on 31.03.2010, 469 NGOs have been affiliated with TNCDW as per the revised affiliation norms listed in G.O.Ms 155 Rural Development and Panchayat Raj (CGS-1) Department, dt.05.09.2007. The new agreement with these NGOs contains many salient features including performance based incentive and greater emphasis on quality and also provides an enabling environment for the growth of community – based organisations like Panchayat Level Federations. These affiliated NGOs are being subjected to performance evaluation annually.

Community Resource Persons

In order to bring sustainability to the SHG movement as well as make it more community based, 5,000 Community Resource Persons (CRPs) have been developed from among SHG members. CRPs undertake capacity building training of the SHGs and provide continuous handholding support to the community-based organisations. They are also used as effective tools of IEC for other Government schemes and are involved in training Social Audit Committee members under MGNREGS programme.

Revolving Fund to SHGs

SHGs become eligible for Revolving Fund (RF) after passing the first credit rating which is undertaken 6 months after the date of formation of the SHGs. It is aimed at augmenting the group corpus and makes them credit worthy to access Bank loan.

Prior to 2006-07, there was no scheme to provide RF subsidy to urban SHGs. The Government announced a new scheme to provide RF subsidy to urban SHGs in 2006-07. During the last 4 years Rs. 87.93 crores have been provided as RF subsidy to 87,939 urban SHGs in the State. Similarly during the last four years 1,93,944 rural SHGs have been provided RF subsidy of Rs. 10,000/- each with the total amount of Rs 193.94 crores. As such during the four years from 2006-07 to 2009-10, RF subsidy of Rs. 281.88 crores along with the Bank credit of Rs. 1,164.23 crores have been disbursed to a total of 2,81,883 SHGs. With the enhanced allocation of RF subsidy by the

Government, the waiting time of the SHGs to receive RF after the credit rating which used to vary from 6 months to 4 years has been reduced to almost zero. During 2010-11, another 65,000 SHGs will be provided RF subsidy. Details of RF sanctioned to the SHGs since 2006-2007 is given in Table- 19.

Table -19 Year- wise Details of RF Disbursal (Rs.in Crores)

Year	No. of SHGs			Financial Assistance		
	Rural	Urban	Total	Subsidy	Credit	Total
2006-07	19,024	5,000	24,024	24.02	36.04	60.06
2007-08	18,563	25,000	43,563	43.56	65.34	108.91
2008-09	1,06,047	43,953	1,50,000	150.00	739.69	889.69
2009-10	50,310	13,986	64,296	64.30	323.16	387.46
Total	**1,93,944**	**87,939**	**2,81,883**	**281.88**	**1,164.23**	**1,446.12**

Credit Linkage

Bank credit is one of the most critical inputs for empowering SHGs and to reduce rural indebtedness. Banks normally extended cash credit of Rs.10,000 to Rs.30,000 to SHGs along with RF subsidy of Rs.10,000 provided by Government. The quantum of credit extended by banks to SHGs was not adequate to meet the credit requirements of all the SHG members.

Therefore the Government have taken special efforts to increase the quantum of credit to SHGs and ensure credit is made available to SHGs in multiple doses. Due to the efforts taken by Government, Banks in the State have started providing minimum of Rs.50,000 as first linkage and minimum of Rs.1 lakh and Rs.1.50 lakhs as second and third linkages respectively.

In order to ensure that the SHGs get timely and adequate financial assistance the Government have taken initiatives to provide repeat loans in the form of second and subsequent doses of credit linkage to the SHGs. The details of credit availed by SHGs are given in Table 20.

Table- 20 Details of Credit Linkage

Sl. No.	Year	Achievement (Rs.in crores)
1	Upto 2001	120.30
2	2001 - 02	97.91
3	2002 - 03	184.65
4	2003 - 04	271.32
5	2004 - 05	490.62
6	2005 - 06	600.44
7	2006 - 07	593.45
8	2007 - 08	804.70
9	2008 - 09	2,174.57
10	2009 -10	2,791.65
	Total	8,129.61

From the inception of Mahalir Thittam, SHGs have been assisted with the cumulative credit linkage of Rs.1,765.24 crores only upto March 2006. But during the last four years alone, credit linkage to SHGs has touched Rs.6,364.37 crores due to the positive interventions made by the Government and the whole hearted co-operation received from the Banks in the State. During 2010-11, the focus of Mahalir Thittam would be on increasing credit linkages to SHGs, particularly repeat loans and a credit target of Rs.3,000 crores has been fixed for the year 2010-11.

To supplement the existing bank credit to SHGs, it is envisaged that PLFs will develop into community level financial institutions catering to the credit requirements of SHGs obviating the influence of moneylenders who are charging exploitative rate of interest. During 2008-09, 102 PLFs under Mahalir Thittam have been sanctioned bulk loan of Rs.27.52 crores by various banks. TNCDW will take necessary steps to further strengthen the financial intermediary role of the PLFs during 2010-11 also.

Panchayat Level Federation

Government of Tamil Nadu have formed about 4.41 lakhs SHGs under Mahalir Thittam implemented through TNCDW over a period of 20 years. The success achieved in the project has prompted the Government to further strengthen the movement and make it sustainable by forming federations of SHGs at Village Panchayat, Block and District level. PLFs have been formed in all the 12,618 Village Panchayats in the State.

The PLF provides a common platform for the SHGs to share their experiences and voice their problems. The PLF can help achieve what individual SHGs cannot, by pooling in their talents and resources and exploiting economies of scale both in production and marketing. PLF can also guide and monitor the functioning of SHGs in a Village Panchayat and also form and train new SHGs. Strengthening of PLFs is the key for achieving sustainability of the SHG movement in the long run.

- Since 2006-07, the Government have taken various initiatives such as providing seed money, instituting Manimegalai Awards to best PLFs and capacity building of office bearers of PLFs. The Government ordered restructuring of PLFs with the objective of making them more inclusive, transparent and participatory and also to improve their governance and sustainability vide G.O.Ms.No:125 Rural Development and Panchayat Raj (CGS-3) Department, dated 21.7.2008.
- In order to accord legal status to the PLFs and facilitate them to access Bank Credit the Government have ordered to register all PLFs under Tamil Nadu Societies Registration Act, 1975. The Government have also vide G.O.Ms.No:111 Commercial Taxes and Registration (M1) Department, dated 17.11.2008 exempted the PLFs from the purview of Section 25 and 42 of Tamil Nadu Societies Registration Act, 1975. This exemption has provided an institutional framework for PLFs to take up income generation activities and benefit from them.
- A detailed action Plan has been drawn up to restructure all the PLFs in the State in three years in a qualitative manner. So far 1,407 PLFs have been restructured under Mahalir Thittam in the State. During 2010-11 a total of 3,780 PLFs would be restructured and further strengthened by providing capacity building to the office bearers and members of both PLF and HLF on Governance and Finance

Management modules. Also, TNCDW will undertake further capacity building of the PLF members and office bearers, on areas like Social Audit, Identification of Business Opportunities etc.

- On completion of six months from restructuring the PLFs are graded based on indicators covering participation, inclusion, governance, transparency, credit discipline and community development initiatives.

Incentive to Restructured PLFs

To encourage the well functioning restructured PLFs, the Government have announced sanction of Rs. one lakh incentive for each successfully graded PLF and allocated Rs.10 crores during 2009-10 for this purpose. Accordingly 1,000 successfully graded PLFs have been sanctioned an incentive of Rs. one lakh each. During 2010-11 another 4,000 eligible PLFs will be sanctioned an incentive of Rs. one lakh each at an allocation of Rs.40 crores.

Bulk Loan to PLFs

Financial intermediation is one of the primary roles of PLF and it is envisaged that PLFs will evolve into community level financial institutions catering to the credit requirement of SHGs. In this regard successfully graded PLFs become eligible for financial linkage and can access bulk loan from the Banks and on lend it to its members.

In few districts bulk loans were sanctioned to the restructured PLFs on pilot basis. The experience of these PLFs showed that PLFs could successfully avail bulk loan from the banks, on lend the amount to member SHGs and repay the loan with interest to the Banks without any default. During 2009-10, 102 PLFs have been provided bulk loan of Rs.27.52 crores by various Banks

Skill Training

The great industrial boom in the recent years has created a heavy demand for skilled manpower in the industrial sector particularly in manufacturing and service sectors offering vast employment opportunities. Skill training is a pre-requisite for exploiting the opportunities offered by the growing economy and to make the unskilled and semi skilled youth employable. In order to equip the rural youth with adequate capacity to compete in the job market and acquire gainful employment, the Government of Tamil Nadu introduced Youth Skill Training in the year 2006-07. This programme has been successfully implemented during the last four years.

During the last four years 56,748 youth have undergone skill training in various trades. The trade-wise details of youth trained under this scheme is given in Table 21.

Table- 21 Trade- wise Number of Candidates Trained

Sl. No.	Name of the Trade	No. Trained
1	IT/ ITES and Computer hardware	10,845
2	Construction Equipments	9,757
3	Driving and Automobile Mechanism	8,786
4	ReadyMade Garments and Textile	6,269
5	Nursing and Hospital Management	5,459
6	Others	15,632
	Total	56,748

The year-wise details of youth trained under this scheme is given in Table 22.

Table- 22 Year- wise Number of Candidates Trained

Sl.No.	Year	No. trained
1	2006-07	5,634
2	2007-08	5,851
3	2008-09	25,123
4	2009-10	20,140
	Total	56,748

During 2010-11 another 25,000 youth will be trained under Youth Skill Training programme at a cost of Rs.20 crores.

Under Enterprise Development Training programme, SHG members who are interested in taking up economic activities particularly in urban areas are trained through reputed institutions. 4,000 women will undergo this training during 2010-11.

Manimegalai Awards

To encourage the well-functioning SHGs and PLFs, the Government announced Manimegalai awards at State and District level in the year 2006-07. Awards are presented to 5 best PLFs and 10 best SHGs at the State Level. One best PLF and 3 best SHGs at the District level are given Manimegalai awards and the best SHG at the Block level is given a certificate. The awards have been presented for the last three years and have been instrumental in motivating the SHGs and PLFs to strive for better performance.

The Government vide G.O.Ms.No:89 Rural Development and Panchayat Raj (CGS-3) Department, dated 05.08.2009 have increased the Manimegalai Award money from Rs.1.00 lakh to Rs 3.00 lakhs for the Best PLFs at State Level and from Rs.50,000 to Rs.1.00 lakh for the best SHGs at State Level as well as for the best PLF at District Level. The Award money for the best SHGs at District Level has been increased from Rs.10,000/-to Rs 25,000/-. The names of the best PLFs which have received State level Manimegalai Award for the year 2008-09 are given in Table 23.

Table- 23: Manimegalai Award for Best PLFs -2008-09

Sl. No.	Name of the District	Name of the PLF
1	Vellore	Yelagiri PLF
2	Namakkal	Ramapuram PLF
3	Thiruvannamalai	Padavedu PLF
4	The Nilgiris	Jaganarai PLF
5	Thiruvarur	Moondramsethi PLF

Award to Bankers

Bankers are playing significant role in the empowerment of women by extending credit to the SHG members for debt swapping, consumption needs and for productive purposes. To honour the Banks as well as individual Bank branches which have shown outstanding performance in extending credit linkage to SHGs in the State, awards at both State and District level have been instituted by the Government. These awards would motivate the outstanding performers and also create a healthy competition among the Bankers.

At State level, 3 best performing Banks and 5 Bank branches are given award. At District level, one Bank and 3 Bank branches get the award. The names of the Banks as well as individual Bank branches which have received State level Bankers Award for the year 2008-09 are given in Table 24.

Table – 24 Bankers Award 2008-09

I. Names of the Best Performing Banks at State level	
First	Indian Bank
Second	State Bank of India
Third	Indian Overseas Bank
II. Names of the Best Performing Exclusive SHG Bank Branches at State level	
First	Indian Bank, Microsate –I, Chennai
Second	Indian Bank, Microsate – II,Chennai
III. Names of the Best Performing other Bank Branches at State level	
First	Indian Bank, Usilampatti , Madurai District
Second	Indian Bank, Pulikarai, Dharmapuri District
Third	Indian Bank, Kaveripattinam, Krishnagiri District
	Indian Bank, Mathur, Krishnagiri District

Issue of Identity Cards to SHGs

The Government have announced that Identity (ID) cards will be issued to all Mahalir Thittam SHGs. The ID cards will help SHGs to gain recognition in society and also have easy access to Government offices and Banks. The ID card will contain group details such as savings, credit rating status, loans as well as member details. ID cards have been issued to Mahalir Thittam SHGs in 11 districts and in remainining 21 districts it will be completed in 2010-11.

Swarnajayanti Gram Yojana (SGSY)

SGSY, a major anti-poverty programme is being implemented since April 1999, with the prime objective of bringing the assisted poor families above the poverty line by ensuring reasonable and sustained level of income over a period of time. This scheme adopts SHG approach and aims to graduate them from micro credit stage to micro-enterprises stage by providing skill development training, bank credit, infrastructure facilities and much needed marketing support to the products produced by them. Government of India and the State Government are sharing the costs in the ratio of 75:25.

In order to ensure that there is greater convergence of activities taken up for the benefit of SHGs in the State, monitoring of the implementation of SGSY scheme has been transferred to TNCDW from 2008-09.

In 2010-11, a sum of Rs. 133 crores is likely to be allocated for the implementation of the scheme with a credit target of Rs. 220 crores. In order to implement the scheme in a more purposeful manner, the following initiatives will be undertaken in 2010-11:

- A sum of Rs. 50 crores will be utilised for disbursing the subsidy component of Revolving Fund to 50,000 eligible SHGs formed in rural areas.
- 6,500 SHGs will be provided with economic assistance with maximum eligible subsidy being 50% of the project cost with a ceiling of Rs.1.25 lakh.

Greater emphasis will be laid to encourage SHGs to opt for major key activities around which suitable clusters can be created at District / Block levels. Necessary infrastructural facilities will be created for these clusters and activity based federations.

Qualitative skill development training through reputed institutions will be imparted to the assisted SHGs.

National Rural Livelihood Mission (NRLM)

Government of India has launched a new scheme called National Rural Livelihood Mission by restructuring the existing SGSY scheme. This scheme is likely to be implemented from 2010-11.

NRLM proposes universal mobilization of BPL households into SHGs, promotion of SHG federations at Village, Block and District level, enhancement of RF subsidy and provision of interest subsidy to SHGs as well as placement linked skill development training for rural youth.

While some of these features are already present in Mahalir Thittam and Vazhndhu Kaattuvom Project, the proposed programme is a major improvement upon the SGSY.

Marketing of SHG Products

Since SHGs do not have adequate capacity, market intelligence and negotiation skills to promote their products, Government have taken various initiatives to support them. To ensure better monitoring and greater co-ordination between different agencies in promotion of SHG products, Tamil Nadu Welfare Society for SHGs has been brought under TNCDW.

A major permanent marketing complex for SHG products is being constructed at a cost of Rs.15.33 crores near Valluvarkottam in Chennai and it is nearing completion. Similarly to create better marketing facilities in rural areas, 90 Village Haats(three per district) are being constructed at the cost of Rs.13.50 crores.

To promote SHG products in urban and semi-urban areas, a calendar of exhibitions has been prepared to conduct exhibitions at State, District and Block levels. During 2009-10, 2 State level, 60 District level and 125 Block level exhibitions were conducted with the total sale of Rs.17.53 crores. During 2010-11, 2 State level, 60 District level and 130 Block level exhibitions will be conducted.

Action Plan for 2010-11 for TNCDW

During 2010-11, TNCDW would focus on the following areas:

- 50,000 new SHGs will be formed among MGNREGS women workers, urban slum dwellers and in areas which have poor coverage of SHGs.
- Revolving Fund along with Bank credit will be provided to 65,000 SHGs and subsidy along with bank credit will be given to about 6,500 SHGs to take up economic activities.
- Credit linkage to the tune of Rs.3,000 crores will be provided to SHGs.
- PLF restructuring would be undertaken in a qualitative manner and 3,780 PLFs will be restructured this year and their office bearers trained.

- 4,000 eligible PLFs will be sanctioned an incentive of Rs. 1 lakh each.
- 25,000 youth will be trained under Youth Skill Training Programme.
- ID cards will be issued to all Mahalir Thittam SHGs in the remaining 21 Districts.
- Efforts will be taken to form activity based clusters and necessary infrastructural facilities, marketing support would be provided to them.

International Fund for Agricultural Development (IFAD) assisted Post-Tsunami Sustainable Livelihoods Programme (PTSLP)

TNCDW is the nodal agency for implementing the IFAD assisted PTSLP. The objective of PTSLP is to build self-reliant coastal communities which are able to manage their livelihoods in a sustainable manner. The Project is implemented at a total outlay of Rs.298.57 crores over a period of 8 years in 114 coastal Panchayats in Thiruvallur, Kancheepuram, Villupuram, Cuddalore, Nagapattinam and Kanniyakumari districts.

The Project envisages the development of community infrastructure, formation of Fish Marketing Societies (FMS), development of Micro enterprises, capacity building of SHGs, skill training for youth and creating awareness on disaster management for coastal school students.

During 2008-09 & 2009-10, staff have been positioned in the Project Management Unit (PMU), six District Implementation Offices (DIOs) and 30 cluster offices to facilitate implementation of project activities. Ten Facilitating NGOs and two Resource NGOs have been engaged in the Project Districts. The Project has completed Baseline Survey of 1.55 lakh households in the project area and based on its analysis Project interventions have been initiated. Under Community Infrastructure Programme, 681 works identified through Micro Plans will be executed during 2010-11. Guidelines for Project funding of Vulnerability Reduction Fund covering individual disaster have been formulated. Structured Survey of 7,414 SHGs has been completed in the project villages and 1,044 weak SHGs have been identified.

So far 7 FMS have been formed (3 in Nagapattinam, 3 in Kanyakumari and one in Cuddalore) and debt relief has been provided for 293 fishermen. Under Coastal School Programme, 30,215 students have been taken for exposure visit and 3,305 teachers have been trained on disaster preparedness to create awareness among coastal school students.

Action Plan for 2010-11:

During 2010-11, IFAD assisted PTSLP would focus on the following areas:

- Under Coastal Area Resource Management, 681 Community Infrastructure works identified through Micro Plans in 114 coastal Panchayats will be taken up and activities for enhancing Fisheries Resource Base will be undertaken.
- Vulnerability Reduction Fund will be put into operation with community participation and Venture Capital Fund will be transferred to PLFs for promoting Micro Enterprises through Bank linkage.
- One Fishermen Federation and Ten FMS with necessary marketing infrastructure will be formed and debt redemption assistance will be extended to the fishermen of these societies. Also ten Fish Landing Centres, one Out Board Repair Centre and one Boat Yard will be established.
- Vocational training for 1,000 youth and necessary capacity building for 1,044 weak SHGs in six project districts will be conducted.
- Capacity Building of 109 PLFs will be taken up after the restructuring process is completed.

The Government have so far provided Rs.30.53 crores for undertaking Project activities. In 2010-11 Rs.37.12 crores have been provided in the Budget for this Project.

WORLD BANK AIDED VAZHNDHU KAATTUVOM PROJECT

Vazhndhu Kaattuvom Project (VKP) is one of the key development initiatives of the Government of Tamil Nadu to reduce poverty and empower the rural poor. The Project provides assistance for productive livelihood activities to poor and very poor people in the village through the Community Driven Development (CDD) approach. The Project is being implemented vigorously in the State from October 2006 onwards. The Project is being implemented for a period of 6 years with an outlay of Rs.717 Crores.

The objectives of the Project are to empower the poorest of the poor, the marginalised and the differently abled and to promote sustainable livelihood for them. The Project develops Community-Based Organisations (CBOs) and strengthens them, enhances the skills and capacities of the poor and promotes transparent governance and social accountability. To achieve these objectives the Project has adopted key non-negotiable principles.

Project Area

The Project is implemented in 2,515 Village Panchayats in 70 backward Blocks spread over 16 Districts (including the newly formed Tiruppur District) covering about 5.2 lakh households.

Table – 25: Details of Project implementation

Phase	No. of Blocks	No. of Village Panchayats	Month of commence ment
I	15	578	October 2006
II	15	585	April 2007
III	20	635	February 2008
IV	20	717	February 2009

Institutional Arrangements

There is a State level Society to implement the Project and to supervise it. In each Project District there is a District level Society responsible for Project implementation. A five member multi disciplinary Project Facilitation Team is constituted at the cluster level to cover 10-15 Village Panchayats. At the Village Panchayat level, the Village Poverty Reduction Committee is vested with the responsibility of Project implementation. The Social Audit Committee at the Village level acts as a guardian of Project's principles.

Project Strategy

The Project follows the following strategy to achieve its objectives:-

Initiation Activities Communication Campaign

The Project undertakes intensive IEC campaign to disseminate information about the objectives of the Project, the non–negotiable principles and the activities of the Project.

Participatory Identification of Poor

The target beneficiaries of the Project, the poorest of the poor, vulnerable and differently abled are identified by the community itself using Participatory Identification of the Poor (PIP) methodology along with social mapping and wealth ranking. It is a simple but powerful tool, which is transparent and verifiable. This methodology has found wide acceptance, better targeting and ownership among all stakeholders.

Institution Building Activities

The Project promotes community organisations like Village Poverty Reduction Committees (VPRCs), Social Audit Committees (SACs), Self Help Groups (SHGs), Panchayat Level Federations (PLFs) and Community Professional Learning and Training Centres (CPLTCs).

Village Poverty Reduction Committee is an inclusive autonomous community organisation formed under the Project predominantly with the representation of the target population. VPRC has the institutional and financial capacity to plan, monitor and support the skill building and to assist differently abled and vulnerable. The VPRC constitutes the Village Panchayat President as the Ex-Officio Chairperson, a woman SHG member from the target population from each hamlet, a PLF office bearer, a representative of the differently abled and two nominated youth members. The VPRC is accountable to the Grama Sabha.

The Social Audit Committee is a social accountability mechanism and reports directly to the Grama Sabha. It is a 5-7 member body that monitors the activities of VPRC, PLF and Economic Activity Federations. Performing the role of a watch dog, it ensures that the Project is implemented in accordance with the Project principles.

Self Help Groups are institutions of poor at village level. The SHGs formed under the Project are from among the left out target poor. Tribal SHGs and special groups for differently abled are also promoted with focus on inclusion, empowerment and collective action. Community SHG Trainers closely monitor the SHGs, providing handholding support.

- Panchayat Level Federations are second level institutions of SHGs that render both financial and non financial services. The PLFs are aimed to provide easy and continuous access to finance at the right time to the SHGs, which is a crucial factor to enable the poor to come out of poverty. PLFs also monitor the formation and development of SHGs.
- Community Professional Learning and Training Centre is an institutional mechanism for the Community Professionals (CPs). It is established and managed by the community themselves. Apart from developing social capital which is key to the sustainability of the Project, CPLTCs provide a platform for community members to share and maximise their learning and experience.

Capacity Building Activities

To build the capacity of the members of Community-Based Organisations in planning, budgeting, implementation, monitoring and managing the Project activities, the Project promotes training through structured modules, exposure visits and internal learning forums.

Financial Linkage Activities

Vulnerable and differently abled identified by the Project are provided individual assistance by VPRC. SHGs consisting of left out target poor, special SHGs formed from among the differently abled and SHGs formed before the launch of the Project are linked to Banks after assessing their readiness and financial discipline through the process of credit rating.

Livelihood Promotion Activities

To augment livelihood and to improve the household income of the target poor, multipronged approach is followed.

The demand supply gap existing among the industries is utilised by providing job oriented skill training to unemployed rural youth. Skill training is conducted through reputed industrial houses leading to employment in Corporate sector or to self employment, Assistance through small loans from VPRCs or through the livelihood corpus fund available with PLFs, thereby promoting individual livelihoods,

To achieve sustainability and scale, Economic Activity Federations (EAFs) that have potential to be financially and institutionally viable are provided capacity building, capital support, linkages and technical assistance to develop business plans and to manage the economic activity.

Consolidation Activities

The Project develops second level institutions like PLFs, CPLTCs and EAFs to provide support and guidance to first level institutions like SHGs, CPs, etc. These institutions would provide sustainability even after the Project withdraws.

Developing Social Capital

The Project has taken efforts to select experienced members of Village Poverty Reduction Committee/SHG to build their capacity to develop them as Community Professionals.

A cadre of home grown Community Professionals (CPs) who have good local knowledge with hands on experience and who can effectively communicate with people, and who are willing to provide their services as trainers to other Project villages or line departments is developed within the Project thereby providing income opportunities and establishing a resource pool within the community which will be always available with the community.

- CPs organise themselves into Community Professional

Learning and Training Centres (CPLTCs) to provide cost effective and quality service based on need.

- CPs who are experienced in various Project activities like conducting PIP process, Community Operational Manual training, funds management, PLF activities are promoted to give specialised assistance.
- Trained Community Professionals are used as effective instruments of IEC of different programmes and training Social Audit Committee of MNREGS, PLF governance training to non-Vazhndhu Kaattuvom Project districts, SHG training in Chennai Corporation, IEC activities under TSC, Health Programmes, etc.

Incentivising performance

Village Panchayats are provided incentives for their pro-poor and supportive efforts in the implementation of the Project. The Village Panchayat incentive fund is based on meeting conditions of transparency, accountability, equity, participation, efficiency of functioning, their response and contribution to Project and to the poor. This helps in building bond between the Community-Based Organisations and the local Government and in the process cementing mutual accountability and transparency in activities between community and local Government.

Impact of the Project

The Project is implemented in four phases. Project activities are going on in full swing in all phases covering 2,515 Village Panchayats. The important accomplishments of the Project are as follows:

Social Inclusion

Focusing on effective targeting of poor, the principle of equity and inclusiveness has been followed in the Project. This has helped in inclusion of the poorest of poor, differently abled and vulnerable in strong community based organisation where they occupy key positions.

- 2,581 community organisations like VPRCs and SACs have been formed and capacitated.

- The ultra poor and vulnerable have been mobilised into 17,927 SHGs.
- 1,489 PLFs have been restructured and registered under the Tamil Nadu Societies Registration Act, 1975. The restructuring process has ensured adequate representation of the target poor thereby giving them a determining role in the decision making process.

Financial inclusion

On successful mobilisation of the target poor into SHGs and imparting training to them, the Project has linked them with formal Banking institutions for credit. Similarly, PLFs are given financial linkage.

- An amount upto Rs.20,000 given as seed money to 14,310 SHGs, from Project fund.
- 10,741 newly formed SHGs provided Revolving Fund to the tune of Rs.60.68 crores and second credit linkage to 1,322 SHGs to the tune of Rs.14.73 crores.
- 9,756 existing SHGs given Revolving Fund of Rs. 47.25 crores and 3,573 existing SHGs given second credit linkage of Rs. 57.18 crores
- 944 PLFs accessed Amudha Surabhi Fund (ASF) to the tune of Rs. 66.6 crores.
- 149 PLFs received sanction for bulk loan from the banks to the tune of Rs. 34.69 crores.

Empowering the marginalized

The Project has been able to reach the marginalised like differently abled, vulnerable and tribals, empower and mainstream them by proactively including them during social mobilisation, institution building and enabling them to access their entitlements.

These efforts have enhanced their quality of life and helped in securing dignity.To have a focused intervention, special fund of 40% of Village Poverty Reduction Committee fund is allocated to exclusively assist differently abled and vulnerable persons for starting livelihood activities thereby improving their socio-economic conditions.

- Nearly 1,19,837 benefits due to differently abled and vulnerable persons have been secured, through convergence with other Government schemes after the intervention of the Project.
- 65,886 differently abled have been mobilised into 6,144 special SHGs and 3,348 SHGs have received Rs. 18.70 crores through Revolving fund.
- National ID cards have been given to 72,123 differently abled persons.
- 94,496 differently abled and vulnerable persons given individual assistance to start small livelihood activity.
- 9,727 people have received assistive devices through Project intervention.
- 4,290 persons have benefited through maintenance grant of Rs 500/- per month and 3,253 persons under Niramaya Insurance.

Empowering the Tribals

In order to empower the tribals, the Project has provided higher allocation to exclusive tribal VPRCs. Higher allocation of Project funds is also granted to tribal families. Tribal community facilitators who are familiar and sensitive to the needs of Tribals are engaged for better facilitation of Project activities.

- 130 exclusive Tribal VPRCs formed.
- 33 Tribal facilitators appointed.

Economic Inclusion

Promotion of Livelihood activities based on local resources and skills is one of the major components of the Project. The Project follows a multi pronged strategy by providing skill training and placement, improving existing livelihoods and introducing to emerging opportunities.

The Project has facilitated the rural youth to upgrade traditional skills, or obtain access to new skills, based on their competencies. This has helped them secure wage employment in reputed industrial houses and enabled them in starting up gainful self employment activities. The Project provides loans to individuals from Amudha Surabi Fund through PLF to start income generating activities. The Project supports formation of economic activity federations around major livelihood activities.

- 62,486 youth have benefited from skill training and out of 46,356 youth who have completed skill training, 37,831 youth are gainfully employed (81% of those who have completed training).
- 43,990 households given loan totaling Rs.44.29 crores from ASF to start individual livelihood activities.

66 Economic activity federations with a cumulative membership of 2,757 persons have been formed and Rs.221.00 lakhs have been released to these federations. The federations have taken up dairy, garment making, floriculture, coir making, goat rearing, etc as income generating activities.

Promoting Good governance & Social accountability

The principles of good governance and social accountability is sine- qua- non for the Project. The CBOs are fully capacitated to adopt the non-negotiable principle of equity, transparency, inclusion, accountability and participation in all activities.

Project level

- Process monitoring is done on a continuous basis by three independent consultancy firms.
- To ensure project funds are utilised for the intended purpose, Professional audit firms have been appointed to audit the accounts of all VPRCs and PLFs.

To ensure compliance to environmental safeguards in all stages of implementation of livelihood Projects an Environmental Resource Agency has been contracted.

Community level

- The SAC performs the role of guardians of Project principles and ensures adherence to non negotiable principles by all CBOs.
- All information relating to Project activities and funds are displayed on the notice boards which are located in strategic places in the villages.

- All major decisions in the Project are taken with the approval of Gram Sabha. CBOs give their periodical report on progress to Gram Sabha.

Community based Insurance Scheme

Project provides a social security measure to target population at affordable rates. The Universal Health insurance scheme which is subsidised by Government of India has been taken up and successfully implemented in selective Blocks. Building on the principle of Project intervention through Community-Based Organisations, this initiative is also managed by community themselves. The Block level federation plays the role of third party administrator and selects the

participating hospitals. This initiative is being extended to all Project Blocks.

HR - Best Practices

Realizing the importance of attracting and retaining good human resources, the Project has adopted innovative HR practices. The Project functionaries are taken on contract and the recruitment takes place through an independent HR agency. The Project lays a lot of emphasis on building the skills of its functionaries through training, workshops and exposure visits. The Project has developed a performance appraisal system that rewards good performance and retains skilled and committed staff.

World Bank Support Missions

The progress of the Project is continuously supported by the periodical visit of the World Bank Support Missions. So far seven support missions of the World Bank have visited the Project and praised it in all successive missions. Some of the observations from the recent missions are given below. It is also noteworthy to mention here that the last support mission has rated the Project Management as "Highly Satisfactory".

"Some of the design and implementation areas that stand out are: inclusion of the very poor, vulnerable, youth, women, tribal and differently abled population in decision making and benefits,......"

– *World Bank Mid – Term Review Mission, February 2009*

"Overall, the Mid term review shows that excellent progress has been made in employment generation and skill training with 30,000 youth trained and 22,000 of them employed with minimum cost to the VKP program. This is a good indication that training provided has been effective. Of those that had been targeted for skills development belonged to the Poorest of the Poor"

–World Bank Mid-Term Review Mission, February 2009

"A remarkable innovation of community to community transfer of experience and knowledge has emerged in the form of Community Professional Learning Training Centres"

–World Bank Mid-Term Review Mission, February 2009

"Achievements under the Project continue in the field of inclusion especially its focus on disability, tribal and most backward communities, and the poorest women as well as on income generation through mobilisation of left-out poor and vulnerable into SHGs and linking them to banks and skills development and employment creation, especially for youth. About 23,300 youth have already benefited from employment. The program has also received very high level commitment of Government of Tamil Nadu"

– Seventh World Bank Implementation Support Mission, December 2009

"Social inclusion remains one of VKP's core pillars and field visits confirmed to the mission that the poorest, vulnerable and marginalised groups are typically being reached, through the Project's initial PIP process and subsequent attention to the left out poor. The mission's field visit to a tribal VPRC in Theni district indicated that good social mobilisation work has been carried out, despite challenges in the tribal villages (e.g., poorer access to services; more remote settings; discrimination from neighboring communities, etc.)"

– Seventh World Bank Implementation Support Mission, December 2009

"Formation and strengthening of village institutions has made good progress, especially in smooth roll out of restructured PLFs in Project villages – not an easy task and this achievement is acknowledged"

– Seventh World Bank Implementation Support Mission, December 2009

"Good progress has been made in functioning of the community professional Centres and providing cost effective service to the communities."

– *Seventh World Bank Implementation Support Mission, December 2009*

Financial Performance

The expenditure incurred under the Project from inception till 31.03.2010 is Rs. 388.44 crores. A sum of Rs.184.14 crores has been provided in the Budget Estimate for the year 2010-2011.

Additional Financing Proposal

The Project has been able to create deep impact in the villages covered by it in a short period of time. This demonstrates the efficacy of Community Driven Development (CDD) approach adopted by the Project. The results of mid-term evaluation done by an independent agency have also shown that the Project has achieved exemplary results in the field and has surpassed the targets set at the beginning of the Project. There is a strong case for expanding activities of such a successful project to other deserving backward Blocks of the State. Considering this, an Additional Financing Proposal for Rs. 950 crores has been sent to the World Bank by the State Government through the Government of India. Additional Financing Proposal seeks to further consolidate the achievements made in the existing Project area as well as to expand the Project to 50 new Blocks, out of which 46 Blocks would fall in 10 new Districts and 4 Blocks would fall in the existing Districts. Government of India has recommended the proposal to the World Bank. The World Bank is expected to approve the proposal soon.

TSUNAMI REHABILITATION SCHEMES

On 26th December 2004, the Tsunami that had originated near Indonesia struck the coastal area of Tamil Nadu and caused heavy damages to the life and property of people. The Government of Tamil Nadu took massive efforts to reconstruct damaged roads and public infrastructure, construct new houses and restore the livelihood of affected people. Many Departments of the Government are implementing the Tsunami Rehabilitation Projects.

In view of the large financial allocation for the projects and physical spread of activities undertaken by the Rural Development and Panchayat Raj Department, a separate Tsunami Project Implementation Unit (TPIU) was set up since 01.08.2005 to monitor the projects implemented by this Department.

The following programmes are implemented by the TPIU through District Implementation Units (DIUs) at district level.

Tsunami Emergency Assistance Project

(TEAP) of the Asian Development Bank (ADB) at an outlay of Rs.292.94 crores with loan and grant assistance for livelihood promotion and infrastructure development. reconstruction of vulnerable houses and for provision of basic amenities.

Emergency Tsunami Reconstruction Project (ETRP) – Vulnerability Reduction of Coastal Community Project (VRCCP) with the assistance of the World Bank at an estimated cost of about Rs.670 crores as credit for reconstruction of vulnerable houses and formation of evacuation routes.

Under these Programmes, the financial expenditure incurred as on 13.5.2006, was only Rs.4.95 crores. Due to the thrust given by this Government to accelerate the pace of implementation, the expenditure under these programmes has increased to Rs.864.84 crores as on 31.3.2010 (TEAP - Rs.292.94 crores and RGRP -Rs.571.90 crores). Also as against the deployment of only 61 persons for the TPIU and DIUs till 13.5.2006, 331 posts have been suitably filled up as on date for better implementation of the projects.

Rajiv Gandhi Rehabilitation Package (RGRP) of the Government of India (GoI) for tsunami affected areas at an outlay of about Rs.716 crores as grant for

Tsunami Emergency Assistance Project (TEAP) funded by Asian Development Bank (ADB)

The project was implemented at an outlay of Rs.292.94 crores. The project commenced on 06.04.2005 and extended upto 31.10.2009. The funds have been mainly utilized for the restoration of livelihood and damaged infrastructure in the coastal habitations. Under this project, 1,602 habitations spread across 257 coastal Village Panchayats in the 12 coastal Districts were benefited.

Livelihood Component

Under this component, the vulnerable sections of the society were provided with Revolving Fund Assistance and Economic Assistance, grant was provided for differently abled persons and capacity building of the community was taken up. The total expenditure under this component was Rs.183.20 crores.

Special Projects: Major initiatives were taken up for capacity building and livelihood related community infrastructure as detailed below:

- An SHG complex has been taken up near Valluvarkottam in Chennai at a total cost of Rs.15.32 crores. This SHG complex is planned to be completed in June, 2010.
- 15 Direct Paddy Purchase Centres have been completed at a cost of Rs.1.62 crores in Nagapattinam and Thanjavur Districts.
- A Handloom Weavers' Cluster with 250 handlooms has been upgraded in Nagercoil at a cost of Rs.61.09 lakhs.
- 9 Bulk Milk Coolers, 37 Milk Parlours and 160 Dairy Co-operative Societies have been established at a cost of Rs.4.06 crores for the benefit of SHGs.
- A Crafts Village in Villupuram district has been established at an expenditure of Rs.67.49 lakhs to promote local crafts.
- 93 Fishermen Societies have been provided with Rs.2.96 crores as working capital assistance.
- Training has been imparted to about 20,000 fishermen and their family members in sea safety measures at a cost of Rs.1.13 crores.

Capacity Building: Under this component, basic orientation training, animators and representatives training, entrepreneurial development programmes and skill upgradation training have been provided to the SHGs to enable them to function as viable groups and to take up various economic activities. Rs.4.47 crores has been incurred as expenditure for the above purpose.

Rural Infrastructure

Roads and Drainages: 610 road works to a length of 699 kms have been completed in the coastal Village Panchayats at a cost of Rs.89 crores.

Public Buildings: Renovation and extension of 196 Village Panchayat office buildings in the coastal Village Panchayats have been completed at a cost of Rs.5.54 crores.

Sanitation

21 short advertisement films have been produced at an estimated cost of Rs.67.28 lakhs for creating awareness on usage of toilets and personal hygiene in rural areas.

Rajiv Gandhi Rehabilitation Package (RGRP) funded by Government of India

The RGRP project is being implemented by the State Government and is funded by Government of India as grant. The project envisages to cover all those vulnerable houses lying within 200 metres from HTL and also the Government built houses under the schemes such as Indira Awaas Yojana (IAY), Singaravelar Fishermen Housing Scheme etc., which are 10 years old as on 01.01.2006 and within 1000 metres from the HTL. Further, this project provides necessary basic amenities in the affected areas.

The following are the major components of the project:-

- Provision of basic amenities in the Non-Governmental Organisations (NGOs) constructed housing sites.
- Construction of NGOs backed out houses.
- Provision of basic amenities in the NGOs backed out housing sites.
- Reconstruction of vulnerable houses.
- Provision of basic amenities in the vulnerable housing sites as per the norms of Anaithu Grama Anna Marumalarchi Thittam (AGAMT).

Provision of basic amenities in NGOs constructed housing sites

The Government have taken up 169 basic amenities such as CC roads, street lights, water supply, sanitation and land filling to the estimate of Rs.57.34 crores at the sites where the NGOs have constructed houses but not provided these basic amenities. 161 works have been completed and an expenditure of Rs.49.41 crores has been incurred as on 31.3.2010.

Construction of NGOs backed out houses

Some of the NGOs initially agreed to take up the construction of tsunami damaged houses in the Districts of Tiruvallur, Kancheepuram, Villupuram, Nagapattinam and Thoothukudi. But, after two years of tsunami occurrence, they have backed out from construction of 2,687 houses. Finally, Rural Development and Panchayat Raj Department had to construct these houses in 17 habitations of the above Districts and Rs.63.09 crores has been incurred as expenditure.

Table - 26 Progress in reconstruction of vulnerable houses and basic amenities under RGRP

(Rs. in crores)

Sl. No	Component	No. of works taken up	No. of works completed	Allocation	Expenditure	% of Expenditure to Allocation
1	Reconstruction of vulnerable houses	18,302	12,665	499.22	377.15	76
2	Reconstruction of NGO backed out houses	2,687	2,687	65.76	63.09	96
3	Basic Amenities					
	i) Roads	976 (638 km)	915 (542 km)	96.09	82.32	85
	ii) Public Buildings	316	291	5.25	4.14	79
	iii) Street Lights	5,699	5,699	2.50	2.50	100
	iv) Sanitation	5,922	5,800	4.70	4.38	93
	v) Other works	307	284	16.66	12.78	77
4	Others (Shifting allowance, Rent, Insurance, etc.)			25.54	25.54	100
	Total	34,209	28,341	715.72	571.90	80

Provision of basic amenities in NGO backedout housing sites

56 basic amenities works have been taken up and completed at the NGO backed out housing sites and an expenditure of Rs.6.08 crores has been incurred.

The basic aim of this Project is the reconstruction of vulnerable houses in coastal areas with disaster resistance features. 18,302 houses (17,207 in situ and 1,095 relocated) have been taken up across 333 habitations and covering 146 coastal Village Panchayats. 12,665 houses have been completed so far (69%) and the remaining 5,637 houses are in progress at different stages. Out of the tendered value of Rs.499.22 crores, the expenditure so far incurred is Rs.377.15 crores (76%). All the pending houses are programmed to be completed before September, 2010.

Provision of basic amenities as per AGAMT norms in the vulnerable housing sites

3,238 basic amenities works such as CC roads, street lights, burial ground / cremation sheds, village ponds, necessary public buildings etc have been taken up as per the AGAMT norms in the coastal Village Panchayats at the tendered cost of Rs.68.14 crores. 3,138 works have been completed as on 31.3.2010 and the expenditure incurred is Rs.52.55 crores (77%). The pending works will be completed before May, 2010.

Other important features of RGRP

Provision of shifting allowance and rent allowance: One time shifting allowance of Rs.1,000/- and a monthly rent allowance of Rs.500/- for 18 months have been given to the in situ beneficiaries of the vulnerable houses. Rs.17.49 crores have been released to 17,207 in situ beneficiaries.

Insurance coverage: A sum of Rs.2.10 crores has been provided by the Government for insuring 20,989 houses against 14 types of natural hazards for a period of 10 years.

State Quality Monitors (SQMs): The State Quality Monitors in the cadre of retired Superintending Engineers/ Chief Engineers have been engaged to ensure quality in the construction of houses and provision of basic amenities.

Provision of hand pumps: 1,002 hand pumps have been provided in the villages covered by RGRP at a cost of Rs.86.07 lakhs from the Central Planning Commission Grant.

Bibliography

Benjamin, J.: *Socio-religious Status of Panchayati Raj in India,* New Delhi, Ashish Publishing, 1991.

Bhai, N.: *Harijan Women in Panchayati Raj,* Delhi, BR Publishing 1986

Calman, J.: *Women and Politics in India,* Colorado, Westview Press, 1992.

Dak, T.M.: *Women and Work in Panchayati Raj,* Delhi, Discovery, 1988.

Erikson, E. H.: *Panchayati Raj and Society,* New York, W. W. Norton, 1993.

Jain, D.: *Women's Quest for Power in Panchayati Raj,* Sahibabad, Vikas, 1980.

Judith, E.: *The Sexual Exploitation of Panchayati Raj,* Cambridge, Polity Press, 1986.

Menon, V. P.: *The Transfer of Power in India,* Bombay, Orient Longman, 1957.

Mohiuddin Khan: 1988, *Development Strategies for Panchayati Raj,* Dhaka, Bangladesh.

Mueller, R.: *Women's Work in Third World Agriculture,* Geneva, ILO, 1985.

Panini, M.N.: *Accounts of Women Fieldworkers Studying their Own Communities,* Delhi, Hindustan, 1991.

Singh, S.: *Role of Women's in Panchati Raj System in India,* New Delhi, Sage, 1995.

Tariq, A: *The Story of the Nehru-Gandhi Family,* New York, Putnam, 1985.

Viitanen, A.: *Women in Home-based Production,* New Delhi, Sage, 1987.

Index

□□□